Thackeray and Women

Micael M. Clarke

Thackeray
and Women

Northern Illinois
University
Press

DeKalb   1995

© 1995 by Northern Illinois University Press

Published by the Northern Illinois University Press, DeKalb, Illinois   60115

Manufactured in the United States using acid-free paper

Design by Julia Fauci   ✪   ∞

Library of Congress Cataloging-in-Publication Data

Clarke, Micael M.

      Thackeray and women / Micael M. Clarke.

         p.   cm.

      Includes bibliographical references and index.

      ISBN 0-87580-197-8

      1. Thackeray, William Makepeace, 1811–1863—Characters—
Women. 2. Women and literature—England—History—19th century. 3.
Women in literature. I. Title.

PR5642.W6FC58 1995

823'.8—dc20   94-36979

           CIP

In loving Memory—

Mary Virginia Lane Keefe

Contents

Figures

Acknowledgments

As anyone who has completed a project of this size knows, help comes in many forms. Among those I wish to thank are Gerald Sorensen, whose seminar first showed me Thackeray's genius and whose advice and criticism have sustained me throughout this project; Dan Majdiak, who encouraged and directed my dissertation; and my readers Dale Kramer and the late Robert Schneider, who, along with the others, gave freely of their time, knowledge, and thought. I wish to thank Robert Colby, who has generously supplied me with encouragement, information, and not a few corrections. I owe much to the help of friends and colleagues, especially Barbara Boyer, Mary Burgan, Richard Burke, Nancy Cirillo, Frank Fennell, Patricia Lorimer Lundberg, Susan Ross, and Nancy Workman, who either read parts of the manuscript or talked it through with me. A grant from Loyola University of Chicago's Research Services Department enabled me to visit collections in England, where I was able to examine certain of Thackeray's letters and diaries. I wish also to thank Alan Kucia, archivist of the Wren Library, Trinity College, Cambridge, for his assistance.

I wish to thank the following publishers for permission to reprint material from early versions of my essays: the University of Texas Press printed "Thackeray's *Barry Lyndon:* An Irony against Misogynists" in *Texas Studies in Literature and Language;* the Indiana University of Pennsylvania Press printed "Thackeray's *Henry Esmond* and Eighteenth-Century Feminism: A Double Vision of Feminist Discourse and Literary Narrative" in *Works and Days: Essays in the Socio-Historical Dimensions of Literature and the Arts;* the Research Society for Victorian Periodicals printed "A Mystery Solved: Ainsworth's Criminal Romances Censured in *Fraser's* by J. Hamilton Reynolds, not Thackeray" in *Victorian Periodicals Review;* and the AMS Press printed "William Thackeray's Fiction and Caroline

Norton's Biography: Narrative Matrix of Feminist Legal Reform" in *Dickens Studies Annual.*

These acknowledgements would not be complete without mention of those who helped with the final preparation of this manuscript. For their excellent advice and professionalism, I would like to thank William Baker, Daniel Coran, and Susan Bean at Northern Illinois University. And for assistance both financial and scholarly, I thank the English Department of Loyola University as a whole, and especially Suzanne Gossett, Chair of the English Department, who has provided counsel and support at key points throughout this project.

Finally, I give loving thanks to my family—my husband, Robert, my daughter, Jennifer, my son, Robert, and my parents, the late Mary Virginia Keefe and William Keefe, and Elizabeth and Robert Clarke.

Note on Documentation

References to Thackeray's works will be given in parentheses in the text. Generally, citations refer to *The Works of William Makepeace Thackeray*, edited by Anne T. Ritchie and Leslie Stephen. For the sake of reader convenience, however, citations of *Barry Lyndon*, *Vanity Fair*, *Henry Esmond*, and *Pendennis* will be taken from more accessible paperback editions.

In addition, quotations from Thackeray's letters will cite Gordon N. Ray's *The Letters and Private Papers of William Makepeace Thackeray*, 4 vols. (Cambridge, Mass.: Harvard Univ. Press, 1945–1946), as *Letters*, followed by the appropriate volume and page numbers.

Thackeray and Women

Introduction

> "Revenge may be wicked, but it's natural," answered Miss Rebecca. "I'm no angel." And, to say the truth, she certainly was not.
>
> —*Vanity Fair*

> You know it has been agreed that at one time of my existence I must have been a woman.
>
> —*Letters* (2: 646)

omen play a major part in every one of William Makepeace Thackeray's novels, if not as central characters, as in *Vanity Fair,* then as representatives of the ethical choices the male central character must make. But Thackeray's women characters are more than mere "signposts"; even in the novels in which a male character is central, as in *Barry Lyndon* and *Henry Esmond,* the effects of gender on individual identity, family, and society are essential components of the work's meaning and values. Thackeray's critique of the relations between men and women provides a continuous and coherent theme that binds all the fiction into a single entity, a Thackerayan universe. As Geoffrey Tillotson put it, "His novels hang together like a dynasty."[1]

This Thackerayan universe has sometimes been misunderstood, however. Especially regarding Thackeray's attitude toward women, critics have always disagreed and still do so today. Peter Shillingsburg, for example, recently took issue with Gordon Ray's influential interpretation of Amelia Sedley's role in *Vanity Fair.*[2] A full-length study of this important aspect of his work is long overdue, and it is my hope that this book will facilitate a new understanding and appreciation of Thackeray's intelligence. To understand Thackeray's ideas on women is to understand the novels better and to recognize, finally, how liberal a Victorian he was: his appraisal of the status of women is comparable to those of Mary Wollstonecraft, John Stuart Mill, and George Eliot.

Thackeray's critique of Victorian gender ideology encompasses not only women's legal disabilities but also the social and psychological effects of gendered patterns of thought and behavior: men learning to like their women to be slaves, as he put it, and women learning to make gods of their men. As the best novelists do, Thackeray explored the interrelations between morality and self-knowledge. His works examine the internalized emotional, intellectual, and ethical systems by which members of a society order their lives.

Thackeray has left few statements to tell us explicitly where he stood on the Woman Question. But by examining the evidence of his readings, letters, lectures, and journalism, and especially by exploring the many parallels between his fiction and his most important relationships with women, we can begin to define Thackeray's views on "female emancipation." And by situating his fiction in its political and cultural contexts, we can make clear the multiple, dynamic relationships between his novels and the nineteenth-century women's movement.

Perhaps the reason Thackeray never made his position on the Woman Question explicit is that he was torn by emotional ambivalence and intellectual skepticism. "'The truth, friend,' Arthur said imperturbably: 'where is the truth?'" (*Pendennis* 649).[3] Yet it was this same skepticism in Thackeray that led him to question his culture's assumptions about gender in the first place. Peter Shillingsburg wrote, "Thackeray's philosophy is revealed in his letters and private papers as a deep and fundamental individual skepticism about causes of every sort. . . . He did not trust institutionalized schemes."[4]

The first literary manifestation of Thackeray's skepticism came in the form of the early satires and parodies. Even in these early works injustice to women is one of his targets. But gradually he developed a broader repertoire of narrative techniques, and his critique of sexism becomes an increasingly complex and subtle component of his novels. Even the most minutely realistic details, such as the brown holland covers on a chandelier or the classical figures on a ticking clock, serve to represent broad social patterns, such as the marriage market, and ultimately to convey judgments on society's values: to declare that injustice to women is an inherent and destructive element of the social fabric.

Another important aspect of Thackeray's novelistic technique, his ironic first-person narrative, is frequently deployed against sexist bias. Not only do narrators such as Arthur Pendennis and Barry Lyndon represent masculine limitations, they also allude to contemporary events in a way that Thackeray's readers would have recognized as indirect political commentary. Over the years, Thackeray's critique of sexism developed in conjunction with his increasing skill as a novelist, and just as his genius helped shape novelistic discourse, I believe that his novels helped transform the gender ideology of his culture.

It is my hope that this work will take Thackeray studies in new directions. The subject of Thackeray's feminist ideas has wide-ranging implications for the role of his novels in the discourse of the age and for understanding the role of the Victorian novel in the history of the women's movement. The works I discuss here are those that speak most clearly of Thackeray's interest in the women's movement and issues of gender. They range from the earliest to the last of Thackeray's writings and form a continuum as patterns are repeated with variations and at increasing depth. The seeds of his more mature ideas can be discerned even in the simplest of his early works: his development as a novelist is characterized by an increase in the complexity, subtlety, and significance of his feminist ideas.

CRITICAL METHODS

This work began quite a few years ago with a seminar on Thackeray taught by Gerald Sorensen. My first seminar report focused on the late Gordon Ray's *The Buried Life*, in which Ray invokes Thackeray's relationships with his wife, his mother, and Jane Brookfield as a key to understanding the fiction. Today, such tracing of "originals" to establish literary meaning is suspect, and for good reason: in moving from biography to a work of art, we are obliged to base our conclusions always on inference; an author's intentions, even if fully realized in the work, are never entirely available to us; and we are in constant danger of confusing the novelist with the novel, which indeed "belongs to the public," as Wimsatt and Beardsley argued in their 1946 "Intentional Fallacy."[5] And yet, the materials of Thackeray's life and the reflections conveyed through his remarks and letters do undeniably shed light on his fiction.

My reading of the relationship between Thackeray's biography and his fiction differs from Ray's: with due respect for the foundation Ray has laid for Thackeray studies, and with care to avoid the pitfalls of the intentional fallacy, I propose that Thackeray was not blinded by sentimental attachment to the key women in his life, but did have rather a sharp, clear understanding of their failings and the underlying causes thereof. Thackeray's life is indeed, as he put it, the "unwritten part" of his novels, and his fiction mediates between the life and the discourse on gender that energized so much of the literature of his age.

One example of Thackeray's transformation of biography into fiction is his use of elements of his wife's insanity. His insights into this personal tragedy anticipate Phyllis Chesler's and Elaine Showalter's twentieth-century analyses of how insanity in women is linked to cultural forces.[6] In *Vanity Fair*, Amelia's character is in part a critique of socially constructed ideas of the feminine; her weakness also consitutes a critique of the masculine socialization that Thackeray had himself undergone. On 3 September 1848, in a letter to his mother, he remarked of Dobbin's falling in love with Amelia: "Good God dont [*sic*] I see . . . my own weaknesses wickednesses lusts follies shortcomings?"[7] Because he was gifted with an extraordinary ability to reflect on his own experiences and shortcomings, Thackeray was able to recognize the ways in which male socialization was implicated in women's problems. This capacity for self-reflection is what enables him to explore gender relations with unusually sympathetic insight.

A feminist reading of Thackeray's novels, juxtaposed against their historical and biographical backgrounds, provides a new understanding of the complex ways Thackeray has inscribed protest against injustice to women in his works. Dobbin's lifetime of devotion to Amelia, for example, can be understood as the expression of an unconscious fear of emotional involvement that is sublimated into gallant idealization of the angelic feminine. Dobbin is a good and noble man, but his relationship with Amelia can be consummated only in disappointment because nineteenth-century English society has, in a thousand subtle ways, so ordered sexual love. It is a theme Thackeray was to dramatize often, and it links Thackeray's life to the gender ideology of his age—and challenges it.

Historical change continually uncovers new meanings in works of literature, just as it continually alters the meaning of a law. And so today an evolving body of narrative and feminist theory provides us with new ways of understanding Victorian literature. Hans-Georg Gadamer describes this process: "The literary critic, who is dealing with poetic or philosophical texts, knows that they are inexhaustible. In both cases it is the progress of events that brings out new aspects of meaning in historical material."[8] Now that we are able to recognize another element of his intelligence, the genius that encompasses strikingly "modern" insights into questions of gender and society, we can begin to analyze Thackeray's writings in terms of our own reevaluations of sexual politics. Because the feminist critique of society has become a part of our shared consciousness, elements of Thackeray's meaning, previously obscure, are now made manifest.

CULTURAL SOURCES OF THACKERAY'S IDEAS

Most people are by now aware that the nineteenth century ushered in modern feminism, and that the changing relations between men and women are, as Ruth apRoberts has said, "*the* subject of the Victorian novel." Thackeray was surrounded by discussions of the Woman Question; it was "in the air." What was true of Charlotte Brontë and John Stuart Mill is true also of Thackeray, that none was an "isolated dissenter from a chorus praising one womanly ideal," and all were read by their contemporaries— and still should be read—"as a response to prior statements in an ongoing public discussion."[9]

Another influence on Thackeray's novels was the "literary apprenticeship" he served by writing for journals that fostered the multiplicity of perspectives embodied in his works. His work with *Fraser's* and *Punch* encouraged Thackeray's natural tendency to satire, and he read voraciously while, as Carlyle said, "writing for his life."[10] Thackeray's early career as a struggling writer brought him into contact with many of his more unorthodox Victorian contemporaries: William Maginn, J. Hamilton Reynolds, Lady Blessington (one of the probable "originals" for Becky Sharp), and the Irish novelist and feminist Sidney Owenson (later Lady Morgan). Other acquaintances included Harriet Martineau, Fanny Kemble, Elizabeth Barrett and Robert Browning, Charlotte Brontë, George Lewes, and John Stuart Mill.

His work for *Fraser's* brought him into contact also with Caroline Norton, whose writings were to provide him with a powerful and very important critique of women's legal disabilities. Norton was not a feminist in the usual political sense, but she was caught in an appalling marriage and found herself becoming a test case by which nineteenth-century British laws concerning divorce, child custody, and married women's property were to be tried. Norton fought brilliantly for Parliamentary reform, both with her pen and in "drawing room politics," and she helped bring about the crucial measures of the Infant Custody Act of 1839 and the Marital Causes Act of 1857. She clearly influenced Thackeray also, for several of his novels reenact well-known incidents from Norton's life. *The Newcomes*, especially, supports the Marital Causes Act (pending before Parliament at the time of its publication) by recreating a "criminal conversation" trial much like the one that made Norton famous. It is ironic that Thackeray, who briefly considered pursuing a legal career, may have had a greater impact on the legal system as a novelist than he could ever have had as an attorney.

Thackeray's extensive readings also informed his thinking about women. Even the "wasted" hours spent reading French novels contributed to the formation of his genius. John Stuart Mill wrote that wherever women are "able to make their sentiments known by their writings," there we find protest against male privilege.[11] Such protest would not have been lost on Thackeray, and his reading included many works written by women. One book found in Thackeray's library after his death, for example, Judith Drake's 1696 *Essay in Defence of the Female Sex*, may help account for his perceptive re-creation of the history of feminist theory.

The complexity of Thackeray's views is compounded by the fact that nineteenth-century feminism is itself so difficult to define. At times, even apparently antifeminist rhetoric served to expand the arena of women's activities—as when John Ruskin urged middle-class women to use their special "womanly" gifts to benefit society, or when Florence Nightingale invoked women's supposed maternal qualities to professionalize nursing for women. But many feminists rejected the essentialism that justified separate spheres: Harriet Martineau, for example, argued that as long as the "male sphere" was the governance of the world, women could help no one—not even themselves—with their supposedly natural gifts.

Mill's response to Ruskin was that neither in affairs of state nor in affairs of the family is queenly power a compensation for the lack of freedom.[12]

Shaped by the conflicting views of his society, Thackeray's ideas evolved in complex ways. His early responsiveness to feminist theory is apparent in a letter he wrote his mother on 1 June 1840, when he was twenty-eight: "Why is it that one does not like women to be too smart?—jealousy I suppose: a pretty selfish race we are truly. And Lady Morgan has shown how cruelly the ladies are kept down" (*Letters* 1: 447). Lady Morgan, born in Ireland as Sydney Owenson, was, like Caroline Norton, one of Thackeray's colleagues at *Fraser's Magazine*. Her book *Woman and Her Master* argues that woman has always been subject to unjust laws that were devised to serve male needs and convenience.[13] Owenson's central thesis is that women should be granted full and equal legal rights because women have always contributed to the advancement of humanity despite oppressive conditions. *Woman and Her Master* attempts to correct the histories that marginalize women by providing examples of female greatness in every age, instances that have survived somehow despite men's control of the historical record. Had women written the histories, she argues, there would be more examples, and had women not suffered such oppression, they would have demonstrated their potential more often.

Thackeray's friendly reference to "Lady Morgan's book" indicates that he sympathized with at least some feminist works. Lionel Stevenson has argued, following up on a hint from Thackeray's daughter, that Lady Morgan was the original for Becky Sharp in *Vanity Fair*. Lady Morgan did indeed begin as a governess, but unlike Becky, she became what Stevenson calls in his preface "our first successful professional woman author." Her character was "ambitious, self-confident, energetic, versatile, proud of her feminine graces and wiles, but not deficient in deeper qualities of determination and feeling."[14] If Lady Morgan is in any way Becky's prototype, then her feminist views would certainly add an extratextual dimension to Thackeray's representation. Perhaps Thackeray especially appreciated Owenson's bold assertion of women's worth because it contrasted so poignantly with his wife's increasing depression and sense of worthlessness.

Disagreement over Thackeray's views of women began with his earliest publications, and it continues to this day. Among his contemporaries, two important women thought very highly of him. George Eliot's admiration is expressed in a letter to John Blackwood, written in 1857, in which she states: "I . . . think of him, as I suppose the majority of people with any intellect do, on the whole the most powerful of living novelists." Charlotte Brontë expressed her admiration for *Vanity Fair* in the dedication and author's preface to the second edition of *Jane Eyre*. Although her early admiration was destined to fade, probably because she came to feel that Thackeray's manner lacked sufficient seriousness, a portion of that dedication bears repeating here:

> Is the satirist of "Vanity Fair" admired in high places? I cannot tell; but I think if some of those amongst whom he hurls the Greek fire of his sarcasm, and over whom he flashes the levin-brand of his denunciation, were to take his warnings in time—they or their seed might yet escape a fatal Ramoth-Gilead.
>
> Why have I alluded to this man? I have alluded to him, Reader, because I think I see in him an intellect profounder and more unique than his contemporaries have yet recognised; because I regard him as the first social regenerator of the day—as the very master of that working corps who would restore to rectitude the warped system of things.[15]

Further testimony comes from Barbara Bodichon, who indirectly expressed her admiration in a letter to George Eliot by citing Thackeray as the summit of literary achievement:

> I can't tell you, my dear George Eliot how enchanted I am. Very few things could have given me so much pleasure [as *Adam Bede*].
>
> 1st. That a woman should write a wise and *humourous* book which should take a place by Thackeray.
>
> 2nd. That YOU *that you* whom they spit at should do it![16]

A contemporary who touched more specifically than either George Eliot or Brontë on the subject of Thackeray's female characters is Elizabeth Rigby, later Lady Eastlake. Her essay "*Vanity Fair, Jane Eyre,* and the *Governesses' Benevolent Institution—Report for 1847,*" is best known today for its attack on *Jane Eyre*'s "pervading tone of ungodly discontent," and Eastlake's simultaneous praise of *Vanity Fair* has prejudiced feminist scholars against Thackeray ever since.[17] (I will discuss this essay in greater detail in connection with *Vanity Fair*.)

Other contemporary reactions to Thackeray's female characters are mixed. John F. Kirk, in an essay in the *North American Review* in 1853, asserts that Thackeray's portraits of women are realistic and natural and, although not as complete as those in *Jane Eyre,* reflect accurately "women who submit, and women who rebel." The reviewer recalls a passage from "Mr. Brown's Letters," in which Thackeray points out that man's inability to understand woman results from suppression: "'We expect falseness from her, and order and educate her to be dishonest.'" Kirk answers charges that Thackeray's good women lack intelligence by asserting that intelligent women find it difficult to be good, and that Thackeray is only portraying the truth: "It is the active and original mind that is most likely to stray beyond the limits which a law, not altogether free from an arbitrary character, has assigned to it."[18]

A review entitled "The Women of Thackeray" that appeared in the *Christian Examiner* in 1860 reveals how relatively free Thackeray was of conventional ideas. The review is a peculiar combination of conservative-romantic attitudes toward "the sex" and sharp Thackerayan insights into the damaging emotional relationships that flow from these attitudes. The reviewer defends Thackeray against the charge that he did not respect women by asserting that he combines truthfulness with reverence for "the sweet divineness of womanhood." Clearly this critic sees gender characteristics as innate, but he or she also recognizes elements of Thackeray's social critique in *Vanity Fair:* "If Thackeray is sharp-sighted to detect the foibles common to the sex, no man has truer sympathy with woman's peculiar trials." This critic is torn between conventional assumptions about women's nature and the reality presented by Thackeray. Thus, although Thackeray has by this time repeatedly demonstrated that feminine submissiveness encourages masculine egoism, because the critic believes that it is "instinctive" for women to admire the men they love, he or she is puzzled: "It is a curious fact in human experience, that the most lovely and devoted of wives are often neglected and unappreciated. . . . Truly the heart of man is a strange thing." Regarding Amelia, the most devoted wife of all, this critic wrote, perceptively enough, "love brings her only unhappiness, but it is an unhappiness which she hugs," concluding that George's death is "one of her greatest mercies."[19] Thus does Thackeray's fiction undercut even the most dearly held beliefs about the sacredness of woman's uncritical devotion.

1. Becky's second appearance as Clytemnestra (*Works* 2: [facing] 429).

Twentieth-century critics are as divided as their nineteenth-century counterparts on the question of Thackeray and women. Some have provided feminist readings of single works. Dorothy Van Ghent's incisive analysis of the "theme of the fathers" in *Vanity Fair* connects Thackeray's portraits of "sick fathers, guilty fathers" to the "general social system of values" that "has determined our conditions of existence and the problems we have to confront." Maria DiBattista, ignoring Lady Eastlake's command that readers take a scissors to Thackeray's illustration of Becky's second appearance as Clytemnestra (see figure 1), uses it instead as basis for her essay "The Triumph of Clytemnestra." In this piece, DiBattista demonstrates a connection "between Clytemnestra's rebellion against the warrior culture that authorizes the sacrifice of her child, Iphigenia, and [Thackeray's] extensive critique of the attitudes toward women and children in the bourgeois, jingoistic, mercantile culture of nineteenth-century England." Similarly, Gordon Ray, Nina Auerbach, and Eve Kosofsky Sedgwick all testify to Thackeray's remarkable "critique of patriarchy" (Sedgwick's words) in their discussions of *Henry Esmond*. Ray wrote that it "might appropriately have been cited by John Stuart Mill in . . . *The Subjection of Women*." And Auerbach wrote, "Thackeray's social acuteness does not elide the dispossession of actual women—in fact, I can think of no mid-Victorian novel more incisively outspoken than *Esmond* is on this subject."[20]

Two twentieth-century essays take a more general view of Thackeray's writings: Katherine Rogers's "The Pressures of Convention on Thackeray's Women" and a chapter in *Corrupt Relations* by Richard Barickman, Susan MacDonald, and Myra Stark. Both of these works conclude that, although Thackeray's early writings challenge established assumptions about women, he became more conventional as he advanced in his career. (It is the purpose of this volume to show that he became, rather, increasingly unorthodox.) Barickman, MacDonald, and Stark argue that the authors they examine—Dickens, Thackeray, Trollope, and Collins—recognized the harm that the Victorian sexual system inflicted, but because these authors benefited from that system, they wrote ambivalent and evasive novels. These critics regard Thackeray as a lesser artist whose later novels enshrine "a kind of male innocence and timidity . . . a retreat from the complexity of the sexual world . . . [so that] the selfish neglect or abuse of women that marks all

the heroes of these novels, done in the service of sentimental idealization . . . becomes almost a mark of nobility."[21] Such a conclusion depends on a reading that ignores Thackeray's irony; his novels offer not a valorization but a critique of such behavior.

Critics are not entirely to be blamed for the confusion over
Thackeray's views. Conflicting and competing versions of feminism are with us still and were even less clearly delineated in
Thackeray's day. Thackeray's achievement is, in part, that he reproduced choices available in the culture—conflicting interpretations of the origins and meaning of masculine and feminine in human life.

THE HISTORICAL REALITIES

Thackeray's novels are historical in the profoundest sense; they
continually demonstrate the degree to which personality is socially
constructed. His is not a determinist view, for characters do make
choices within a context in which multiple interpretations of their
experience are available. But there are "dominant" and alternative
interpretations, and social pressures combined with emotional factors play an important role in the characters' choices. Henry Esmond, for example, changed both his politics and his religion as
his emotional needs led the way. Thackeray's strength lies in depicting the individual, private experience of "social emotions." His
characters often find the normative roles that the dominant culture assigns them uncomfortable, and they respond in a variety of
ways: some learn hypocrisy, as Becky Sharp does; some accept isolation, loneliness, or defeat, as Rosey Newcome and Clarissa de
Viomesnil do; and some rebel, as do Amelia Sedley and Ethel Newcome. Therefore, one aspect of Thackeray's superb historicism is
the nuanced re-creation of what is now called social discourse systems.

Much of the historical development of the women's movement
in Victorian England is straightforward—feminist ideas were advocated, they were gradually accepted, and changes occurred,
such as the establishment of Queen's College. But there are also
paradoxes in the way women's equality advanced. One paradox is
that some women achieved power and freedom by taking advantage of—manipulating rather than resisting—conservative essentialist views of women's nature. Mary Poovey demonstrates that

both Caroline Norton and Florence Nightingale did this to some degree. Another paradox is that, as social structures became more organized, some kinds of informal status previously available to women (as midwives, for example, or shopkeepers, or Methodist preachers) disappeared as men moved into positions of authority in new systems of medicine, business, and religion. A third paradox is that concepts of male and female in the nineteenth century came increasingly to be defined in terms of opposition and mutual exclusivity, so that real women frequently invalidated accepted concepts of "true womanhood."[22]

The final paradox is that there was undeniably a degree of freedom available to women who wished to pursue it, and who had the good fortune of either an independence or a generous, enlightened, or cooperative family. M. Jeanne Peterson's *Family, Love, and Work in the Lives of Victorian Gentlewomen* provides an impressive range of examples of her proposition that not all Victorian women were oppressed, and that some were extremely successful in political, artistic, and social arenas.[23] Peterson does not deny the exclusion of women from educational and public structures that gave professional training, promotion, and power almost exclusively to men, and she acknowledges also that in the middle classes, where men's identities depended on public achievement, women were more restricted than in the upper classes. But her book also suggests that some oppression was actually self-imposed—testimony to the power of gender ideology on the psyche, perhaps, and to the complexity of the phenomena Thackeray portrays.

An increasing recognition among Victorians of the importance of childhood experience, which was to culminate in Freud, led to increasing pressure on mothers. As Erna Olafson Hellerstein, Leslie Parker Hume, and Karen Offen point out in *Victorian Women,* there was "a growing feeling for the importance of a personal relationship between mother and child."[24] The domestic ideal grew out of traditional prescriptions for women's duties that may have originated in biology but were usually associated with the idea that women's lives ought to center on children and home and be ruled by a husband.

At the same time, due to industrialization, urbanization, and the growth of a vast, prosperous middle class, women's roles became more sharply distinguished from those of their male counterparts. For example, trade became a complex urban phenomenon, in which women were less likely to take part than in the older, local shops that they could not only work in but run. Thus, women's ignorance of the family's finances increased their dependency (as is the case with Amelia Sedley and her mother). At the same time, some traditionally female functions were professionalized and brought under masculine authority—most notably "childbirth, sexuality, and the raising of children" but also health care in general.[25]

An important influence on family life was the fact that women had so few alternatives. Some single women such as Harriet Martineau enjoyed their freedom (Martineau expressed relief at having escaped marriage). But most women had to choose between economic and social marginalization and a marriage in which they had virtually no legal rights. In fact, the Seneca Falls Declaration of 1848 proclaimed married women "civilly dead."[26] And so, economic motives sometimes operated to pressure women into loveless marriages, where abuses of a husband's legal privileges would be more likely: Thackeray's Clara Newcome is but one example.

How often in actual life did a man like Barnes Newcome cast off a mistress and illegitimate children when he married? Examples abound, in life and in literature. Thackeray's father in India did exactly that; Charlotte Brontë's Rochester had several former mistresses and an illegitimate child as well as a mad wife, as he engaged Blanche Ingram in a pseudo-courtship and proposed marriage to Jane Eyre. From *Catherine* on, Thackeray's works reflect the reality that marriage provided social, sexual, and economic advantages for men, whereas it was the only profession open to women and, furthermore, a lottery in which they had little or no recourse if they bought a losing ticket.

Many marriages were indeed happy, as Peterson's book *Family, Love, and Work* reminds us, but happiness in marriage is sometimes compromised by factors external to the marriage itself. Economic dependence, as Wollstonecraft points out, fosters feelings of vulnerability and uselessness: "Confined, then, in cages like the feathered race, they have nothing to do but to plume themselves, and stalk with mock majesty from perch to perch." Thus, a sense of powerlessness may have helped fuel women's considerable involvement in social reform movements. The Women's Christian Temperance Union, and voluntary motherhood and social purity reform societies, all, in Hellerstein's words, "sought to convert men to female ideals of temperance and chastity . . . in the interests of all women. A direct call for egalitarian marriage appeared at mid-century."[27] The "cult of motherhood" formed part of the domestic ideal and served to elide the reality that a poorly educated, dependent, often unhappy woman does not make a good mother. Wollstonecraft knew it, and Thackeray demonstrates it repeatedly. The ideal also served to keep women away from pursuits and occupations that might have satisfied their longing for what Simone de Beauvoir in *The Second Sex* rightly calls "transcendence," that is, participation in human community.

Women's emotional experiences differed with each individual, of course: marriage, children, sexuality, emotional satisfaction, all depended to some extent on individual circumstances. Nineteenth-century sexual attitudes, for example, were far more varied and complex than self-congratulatory twentieth-century stereotypes of Victorian prudery and repression admit, and—as Foucault's *History of Sexuality* implies—perhaps more admirable as well.[28] But broad social patterns and ideology are amenable to some generalizations that make a critique possible. Thackeray's novels present psychologically individuated characters interacting with broad cultural and historical forces. This is why he so frequently employed female characters in unlike pairs (Becky and Amelia, Beatrix and Rachel, Helen and Laura, Ethel and Clara). As different as they are, each woman labors under the same disadvantages: enormous economic pressure to marry; condescending, "gallant," and subtly hostile men; and an ancient tradition of the angel-demon dichotomy that locks women into their respective roles.

As we have seen, the domestic ideal exerted increasingly intense pressure, as women's work became more removed and even remote from the public life of the community. At the same time, the concept of work changed to mean wage labor, and so the unpaid labor of women in their homes could be redefined as instinctual, self-rewarding, and finally as not working at all. But, in another development, the growth of the market economy enabled some women to move out of the home and into public life as nurses and teachers—ironically, by invoking the ideology that pronounced women to be naturally suited to such work. Thackeray's novels reflect these complex realities. *Vanity Fair* is about two women's "careers": after a poor education came a choice between marriage or governessing. And Thackeray's last two novels, *Philip* and *Denis Duval*, feature women characters who work as nurses and midwives. Caroline Gann in *Philip* even employs chloroform (which she carries in her pocket to assist women in childbirth) to "knock out" a threatening adversary.

The female reproductive system, a subject that was critically important and nonetheless virtually taboo, generated many measures regarding women, including the debate over women's education and work. Theories about the fearsome complexity and fragility of this system underlay many of the exclusions and restrictions women encountered in their attempts to enter higher education.[29] Fear of female sexuality sometimes was expressed as outright denial. Obviously, men as well as women were constrained by this gender ideology, and women were sometimes able to manipulate it to their advantage, but it served primarily to bar women from access to power-conferring institutions such as law, medicine, religion, and higher education.

For women, according to Poovey, qualities defined as "naturally" feminine included domesticity, the maternal instinct, selflessness, passivity, a weaker sexual drive, and the innate capacity to serve as man's "moral hope and guide." And yet, such ideals were continually threatened by the emergence of contradictions— women in childbirth, the "most natural and feminine of acts," would express sexual excitement. And the domestic ideal that authorized women to express maternal instincts as nurses and governesses provided them also with an opportunity to be aggressively capable in the public sphere.[30]

There are many remarkable parallels between Poovey's *Uneven Developments* and Thackeray's fiction: both explore maternity, nursing, governessing, the profession of writing, laws that validated male power over women, and the spectrum of restrictions inherent in the idealization of the feminine. Poovey even devotes a chapter to Caroline Norton's rhetoric and another to the Victorian governess. Many of the deductions and conclusions that illuminate her analysis of Victorian gender ideology could have been gleaned from Thackeray's fiction. It is my purpose in this volume to show that, over a century ago, Thackeray's novels were already providing a brilliant analysis of the gender ideology of his age— not merely reproducing the assumptions that authorized the subjection of women but reproducing in order to oppose them.

An Overview of Feminist Positions

In his ability to incorporate conflicting views into his fiction, Thackeray is like Dostoyevsky as Bakhtin describes him:

> [He] possessed an extraordinary gift for hearing the dialogue of his epoch, or, more precisely, for hearing his epoch as a great dialogue. . . . He heard both the loud, recognized, reigning voices of the epoch, . . . as well as voices still weak, ideas not yet fully emerged, latent ideas heard as yet by no one but himself.[31]

The voices that Thackeray heard cannot be broken down into simple feminist and antifeminist categories. Feminism itself has undergone so many historical changes and encompasses today such a variety of schools that some scholars eschew the word *feminism* entirely and prefer terms such as *the woman question, the women's rights movement,* and *the emancipation of women.* Thackeray does not choose among the various feminist theories but consistently incorporates elements of many.

For those readers unfamiliar with the various currents and contradictions of the feminist theoretical debate, a brief overview will be helpful. Rosemary Radford Reuther's *Sexism and God-Talk* provides one of the clearest analyses. Reuther categorizes all views on the relations between men and women into three major groups: romantic, liberal, and eschatological. *Romantics,* in Reuther's analysis, are united in their view that the differences between male and female are "natural." Conservative romantics believe that woman's "nature" is fragile and that women best preserve their qualities of altruism and purity by avoiding the world of competition and power and staying in the home. Some conservative romantics believe that it is natural for men to rule women; others would argue merely that women and men should have separate spheres in which each rules. Reformist romantics, on the other hand, argue that women's innate virtues should be brought into the public sphere in order to help reform corrupt (masculine) social institutions. We can see here how easily the language of romanticism can be invoked to advocate reformist feminism, which urges that women be given the opportunity to "clean up" society and to bring their "nurturing" talents to schools, hospitals, and political institutions. Because romantic feminists believe that women have peaceful natures, for example, "peace on earth represent[s] the millennial vision of reformist-romantic feminism at its highest." But this is not the end of the romantic spectrum. Radical romanticism, as Reuther describes it, is "pessimistic about the possibilities of converting male nature to female goodness." Thus, radical romantic feminism "repudiates male culture . . . and withdraws into the female sphere as a separatist enclave of female values."[32]

Reuther's second major category, *liberalism*, differs from romanticism in that it "rejects the classical tradition that identified nature or the order of creation with patriarchy." In liberalism, "All human beings, male and female, share a common human nature, characterized by reason and moral conscience. . . . From this . . . flows [*sic*] equal rights in society." Male privilege, liberalism asserts, is based on historical injustice, which has distorted the original equality of all people, and on false concepts of male superiority. Thus it is *equality* that is "mandated by nature itself."[33]

Ruether's third category, the *eschatological*, provides a useful approach to Thackeray, whose extremely pious Evangelical mother constantly attempted to influence his ideas. Mrs. Carmichael-Smyth did not effect the conversion she intended, but she did contribute to his understanding of sexuality and morality. Evangelical Protestantism such as Thackeray's mother practiced worked to encourage the development of an ethic of internalized moral authority and "personal questioning of goals and achievements" in the first half of the century that in turn led to an emphasis on the importance of education in the second half.[34]

Some elements of his mother's thinking have emerged in Thackeray's works as what Reuther terms eschatological feminism, which, like patriarchal antifeminism, equates the subordination of women with the Fall. However, it differs from patriarchal antifeminism in that it does not view the Fall as proof of women's inferiority, nor does it equate women's subordination with divine justice, as punishment for Eve's role. Rather, the subordination of women is viewed as a part of our suffering and sinful mortal existence: "Whether divinely mandated or the result of sin, patriarchy is of the nature of historical existence." Thus, eschatological feminism tends to accept the inequality of men and women as inevitable, to be transcended only in heaven. It insists on spiritual equality but "has no message of equality of women in the world." It invites women not "to change the world, but to leave it."[35]

Such views characterize certain pious women in Thackeray's works: characters such as Madame de Florac in *The Newcomes,* who has achieved a saintly resignation to her sufferings, yet still can ask, "Is it written eternally that men are to make slaves of us?"[36] Much of *Vanity Fair* serves as reiteration of the idea, expressed in Ecclesiastes, that suffering and sorrow, including the particular sorrows of women, are an inescapable part of mortal life. Thus, Thackeray shares with eschatological feminism the sense that a patriarchal order is immoral, and perhaps at times, he also shares in its resignation, its reluctance to attempt political change.

Thackeray avoids aligning himself with any single feminist theory, however, in part because he avoids all systematic approaches, and in part because none of the approaches outlined above contains all of the truth. Linda Alcoff's fine essay "Cultural Feminism versus Post-Structuralism" describes the strengths and weaknesses of each kind of feminist thought by contrasting what she terms cultural feminism and poststructuralism. According to Alcoff, "cultural feminists" define and appraise women according to their known attributes and activities. Thus, a lack of aggression may be reified into peacefulness. Cultural feminists include those who subscribe to essentialist definitions of women based on female physiology as well as those who look to feminine culture and tradition for the source of "female essence." Cultural feminism has benefited women by suggesting the genuinely positive attributes of women's culture, but as Alcoff points out, any feminist theory that attempts to define woman necessarily invokes "a homogeneous, unproblematized, and ahistorical conception of woman." Such universalizing conceptions can validate the dominant culture's assumptions about gender and support a normative definition: "cultural feminism . . . . is in danger of solidifying an important bulwark for sexist oppression: the belief in an innate 'womanhood' to which we must all adhere lest we be deemed inferior or not 'true' women."[37]

A fundamental problem in cultural feminism is that any working definitions of "Woman" have been "overdetermined" by male supremacist culture. John Stuart Mill recognized that no one "knows, or can know, the nature of the two sexes, as long as they have only been seen in their present relation to one another. . . . What is now called the nature of women is an eminently artificial thing—the result of forced repression in some directions, unnatural stimulation in others." Consequently, poststructuralists reject essentialist definitions of women to argue that humans are determined by social discourse systems. "Woman," they argue, is a socially constructed fiction that feminists must dismantle. Although poststructuralists have been a positive force in the women's movement, in that they have demonstrated some of the ways in which social discourse constructs gender, yet (Alcoff points out) poststructuralist feminism "threatens to wipe out feminism itself": it is not enough to dismantle the concept of woman, for feminists must address the realities of women's lives and maintain a sense of what a better world would be like.[38] Thus, the two dominant tendencies in feminist theory, essentialism and nominalism, are both useful, but both inadequate.

Any solution to the inadequacy of these two approaches must involve consciousness of the historical, biological, and cultural forces at work in human life. It is the self-analytical power of all women, according to Alcoff, to "think about, criticize and alter discourse" that distinguishes the feminist from the antifeminist woman, even if in other respects their lives seem identical. From this consciousness will come an element of self-determination at least in the way we understand our identities, even if other factors cannot be changed. Drawing on the work of Teresa de Lauretis, Alcoff emphasizes that women have this power because each interprets or constructs an identity "'within the horizon of meanings and knowledges available in the culture at given historical moments, a horizon that also includes modes of political commitment and struggle.'"[39]

It is just such a "feminist conceptual horizon" that Thackeray provides. His work testifies that "universal" concepts of womanhood are to some degree culturally determined; he also recognizes that, arbitrary as they may be, cultural definitions cannot easily be escaped by women whose lives are constrained by the actualities of biology and of legal, economic, and social systems that are grounded in, and reinforce, those definitions. Thackeray's works establish a sense of gender that is neither nominalist nor essentialist but furthers our ability to understand gender in its historical dimension in the way Alcoff finally advocates:

> Gender is not a . . . given thing but is, instead, a posit or construct, formalizable in a nonarbitrary way through a matrix of habits, prac-

tices, and discourses. . . . it seems both possible and desirable to construe a gendered subjectivity in relation to concrete habits, practices, and discourses while at the same time recognizing the fluidity of these.

Although worlds removed from Thackeray in style, Alcoff's words aptly summarize his intellectual position. Even Coventry Patmore, best known to feminists as author of *The Angel in the House,* recognized Thackeray's prescience: "We are all of us disciples of that school of the new science of moral anatomy, of which Mr. Thackeray is the master; and it is emphatically true of him, as of all other great writers, that he is only 'outrunning the age in the direction which it is spontaneously taking.'"[40]

1/ The Formative Years

A perilous trade, indeed, is that of a man who has to
bring his tears and laughter, his recollections, his personal griefs and joys, his private thoughts and feelings to
market, to write them on paper, and then sell them for
money.

—*English Humourists:* "Sterne" (*Works* 11: 319)

[C]ould we know the man's feelings as well as the author's thoughts—how interesting most books would
be!—more interesting than merry. I suppose harlequin's
face behind his mask is always grave, if not melancholy.

—*Pendennis*

As a young man, Thackeray endured years of anxiety, sorrow,
loss, and failure. But this is not to say he was continually miserable;
despite the troubles that pursued him, Thackeray managed to
dine well and in good company, to travel, and to develop his remarkable gift with words. The title of the first volume of Gordon
Ray's biography, *The Uses of Adversity,* sums up one of the consistent
patterns in Thackeray's life: his genius throve in adversity. Whenever he encountered people or endured events that gave him
pain, he turned that pain into fresh and original insights. His
wife's madness and its consequences were among the most powerful influences on his thought, but many other factors contributed
to the whole, including the loss of his fortune, which drove him to
writing for a living, and the more particular fact that he wrote for
Fraser's and *Punch,* which helped him early on to develop his gifts
for satire, parody, and irony. Part of Thackeray's political liberalism stems from what Ray terms the discrepancy between "the treatment that he expected from society and the treatment that he received."[1] His experience of comparative poverty, after having been
raised a gentleman, made him both an insider and an outsider, a
snob and the receiver of snubs.

Love and Family, Ideals and Reality

The story of his mother's frustrated love haunts many of Thackeray's works—most poignantly in Madame de Florac's lifelong unfulfilled love for Colonel Newcome—and is always presented in a way that condemns the marriage market. His mother's story goes some way toward explaining why one of Thackeray's recurring preoccupations is the "stormy region of longing passion unfulfilled"[2]—but of course his own life supplied sufficient examples.

In the winter of 1807–1808, Thackeray's mother, Anne Becher, fell in love with an "ineligible" younger son, Henry Carmichael-Smyth. When Anne, then fifteen, refused to stop seeing him, her grandmother locked Anne in her room. Anne secretly attempted to send Henry letters, but she was found out. Anne's grandmother told her Henry had died, and she returned Henry's letters unopened with a note stating that Anne no longer cared for him. Anne's silence would have appeared to confirm the lie. Several months later, the grieving Anne was sent to India to seek a more acceptable husband, and in 1810 she married Thackeray's father, Richmond Makepeace Thackeray, son of Amelia and William Thackeray and wealthy secretary to the East India Company's Calcutta Board of Revenue.

Two years later, Anne and Henry met again in India: Richmond had invited him home for dinner. After their shocked meeting, Richmond was informed of what had happened, and in some manner not explained in the family chronicles, he was never to be the same toward his wife again. Three years later Richmond Thackeray died, and Anne married her first love.[3] Ironically, after all the suffering that had been caused by his apparent lack of prospects, Henry inherited a handsome fortune.

If Richmond's changed feelings toward Anne were caused by jealousy, this would have been an example for Thackeray of the sexual double standard. Before Anne arrived in India, Richmond had been keeping an Indian mistress, Charlotte Rudd, and had an illegitimate daughter, Sarah. East India Company rules forbade marriage to Indian women, but what Gordon Ray calls "concubinage" was so common that by 1782 the British had found it necessary to set up an orphanage for the children of such unions. Anne Thackeray was named Sarah Rudd's guardian in her husband's will. In addition, Henry Carmichael-Smyth's brother Charles had a "natural" son whom he brought back to England,

and Richmond Thackeray's sister married a judge with eight illegitimate children. These Englishwomen were not naive; they must have understood their position in the marriage market.

Thackeray was to use his family's Indian background frequently. His father's situation is reminiscent of *Vanity Fair*'s Jos, whose wealth comes from exploiting the Indian populace, and whose greedy consumption of food and drink has struck some critics (Dorothy Van Ghent, for example) as a metonym for the British empire. *Vanity Fair* also contains pathetic references to young girls being sent to India to hunt for husbands, and the elder Sedley's coarse jokes about a "black Mrs. Sedley" imply the author's condemnation of the racial and sexual imperialism embedded in Thackeray's own family history.

One of the most important forces in developing Thackeray's understanding of gender issues was the central sorrow of his life, his wife's insanity. At twenty-three, Thackeray fell in love with Isabella Shawe—charming, gentle, seemingly without passion—but he believed that she would blossom under his tutelage. On 3 July 1836, he wrote her, "Your own heart has never as yet had fair play, and [at home] where your words are questioned rudely, and your feelings scarcely permitted to shew themselves, there is no wonder that a certain habit of coldness & indecision should have sprung up" (*Letters* 1: 316). From the beginning, Thackeray's attitude combined indulgence, perhaps even a bit of condescension, with insight: here, with an empathy worthy of Mary Wollstonecraft or George Eliot, he ascribes Isabella's faults to her upbringing. At first, William and Isabella Thackeray were happy, but gradually Isabella's emotional dependence became an issue. One of Thackeray's sketches of early married life shows him walking with a child-sized woman (see figure 2). Thackeray complains in his letters that she often interrupted his writing, and her continued helplessness became more and more disillusioning. The cycle of unhappiness was completed by the increasing frequency of Thackeray's absences from home and perhaps by his emotional absence as well.

After the birth of their first child, Anne, Isabella became despondent, but her mother had suffered similar postpartum depressions, and when Isabella recovered it was assumed that all was well. However, their second child died after only eight months of life, and again Isabella became despondent. Again she rallied with

2. Thackeray and wife: A caricature of early married life
(Ray, *Uses of Adversity* [following] 238).

time, however, or so it seemed to Thackeray, and her third pregnancy was healthy and happy. But after the birth of the baby Harriet, Isabella sank again into depression, and this time she never
recovered.

In 1840, under great financial and emotional pressure, Thackeray decided to travel to Belgium to write a series of essays similar

to *The Paris Sketchbook*. Readers seldom forget the haunting scene Thackeray painted of that leave-taking, when Isabella, inexplicably, began to laugh (*Letters* 1: 475). Thackeray did not become aware of the extent of Isabella's mental illness until later in 1840, when he took her to Ireland in the hope that Mrs. Shawe could help her daughter. During the passage on the boat, Isabella lowered herself into the sea from a water closet, and she was spotted some time later, floating Ophelia-like, indifferent to danger. According to Monsarrat, this was only one of many suicide attempts.[4] In October 1840, Thackeray looked back on that period and wrote:

> O my God what a dream it is! I hardly believe it now I write. She was found floating on her back. . . . This it was that told me her condition   I see now she had been ill for weeks before, and yet I was obstinately blind to her state, and Powell & the surgeons must tell me that there was not the slightest reason to call a physician, that nothing was the matter with her. (*Letters* 1: 483)

Thackeray went to extraordinary lengths to help Isabella and was always to regret his earlier neglect. Another significant incident, which Thackeray did not know about at the time, was more ominous. One day, while walking on the seashore with her daughter Annie, Isabella pushed her child into the water in what seemed an attempt to drown her. Then, again for no apparent reason, she pulled Annie back onto the beach. Thackeray was to include a similar scene in his last, unfinished novel, *Denis Duval*.

Thackeray did know, however, that Isabella was a danger to herself, and for several months he tried to take care of her himself rather than commit her to an institution. His letters speak of long, miserable days with frightened children, a demented wife, and bitter tongue-lashings from a mother-in-law who refused to help him because, she said, he had taken away a sane daughter and brought back an empty used-up shell of a woman. He wrote of sleeping with a ribbon tied from his waist to hers, so that if Isabella got out of bed, Thackeray would be awakened to continue his watch over her. When the strain became too much, he hired someone to help him, and he marveled at how cheerfully a woman could cope, for ten francs a week, with work that had broken him. Finally, the difficulties of his life and the hopelessness of Isabella's condition forced Thackeray to place her in a private home.

Isabella's insanity is associated with what seems a complete absence of self-regard—a "feminine" quality that may have first manifested itself charmingly in her gentle helplessness and deference, but that Thackeray later was to recognize as an "amiable slavishness" much like Amelia Sedley's in *Vanity Fair*. Thackeray described a visit to Isabella in her new residence: "She kissed me at first very warmly and with tears in her eyes, then she went away from me, as if she felt she was unworthy of having such a God of a husband. God help her" (*Letters* 2: 3).

Isabella's illness had many consequences, direct and indirect. First, it made Thackeray dependent on the assistance of women. Appeals to Isabella's mother were rebuffed, but several women helped him generously. His step-sister Mary Carmichael provided a loan (as Laura Bell, Ethel Newcome, and Caroline Gann all provide money to young men in the novels). His servant Brodie postponed her wedding to care for the family. And his mother spent years helping Thackeray to raise his daughters (though not without many volatile religious disagreements).

Another effect of Isabella's "living death" was that, despite his mother's continuous pleas to let her take full charge of the girls, Thackeray reserved to himself some of the parental roles usually filled by a mother. He dismissed or lost a number of governesses because they were to his mind not intelligent enough to teach his daughter Annie, who he feared was "going to be a man of genius" (*Letters* 2: 240–41). In fact, he had so much difficulty in keeping a governess that he developed something of a shady reputation in that respect. Thus, when Charlotte Brontë dedicated the second edition of *Jane Eyre* to Thackeray, it was said that *Jane Eyre* had been written by one of Thackeray's rejected governesses, and that he, with his mad wife (of whom Brontë knew nothing when she dedicated the book), was Rochester. The incident was embarrassing to both Brontë and Thackeray. At issue in Thackeray's dealings with governesses were questions of women's intelligence and the system of education in which their minds had been formed—a system Thackeray frequently compares to Chinese foot-binding. Thackeray became more aware than most Victorian fathers of the cultural "programming" involved in raising a girl. He did not wish to raise "liberated" daughters—he certainly did not want them to be like American women, he wrote—but he did recognize that for his older daughter to use her remarkable intelligence to the full would make her something of a "man of genius."

A third effect of Thackeray's "bachelorhood" was social. Thackeray was naturally attracted to society, and even in the early years of his marriage, he seemed to do his best work in clubs and hotel rooms. After Isabella's breakdown his home was empty, and he happily accepted any dinner invitation, preferring even the dullest company to eating alone. And there was a deeper need for intelligent women's companionship, which drew him to the drawing rooms and dinner tables of the best London hostesses, among them Anne Procter, Jane Brookfield, and Caroline Norton.

His heart, which "priceless jewel" he longed to confer on someone (*Letters* 2: 813), needed a loving relationship with a woman, but Thackeray was restrained from actually having an affair by several things. First, he had moral reservations about sexual liaisons outside marriage. He prayed, in his journal and letters, for the power to control his passions and become a good father and mother to his children, to "give them good and honest example: keep them out of misfortunes wch result from my Fault: and towards them enable me to discharge the private duties of life" (*Letters* 2: 31). Lust was one of the temptations (in addition to drinking, gambling, and keeping late hours) that he named in his diary as he resolved to discipline his life and do his duty for his family. Thackeray wrote his mother that if some woman did accept that inestimable treasure, his heart, he would despise her, and "the very day of the sacrifice would be the end of the attachment" (*Letters* 2: 813). He was torn between skepticism—recognizing the hypocritical and even in some ways immoral characteristics of the Victorian sexual ethos—and admiration for the moral and social order it was intended to promote. Like his Evangelical mother, he deplored the sexual double standard that endowed men with a kind of glory for "ruining" women; some of his works make clear the devastating price women paid when men "conquered."

But there was also what Ray calls a "Bohemian side" to Thackeray's life (which will never be known, but which he may have paid a high price for), and as a young man he contracted a stricture of the urethra that may have been caused by gonorrhea. His "old enemy . . . the hydraulics" caused him to suffer for the rest of his life. These hydraulics problems, along with anxiety, overwork, spells that were probably recurring episodes of typhoid and malaria, and his penchant for dining out and "jollifying," all led to his dying early at the age of fifty-two.[5]

After Isabella's illness, Thackeray transferred much of his need for affection to Jane Brookfield, the wife of his friend William. As Thackeray gradually fell in love with Jane, she encouraged him by speaking of her own unhappiness, and Thackeray came to feel that she was being badly treated by her husband. Gradually his friendship with William changed to contempt and a mutual antagonism fueled by jealousy, although their outward behavior remained cordial. Thackeray's fictional portraits of unhappy marriage tend to side with the women's perspectives, and it is important to recognize how strongly his perspective was influenced by Jane Brookfield. Rachel Castlewood's marriage in *Henry Esmond,* for example, is based on the Brookfield marriage. Indeed, Thackeray took a certain pleasure in the public controversy over *Esmond,* remarking, "How mad poor Tomkins [William Brookfield] must be at the press selecting those passages. He will treat her better after though."[6]

It is not clear whether Jane Brookfield ever loved Thackeray—she seems to have been too fearful or too cautious to resist her husband's will for long, and in 1851 she wrote Thackeray a letter breaking off their friendship because her husband had so ordered it. Thackeray felt he had been taken for a fool, that he had trusted in someone who had never cared for him. Much of the rage and anguish he felt at that time manifest themselves in *Esmond,* first as a loss of faith in romantic or sexual love, and second, in the sense the book gives of Esmond's being either disingenuous or imperceptive regarding his own relationships with women. But on some level, Thackeray knew that the break with Jane Brookfield was for the best. Neither of them had ever intended to abandon home and children, or to shatter hard-won social and (in Thackeray's case) professional standings. Thackeray well knew that for them love would not thrive in conditions of social isolation or financial hardship—and probably sexual guilt. Until the break in 1851, however, Thackeray's friendship with Jane Brookfield provided him with warm admiration, an intimate friendship, intellectual companionship, and personal knowledge of the woman's position in an unhappy marriage, which all helps to explain why Thackeray—who, after his ordeals with his wife, his mother-in-law, and Jane Brookfield, might easily have become a bitter misogynist (men have done so with less cause)—in fact became a member of the "women's party" in his writings.

SOCIAL AND PROFESSIONAL CONTEXTS

Thackeray's relations with women are not the only biographical facts to be taken into account, however. His spirit was shaped also by considerations of class, money, and the necessity of finding a profession. Raised as a gentleman, with gentlemanly expectations of a lifelong supply of theater tickets and new kid gloves, Thackeray began by spending at least £157 in his first term at Cambridge. Then unavoidable misfortune and a series of reckless actions drove him into a poverty that was to spur his writing until the success of *Vanity Fair* relieved the worst of his financial anxieties.

His weakness for gambling, added to a taste for good things, drained some of his fortune. One morning, while still an undergraduate at Cambridge, he withdrew £1,500 from the family account to pay gambling debts. Leaving Cambridge after a year and a half, undecided about what to do with his life, Thackeray traveled to Weimar, continuing the disastrous "career of falling in with charming rogues," both male and female, that had caused him so much trouble at Cambridge. In 1831 he returned to London to study law but found the work entirely alien to his temperament. He described it as "one of the most cold blooded prejudiced pieces of invention that ever a man was slave to" (*Letters* 1: 182). Gradually his resolve evaporated, he lapsed once more into gambling, and, finding himself in the hands of the lenders, he became one himself.[7]

In 1832 the great Indian banking houses collapsed, and his fortune, which Monsarrat believes amounted to £11,325—money left him by his father, which he had expected to inherit when he reached the age of twenty-one—all either evaporated in the collapse or was stolen by his trustee uncle. And yet, he wrote a year later, "I believe I ought to thank heaven for making me poor" (*Letters* 1: 271). Thackeray continually grappled with the "dark side" of the values he held most dear. His training for a life of gentlemanly ease had given him all the benefits of a privileged member of a powerful empire—a good education, a love of art and literature, travel, and a broad cultural and historical perspective. And all those benefits led, in this thoughtful man, to a questioning of the system that could provide benefits to only a few and leave so many others in a state of ignorance and misery.

As a young man, Thackeray called himself a Republican who wanted to see the "bloated aristocracy blasted to the . . . winds," and for some six months Thackeray wrote for the radical *Constitutional,* but unlike his parents, Thackeray could not long adhere to a stance of political radicalism.[8] Privately he came to feel the Radicals "bigoted and despotic" and complained that they forgot the value of civilization. Thackeray worked with the Whigs in support of the Reform Bill of 1832 at the same time that he admired and defended the Tory Duke of Wellington. With what Monsarrat calls his "exceptionally pronounced doubleness of vision," Thackeray found the revolutionaries tyrannical, the Whigs blind and selfish, and the Tories snobs, fitting targets for his ridicule: when Lady Londonderry complained in the *New Monthly Magazine* that few things are more annoying than being awakened by one's maid at four in the morning, Thackeray pointed out in *Punch* that the maid might have been even more annoyed at having to rise at three.[9]

In his brief flirtation with politics, Thackeray came to reject any system of ideas that fostered complacency and political if not religious "excommunication" of those who disagreed. He viewed revolutions as the substitution of one kind of tyranny for another. He believed, as Pen says in *Pendennis,* "Make a faith or a dogma absolute, and persecution becomes a logical consequence" (ch. 61: 646). Thackeray's forays into politics gradually honed his views so that by the time he ran for Parliament in 1857, he could run only as an Independent. Through all this, his youthful high spirits seem undimmed. He still loved the theater and enjoyed a rich social life, including the company of some talented, intelligent men and women such as Fanny Kemble, Harriet Martineau, Arthur Hallam, Edward Fitzgerald, Alexander Kinglake, and Alfred Tennyson.

Freed by poverty and misfortune from the demands of respectability, Thackeray plunged into the relatively disreputable careers of journalism and art. He bought a newspaper, the *National Standard,* wrote prodigiously for it, and at the end of three months, losing money with every issue, shut it down. For a while, Thackeray turned to art, engaging teachers in London and then in Paris, where he met Isabella Shawe. His relationship with Isabella was soon to be as disastrous as his professional career, but he chose her in spite of (or perhaps unconsciously because of) her apparent weaknesses and faults, just as he had in some ways precipitated the financial disasters that required him to develop his talents and intelligence. These events forced him to write, and they infused his work with the tone of ironic self-criticism that is so characteristic of his style. It was while he was most passionately attached to Isabella and hoping to marry her that Thackeray began to define himself as an author. In 1836, he published *Flore et Zephyr,* and through his step-father's generosity in supplying his salary, had himself appointed Paris correspondent for a radical daily, the *Constitutional.* Then Thackeray returned to Paris and, flying in the face of Mrs. Shawe's hostility and Isabella's strange passivity, married Isabella Shawe on 20 August 1836.

In both marriage and work, Thackeray came to question his early enthusiasms. His writing for the radical *Constitutional,* now more financially necessary than ever, concealed a growing disenchantment with radical politics, and his early enthusiasm for his charming but childish and passive wife gradually eroded too, so that soon Thackeray came to question why it was that men preferred "milk-and-water women" (*Letters* 1: 460). If Isabella was Thackeray's Amelia Sedley, he was soon to meet his Becky Sharp, however. The years from 1837 to 1847 saw Isabella gradually decline into insanity, and Thackeray took up a variety of lines of writing in a desperate attempt to stay afloat financially.

While writing for the conservative *Fraser's Magazine,* Thackeray met Caroline Norton, a probable "original" for Lady Lyndon, Becky Sharp, and Clara Pulleyn Newcome, and a key figure in reforming English laws regarding marriage and divorce, child custody, and married women's property.[10] Norton was to provide Thackeray with much material for his novels.

Thackeray's letters and diaries provide some glimpses of their relationship. In 1845, Norton arranged for Thackeray to dine with Lord Melbourne, who thought he was a clergyman. In 1847, Thackeray wrote to thank Norton for a book, to apologize for making impertinent remarks about her appearance in his "Grumble about the *Christmas Books,*" and to promise a visit (*Letters* 2: 229, 263–65). In the same year, Jane Brookfield advised her husband against accepting an offer to share a house with certain friends, warning him against the effect that such company would have on his reputation as a minister, and significantly (perhaps in jealousy) pairing Norton's name with Thackeray's: "Cannot you call up visions of cosy little Sunday dinners with *Mrs. Norton*, Mr. Thackeray, & Mr. and Mrs. Wigan?"[11] Thackeray's diary records a remark made shortly after 10 March 1847 by "C.N.," presumably Norton, which is very much in the spirit of *Vanity Fair:*

> I tried in vain to convince the fine folks at W. Fox's that revolution was upon us: that we were wicked in our scorn of the people—they all thought there was poverty and discontent to be sure, but that they were pretty good in themselves; that powder and liveries were very decent & proper though certainly absurd—the footmen themselves would not give them up C.N. said. (*Letters* 2: 30–31)

And in 1848, Thackeray attended a party at the Duke of Devonshire's with Norton, "she sitting bodkin in her own brougham, and indeed there are very few more beautiful bodkins in the world" (*Letters* 2: 373 n. 93). Lionel Stevenson maintains that Norton "pushed" Thackeray in his career as writer, by introducing him to influential people, and states that Thackeray was still seeing her as late as 1862.[12]

Existing evidence indicates that Thackeray's relationship with Norton was a friendship, spiced perhaps with a feeling of mutual attraction, but not a love affair. Both had other, deep emotional involvements at various times—Norton with Sidney Herbert, and Thackeray with Jane Brookfield—and although Norton delighted in being unconventional, she was more interested in society than in seduction. And Thackeray's letters and diaries indicate that for him, a sexual relationship would have ended the friendship. However, Norton was a witty, intelligent, and elegant woman whose dinners must have been delightful to the lonely, restless, and cash-strapped Thackeray. Lady Eastlake remarked once that Norton used her eyes "ably and wickedly" and later went on to describe Norton's charm in terms that evoke Becky Sharp and indicate why Thackeray would enjoy Norton's company:

> She is a beautiful and gifted woman: her talents are of the highest order, and she has carefully cultivated them—has read deeply, has a fine memory, and wit only to be found in a Sheridan. No one can compare with her in telling a story—so pointed, so happy, and so easy; but she is rather a professed story teller. . . . [S]he is a perpetual actress, consummately studying and playing her part, and that

always the attempt to fascinate—she cares not whom. Occasionally I got her to talk thinkingly, and then she said things which showed great thought and observation.[13]

Alice Acland makes the parallels between Becky and Caroline explicit:

> In the almost flamboyant effect of her personality [Caroline Norton] was very far removed from the ideal feminine type of the day. The pure, gentle, timid, docile woman—a type soon to be crystallised in the person of Amelia Sedley—held a high place then in the public imagination. It was impossible for Caroline to model herself on the lines of such doves with folded wings. And because she could not pretend to be an Amelia Sedley, many people thought she must be a Becky Sharp instead.[14]

Norton's satirical remarks against the sacred icons of nineteenth-century England must have struck a responsive chord in Thackeray. And so it is not surprising (especially in light of other influences such as his wife's insanity and Jane Brookfield's unhappy marriage) that Thackeray, captivated by this Becky Sharp with a heart, took up the causes that Norton fought for and made her a recurring figure in his fiction.

Caroline Norton was indeed a subject for literature. Allusions to her life and character appear in a number of works, and Meredith's *Diana of the Crossways* (1885), based on Norton's life, invokes Thackeray's spirit in the first chapter:

> A great modern writer, of clearest eye and head, now departed, capable in activity of presenting thoughtful women, thinking men, groaned over his puppetry, that he dared not animate them, flesh though they were, with the fires of positive brainstuff. He could have done it, and he is of the departed! Had he dared, he would (for he was Titan enough) have raised the art in dignity on a level with history.[15]

In 1827 Caroline Sheridan, then nineteen, married George Norton "for practical reasons."[16] Her mother was a widow with seven children, and he seemed a good match in the "marriage market" that Thackeray so frequently attacks. The marriage soon fell apart. Beginning in about 1830, William Lamb, Lord Melbourne, then Home Secretary, became a daily visitor to Norton's home. Melbourne arranged a government post for George Norton, which he was to enjoy as a sinecure for the rest of his life. (One is of course reminded of Becky, Rawdon, and Lord Steyne.) But in 1836, impelled by jealousy, greed, and political expediency, George filed suit against Melbourne for "criminal conversation." We will probably never know what Caroline's relationship with Melbourne was. At the trial, George Norton's witnesses were so patently unreliable that Melbourne was acquitted by a jury that never even left the box to deliberate. Today, Caroline's cry of "I am innocent!" haunts her writings, just as Becky's cry haunts the conclusion of *Vanity Fair*.

Norton's situation demonstrated the powerlessness of women under the law. Because she had been judged innocent in the "criminal conversation" trial, George could not divorce her (it was necessary to prove a wife's adultery to obtain either an ecclesiastical separation or a civil divorce). And because Norton, afraid of losing her children, had returned to George after he had been violent and unfaithful, she had "condoned" his behavior and could not divorce him. Years later, in *English Laws for Women*, she wrote, "These boys having been the gleam of happiness in my home, it was not to be supposed I would give them up without a struggle, because it was so 'written in the bond' of English law."[17] So, instead, she fought the law.

Caroline's campaign was conducted on two fronts. Socially, she used her influence with literary and political men to enlist supporters such as Serjeant Talfourd, who in 1836 (the year in which Thackeray married) introduced an Infant Custody Bill into the House of Commons that offered mothers of children under seven the right to petition for a custody hearing—a limited improvement but a beginning. To gain political support, she wrote and published at her own expense a pamphlet entitled *Separation of Mother and Child by the Custody of Infants Considered* (1837). It was, in Acland's words, the "First blow in her long battle for legal reform."[18] In August 1838, while Talfourd's bill was being debated in the House of Commons, Norton was attacked in the *British and Foreign Review* as a "she-devil" who was sleeping with Talfourd in exchange for his support. In February 1839, Nathaniel Ogle responded with a long article defending Norton and advocating the Infant Custody Bill, which appeared in *Fraser's* simultaneously with portions of Thackeray's *Catherine*.

In the summer of 1839, the Infant Custody Bill became law.

Women had been granted an infinitesimal opportunity to keep their own children, but Norton's victory was not to benefit her at all: George had sent their children to his sister's home in Scotland, where the new law did not apply. Norton wrote in *English Laws for Women* that one son was flogged for reading a letter from her, and the other was stripped, tied to a bedpost, and whipped by George's sister for some other offense. Tragically, the youngest boy died after a fall from a horse while his mother was still struggling to gain custody. In a letter to a friend, she reflected, "It may be sinful to think bitterly at such a time. . . . But it is not in the strength of human nature not to think, 'This might not have happened had I watched over them!'"[19] Thackeray was to include the incident, with some modification, in *Barry Lyndon.*

That Ogle's defense of Norton and the Infant Custody Bill appeared in *Fraser's* in February 1839, simultaneously with Thackeray's *Catherine,* epitomizes the connections between Thackeray's personal and professional lives: while his sweet feminine Isabella (forerunner to Amelia) was sinking into madness, his combative colleague Norton (forerunner to Becky) was battling for the rights of women, in the papers and in the courts. As metonym for female rage and mental derangement and as satire on literary representations of women, *Catherine* provided implicit commentary on the social system in which Thackeray found himself mired. W. C. Brownell remarked once that Thackeray had "the most interesting personality, perhaps, that has expressed itself in prose."[20] As we begin to know that personality better, we come to agree with Elizabeth Drew, that "[i]t is impossible as we read Thackeray today not to be convinced that he had the greatest contempt for the opinion of his day as to what made a 'good woman.'"[21]

2/ Early Works
A Foundation in Parody

For a man, remorse under these circumstances is perhaps uncommon. No stigma affixes on *him* for betraying a woman. . . . The game, in fact, and the glory, such as it is, is all his, and the punishment alone falls on her.
—*Catherine* (*Works* 24: 39–40)

This supreme act of scoundrelism has man permitted to himself—to deceive women. . . . [I]ndeed one may sympathise with the advocates of women's rights.
. . . We have read of that wretched woman of old whom the pious Pharisees were for stoning incontinently; but we don't hear that they made any outcry against *the man* who was concerned in the crime. Where was he? Happy, no doubt, and easy in mind, and regaling some choice friends over a bottle with the history of his success.
— *Shabby Genteel Story* (*Works* 18: 52)

Every man imprisons his wife to a certain degree; the world would be in a pretty condition if women were allowed to quit home and return to it whenever they had a mind. In watching over my wife, Lady Lyndon, I did no more than exercise the legitimate authority, which awards honour and obedience to every husband.
—*Barry Lyndon*

His early writings reveal Thackeray's development on two fronts. As book reviewer, editor, and writer of some 450 pieces (sent to at least twenty-two periodicals), particularly as a "regular" for *Punch* and *Fraser's,* he developed an apparently innate gift for parody into a critique of language, style, and voice in the novel.[1]

At the same time, Thackeray's understanding of the situation of women deepened and grew against a background in which his wife sank ever deeper into depression, while friends such as Caroline Norton and Lady Morgan succeeded in making women's status a major public issue.

The path that Thackeray follows may be summarized as leading from a rejection of the "romanticalities" of much of the popular fiction of his day toward a redefinition of realism (influenced to some degree by the work of contemporary women writers) that culminated in both a strong sense of what makes fiction "true" and a recognition that much bad fiction, bad morality, and bad law include as a fundamental element the devaluation of women. Thackeray's gift for parody emerged, according to Wheatley, from "his sensitivity to the connections between popular romances and social order." *Barry Lyndon* represents the culmination of Thackeray's early parodies, and so deeply immersed is it in the language and assumptions of his culture that many people thought Thackeray meant Barry to be likable. It is my purpose in this chapter to explore the factors in Thackeray's life and in the development of his art that brought him to such a point that, by 1844, he could write a fierce parody linking a literary subgenre—the criminal romance—to laws, customs, and beliefs that gave men almost unchecked power over women. It is true, as Wheatley points out, that "Parody . . . is both conceptually and biographically fundamental to Thackeray's career as a novelist."[2]

THACKERAY'S PHILOSOPHY OF THE NOVEL

> Many points of view, many typical moods which are given superior body and form in the novels appear in the reviews, burlesques, and narratives which make the bulk of his early journalism. There is no sudden break in the stream of his development; he did mature, however, and the process of that growth is worth following.[3]

Thackeray's *Fraser's* reviews and even *Catherine* itself join with other pieces in the magazine to articulate and shape a philosophy of fiction, a "*Fraserian* perspective," as it were, that Thackeray found congenial, and mined and developed. Miriam Thrall points out that the Fraserians delighted in "ridiculing in particular the mixture of unsound moralizing with flamboyant romance" and "lampoon[ing] the tendency in the fiction of the day to ascribe refinements and sensibilities to a character in the underworld, without regard for either reality or common sense."[4] Peter Shillingsburg notes that Thackeray sometimes served as agent or editor for friends (even for his mother on one occasion), and one of the pieces he submitted to *Fraser's* on behalf of a friend has been mistakenly attributed to Thackeray himself. This piece, and another that has been linked to it by an internal allusion, while not entirely "Thackerayan," do however provide a window into Thackeray's intellectual world. These are "Hints for a History of Highwaymen" (March 1834), and "William Ainsworth and *Jack Sheppard*" (February 1840), both by John Hamilton Reynolds.

In his early life Reynolds (1796–1852) was a Romantic poet and friend of Keats. Anne B. Procter, in a letter to Thackeray, recalls Reynolds as a young man: "so merry—so good—working so hard for his Mother & Sisters" (*Letters* 3: 127). Later in life he became a lawyer and satirist and began parodying the Romantics. In 1838 he moved to the Isle of Wight where, the *Dictionary of Literary Biography* tells us, "failing health and failing fortune somewhat soured his temper and sharpened his tongue." In 1840 Thackeray submitted Reynolds's review of *Jack Sheppard* to John Fraser with a note mentioning that "[he] would be a capital aid to your Magazine."

Reynolds begins the *Jack Sheppard* review by reminding the reader that in "Hints for a History of Highwaymen," he had criticized Cooper's *Red Rover* and Byron's *Corsair* as "flattering, pretty pictures of the beastly, brutal bucanier."[5] Now, Reynolds continues, he sees with regret that Ainsworth is doing the same thing: encouraging criminality by investing it "with all the interest and the graces of romance" (228). Reynolds compares Ainsworth's characterization of Jonathan Wilde in *Jack Sheppard* to Fielding's *Jonathan Wild* (another source for Thackeray's *Barry Lyndon*) by juxtaposing lengthy passages from both books. He does not comment on these at first, except to say that although it may not be "fair to bring Fielding into the ring against Ainsworth . . . it was the latter who provoked the challenge" (236). Ainsworth's book, writes Reynolds, is "marvelous, and terrible to read," "sometimes ineffably laughable," and "rather droll" (240). For in Ainsworth, Jonathan Wild does things in earnest—for example, "snivelling over recollections of bygone love"—that in works by artists "who know what they are about," he is made to burlesque (240). "We must insist on it," writes Reynolds, "that our thieves are nothing more than thieves, whom it is hopeless to attempt gilding over with the graces and glories of chivalry" (240).

Reynolds contrasts Ainsworth's description of Jack Sheppard's last meeting with his mother with that given in the *Newgate Calendar*. In Ainsworth, when Jack Sheppard knocks on his mother's door, she, thinking that Sheppard is a man who intends to ravish her, stabs herself and lies dying on the floor as she takes a pathetic, lingering, final leave of her son. But the version of this incident given in the *Newgate Calendar* portrays Sheppard's mother (whom Thackeray calls in *Catherine* "his gin-drinking mother, that sweet Magdalen!")[6] as more concerned about her next drink than about her son. But Reynolds goes further, to demonstrate an even deeper irony: Jack Sheppard's actual letters, though not elegant, reveal a caustic wit and an originality far greater than Ainsworth's, for Sheppard, thief though he is, had not turned his hand, "like the ingenious persons who write such works, to thieving in the literary line" (241).

Reynolds concludes with some reflections on the society that first creates the Jack Sheppards, and then puts them to death:

> Can there be found a more forcible illustration at once of the brutality and the inefficiency of the criminal jurisprudence of England . . . than the life of this unhappy lad? . . . From the agents of the police, "who made the culprits first, and then who slew them," to the fee-sucking attorney and the blood-sucking informer; from the jury, selected from those classes in which infractions of the rights of property are held to be offences of the deepest die, and who never scruple to sacrifice life or any thing else for the protection of "trade," to the judge and lawyer, hardened by a constant dabbling in death . . . from the fountain, in short, to the finisher of the law, never does a thought seem, in the days of Jack Sheppard, to have crossed the minds of any one among them that they were not performing the mission for which they were sent into the world, by rearing, training, bagging, hunting, worrying, and throttling criminals, as if they were vermin. (242)

The blame for such suffering, Reynolds states, extends to writers like John Gay, who visited Sheppard in prison and made him the subject of a satire, *The Beggar's Opera,* a diversion for the more fortunate who give no thought to their responsibility toward their fellow creatures. Authors, he contends, would do society a far better service if they gave the Jack Sheppards of the world a word of encouragement or instruction, or called public attention to the injustices of the law.

Reynolds's review makes explicit the ideas underlying Thackeray's parodies. He too recognized that sentimental fiction prevents analysis of social problems and, even worse, reinforces the ideas on which unjust practices are based: both women and the poor are punished and rewarded in such works by the benevolent patronage of their "betters," who are in actual life intimately bound up with the conditions that made them poor and desperate in the first place. In an 1845 review of Charles Lever's *St. Patrick's Eve,* Thackeray wrote:

> Has any sentimental writer organised any feasible scheme for bettering the poor? . . . At the conclusion of these tales . . . there somehow arrives a misty reconciliation between the poor and the rich; a prophecy is uttered of better times for the one, and better manners in the other; presages are made of happy life, happy marriage and children, happy beef and pudding for all time to come. . . . This is not the way in which men seriously engaged and interested in the awful question between rich and poor meet and grapple with it.[7]

And so Thackeray set out to find a better way to grapple with it.

This is not to say that the popular literature of his day had no value for Thackeray or for the development of the novel. Vineta Colby's *Yesterday's Woman* makes it clear that the popular nineteenth-century novel has had lasting influence: for example, by "reducing the heroic proportions of . . . individual characters, [it] gave them new importance and dignity as human beings."[8] Colby enables us to read Thackeray in the context of a substantial body of women writers who were, as he was, engaged in defining realism, authors such as Hannah More, Maria Edgeworth, and Harriet Martineau. Although critic E. S. Dallas in the 1860s cited Thackeray as the "supreme example" of nineteenth-century realism, credit is due these women writers who may be little known today, but whom Thackeray read and presumably learned from.

The new mid-nineteenth-century novel at the same time foregrounded women, and it transformed "type characters" into characters typical of a social class, thus raising issues of class divisions and values that were to become an important element in Thackeray's social realism. The silver fork novels were, as Colby points out, "a bridge between upper-class romance and middle-class domestic fiction. No student of English social history can ignore their value as records of the transformation of popular ideals, tastes, and values from a court center to a home center."[9] And although Thackeray parodied Mrs. Gore, he respected her veracity and wrote to her: "Cruel woman! Why do you take off our likenesses in that way?" (*Letters* 3: 74). Two other popular works, Bulwer-Lytton's *Paul Clifford* (1830) and Harriet Martineau's *Illustrations of Political Economy* (1832–1834) can still be appreciated today as early examples of realistic fiction that conveys a social critique.[10]

Women's writings and women's issues merged with Thackeray's genius, and together had an enormous impact on the development of the novel. John Loofbourow states that "Thackeray's writing is a major factor, [like an] irreversible diversion, by a genetic mutation, of a continuous process of evolution." The profound differences between the eighteenth-century novels of Smollett, Fielding, and Defoe and the modern novels of Forster, James, and Woolf, he maintains, can be traced to Thackeray's writings, in particular to his extraordinary power of employing and interrogating social conventions in and through the textures of narrative: "Thackeray was mainly concerned with exposing the delusions expressed in artistic conventions themselves—the sequence of idealized poses or poeticized fantasies, the literary modes associated with social or psychological artifice."[11] Here it becomes clear why Loofbourow's evolutionary metaphor is appropriate, for the fashionable fiction of the time was bringing the novel forward into new areas of realism, social awareness, and recognition of women's interests, while retaining strong traces of romance—of sentimentalized ideas of good and evil, of material rewards for moral virtue, of the marriage-ending as the summit of happiness for women. Thackeray was to establish techniques that would take the novel into the twentieth century.

Thackeray's early reviews express his recognition of the ethical power of that most delightful of indolent pastimes, the novel. In a review written in Paris in 1839, "On Some French Fashionable Novels: With a Plea for Romances in General," he argues:

all who from laziness or principle, are inclined to follow the easy and comfortable study of novels, may console themselves with the notion that they are studying matters quite as important as history. . . . [For] the novelist has a loud, eloquent, instructive language, . . . sham histories [are] much truer than real histories; which are, in fact, mere contemptible catalogues of names and places, that can have no moral effect upon the reader. (*Works* 22: 95–96)

Novels, he felt, give one a more intimate picture of the life of a people than histories, which record only outward show; novels contain "true character under false names" (99). Thus, rather than deny the "truth" of fiction, Thackeray argued that it best represents the double reality of history and private life. Not only is the novel a superior form of history, it is a moral system as well, "cheap and delightful" (99). But the lesson conveyed is not always the one intended; novels also give "unconscious testimony" (109) to the assumptions and attitudes of the writer, which are so deeply ingrained in the writer's mind and character that they become the "moral" of the tale without the author's knowing it.

Another of these early reviews, "Half-a-Crown's Worth of Cheap Knowledge," published in *Fraser's* in March 1838 (*Fraser's* 17: 279–90) demonstrates that Thackeray was already connecting class issues with literature. The review discusses fifteen works published for a lower-class audience, all purchasable for half a crown—thus, "cheap knowledge." Thackeray begins by reminding his (presumably) middle- and upper-class *Fraser's* readers how little they know of the majority of their fellow Englanders, compared to whose "vast mass of active, stirring life," they are but "an insignificant speck" (280). Only the "admirable 'Boz'" has given any real account of the life of the poor, while other writers such as Bulwer and Hook give accounts that are either "entirely fanciful" or that contemptuously fail to "penetrate beyond Mecklenburgh Square" (280). He suggests that a collection of cheap reading such as he has just bought will help alleviate this extraordinary ignorance, and thus he sets about his task of edification.

Thackeray finds, by perusing the literature of the poor, that Radicalism is not the political creed of the common people and is not the threat to the country that some say it is. Only one of the fifteen publications is political, *The Poor Man's Friend,* and it is essentially an advertisement for the *London Dispatch:* in other words, a humbug. The other is a well-executed Temperance publication that gives a "wholesome" account of the horrors and wretchedness of poverty, for which (Thackeray reminds the readers) credit is due to the "'poor man's friends' who sit on the ministerial benches" (*Fraser's* 17: 283). The other works include at least two plagiarisms; a witless, dull fiction in which Queen Victoria and her court engage in a snowball fight; and other works, some harmless amusements and some ribald or obscene. And so, thanks to the spread of literacy, wrote Thackeray, "Where we had one scoundrel we may count them now by hundreds of thousands" (290).

This review expresses several ideas that fuel Thackeray's writings: that the privileged have a responsibility to the powerless, that reading materials do not necessarily improve but often merely reflect their readers' ideas and interests (sometimes even lowering them) and that a thoughtful examination of a people's literature will make those ideas manifest. Wheatley has remarked (and it is true of Thackeray's reviews as well) that Thackeray's parodies set up both an aesthetic and a moral standard: there is a language that is not only the language of intelligence, but of "good sense"— and part of good sense is to abhor both lower-class criminality and upper-class exploitation.

Dickens comes off well as "the admirable Boz" in this review, but a better understanding of Thackeray's views on Dickens can be gained from the conclusion to *Catherine*. Although Thackeray's more direct attacks on Dickens and Ainsworth were deleted from most subsequent editions, his views are clearly expressed in the original *Catherine*, published in *Fraser's Magazine*. In "Catherine: A Story—Chapter the Last," Thackeray openly "pans" the work of his contemporaries. He begins by acknowledging Dickens's literary power, evident in *Oliver Twist*, but characterizes that power as dangerous, for it induces "pity and admiration" and even love for "a set of ruffians whose occupations are thievery, murder, and prostitution" (*Fraser's* 21: 211). *Oliver Twist* is, it is clear, exactly the kind of writing Thackeray had just condemned in the preceding paragraphs as pleasant poison.

And now, Thackeray goes on, Dickens having created a taste for such work, "something more extravagant still" appears in Ainsworth's *Jack Sheppard*. Although the works of Dickens and Ainsworth may seem to resemble the great criminal romances of the past, works such as Fielding's *Jonathan Wild* and Gay's *Beggar's*

Opera, they do not convey the same moral intelligence. The older criminal romances are redeemed by qualities that Dickens and Ainsworth lack: *Jonathan Wild* by Fielding's "grand and hearty contempt" for the criminal Wild, and *Beggar's Opera* by Gay's satire against the rich and powerful. Both of these novels provide a moral "for those who will take the trouble to find it" (*Fraser's* 21: 211). But today, though much is worthwhile in Dickens, Thackeray exclaims, "in the name of common sense, let us not expend our sympathies on cutthroats, and other such prodigies of evil!" (*Fraser's* 21: 211) These remarks are consistent with Thackeray's *Times* article on Fielding (2 September 1840), in which he criticized Ainsworth as having written "a book quite absurd and unreal, and infinitely more immoral than anything Fielding ever wrote."[12]

It may be said that writers such as Bulwer-Lytton, Ainsworth, and Dickens inspired Thackeray in a negative way, that is to say, inspired him to oppose the values implicit in the style and structure of their novels. During his second American tour, *Lippincott's Magazine* quoted Thackeray as having remarked apropos of Dickens: "'Genial, yes, . . . but frank'—and a twinkle came from over the spectacles—'well, frank as an oyster.'—'Dickens . . . is making ten thousand pounds a year. He is very angry at me for saying so, but I *will* say it, for it is true. He doesn't like me: he knows that my books are a protest against his—that if the one set are true, the other must be false.'" And so another element in the development of the novel, what Thrall termed the "terrific hue and cry" that arose against Ainsworth's and Dickens's popular romances, helped Thackeray transform the novel, in Sutherland's words, from "sloppy romance" to "solid realism."[13] Thackeray's novels were indeed a protest, as he said, a protest against an entire system of false social values, including false ideas of male honor and female virtue, and of the role of the novel in shaping a culture. His first "criminal romance" features a murderess, Catherine Hayes; his first "sentimental romance" features a fallen woman; and his first novel-length, first-person narrative is told by a misogynist who blames all the world's evil on women.

WOMEN AS AUTHORS AND AS CHARACTERS

Catherine began as a challenge to the criminal romance, which, as

Thackeray wrote in "On Some French Fashionable Novels," abounded in "gay and agreeable cut-throats, otto-of-rose murderers, amiable hackney-coachmen, Prince Rodolphs and the like, being representatives of beings that never have or could have existed" (*Works* 22: 94–95). Thackeray called the novel his "*Catherine* cathartic"[14] because he intended it to counteract the "poison" of criminal romance by producing a "wholesome nausea" in response to the Newgate novels, with their sentimentalized and glamorized criminals (*Works* 24: 193). He specifies this purpose early in the novel:

> And here, though we are only in the third chapter of this history, we feel almost sick of the characters that appear in it. . . . But how can we help ourselves? The public will hear of nothing but rogues; and the only way in which poor authors, who must live, can act honestly by the public and themselves, is to paint such thieves as they are: not dandy, poetical rose-water thieves; but real downright scoundrels. . . . They don't quote Plato, like Eugene Aram . . . or die whitewashed saints, like poor "Bis Dadsy" in *Oliver Twist*. No, my dear Madam, you and your daughters have no right to admire and sympathise with any such persons, fictitious or real. . . . Keep your sympathy for those who deserve it. (*Works* 24: 50)

Thackeray's early parodies were directed against what he saw as an essential dishonesty in the sentimental novel: it purported to sympathize with the poor, but in reality manipulated middle-class sentiment to gain a market and, in doing so, reinforced false conceptions of class and justice. Women characters especially, both good and "fallen," were presented in ways that obscured the responsibilities of society. Thackeray's parodies were motivated by a desire to reform the literature that influenced public consensus on economic and political matters. Always sensitive to the subjectivity of the human mind, Thackeray recognized that conscience and moral choice depend on beliefs and value systems that are culturally constructed. His works repeatedly question how social attitudes affect private behavior and how they may cause either good or evil.

It is a Thackerayan quality—and indeed a characteristic Victorian postromantic intellectual stance—to distrust subjectivity and to demonstrate through narrative that our perceptions and judgments are too often based on social training or self-justifying emotion. Jerome Buckley noted in *The Victorian Temper*, "Almost every Victorian thesis produced its own antithesis, as a ceaseless dialectic worked out its designs."[15] In his distrust of both empiricism and of the subjective, Thackeray anticipates modernism: he was acutely aware of the way personality, including gender-associated characteristics, may be socially constructed.

Thackeray's early portraits of women provide ambiguous material for a feminist analysis. At first glance, his female characters seem to reinforce feminine stereotypes: Catherine Hayes is a murderess, Caroline Gann is a "fallen woman," and Lady Lyndon loves the man who abuses her. But it is with such characters that Thackeray begins to tackle the question of what it means to be a woman. For example, all of his female characters fall victim to the "sexual marketplace." Mary Ancel promises marriage to a stranger in order to save her father from execution; in the end she outwits the man but would have killed him on their wedding night had her stratagem failed. Catherine Hayes and Caroline Gann are seduced and abandoned by sexual entrepreneurs to whom (as Thackeray says in *Catherine*) the game belongs. And Lady Lyndon is pursued for her money, just as Catherine had been pursued for her sexual attractiveness, with that "desperate, greedy eagerness and desire of possession, which makes passions for women often so fierce and unreasonable among very cold and selfish men" (*Works* 24: 20).

These stories also establish another pattern: sweet, "feminine" women like Caroline Gann are mentally and emotionally too weak to resist a domination that demands, as John Stuart Mill put it, not only their obedience, but their sentiments. These women, lacking what Mill would call the power of self-government, approach very near to madness. That the pattern originates in Thackeray's wife's personality is inescapable; by 1840, Isabella was repeatedly attempting to kill herself.[16] On the other hand, women who rebel become destructive: Mary Ancel's plan to kill the husband who is being forced upon her makes her the first of Thackeray's women characters to turn to violence; Catherine Hayes and Becky Sharp follow in ever more complex versions of the same story, the story of a woman pressured by economic and political powerlessness to marry where she does not love. Robert Colby states:

> *Catherine* does not reveal a novelist suddenly sprung forth in full power . . . but one struggling to be born. . . . Despite [its flaws], *Catherine* repays careful reading, if for no better reason than to see Thackeray exploring his *metier* as a writer and anticipating the path that he was to follow.[17]

Catherine appeared at the same time that Caroline Norton's Infant Custody Bill was being argued in Parliament, and the women's movement was being debated in articles such as "Woman and the Social System" (*Fraser's* 21: 698–702), or "Criticism on Women" (*Westminster Review* 32 [1839]: 454–75). The first article argues that women fare better under Christianity than they would under socialism and demonstrates to a modern reader that the debate about women, property, family, and religion had advanced to what seems a remarkably modern stage by 1840. Although Thackeray probably agreed in preferring Christianity to socialism, the article may have inspired the "corrective" opening sentence of *Barry Lyndon* in the January 1844 issue of *Fraser's,* which parodies Judeo-Christian representations of women as the source of all human sin and suffering.

By the time *Catherine* began to appear, Harriet Martineau's "radical" *Society in America* (1837) "with its indictment of female oppression," had been out for two years. Thackeray dined with Martineau and John Stuart Mill some time in the early 1830s. One can't help but speculate upon what effect these two thinkers might have had upon the very young Thackeray, but little is known. They did not meet again for another twenty years, and although Martineau claimed to be "unable to read *Vanity Fair,* from the moral disgust it occasions," she pronounced *Henry Esmond* "*the* book of the century."[18]

Many of Thackeray's comments (like those from *Catherine* quoted above) are addressed to women readers, and he recognized the growing influence of women writers as well. Early reviews and comments in his letters and fiction show that he was reading, at the very least, George Sand, Maria Edgeworth, Lady Morgan, and Frances Trollope. At this early stage in his career, Thackeray's attitude toward writing women seems somewhat ambivalent. His essay "Madame Sand and the New Apocalypse," for example, published in the same *Paris Sketch Book* that contains "Mary Ancel," praises George Sand's talent and intelligence but discounts her ideas on the *ad feminam* grounds that her irregular life should make any reader distrust her philosophy of marriage, which according to Thackeray was that "the laws of marriage . . . press very cruelly upon unfortunate women" (*Works* 22: 232). It was, however, a philosophy that Thackeray was to express in his own later fiction. And in a review included in "Our Batch of Novels for Christmas, 1837," published in *Fraser's* in 1838, Thackeray criticized Frances Trollope's *The Vicar of Wrexhill,* partly on the grounds that a woman, "having very little, except prejudice, on which to found an opinion, . . . makes up for want of argument by a wonderful fluency of abuse. A woman's religion is chiefly that of the heart, and not of the head" (*Fraser's* 17: 79).[19] Even as a young man, Thackeray took pains to avoid unfair generalizations against women as a class. His dismissal of women's opinions, for example, is ameliorated by the recognition that women's intellectual training was deficient; the idea is implied by Thackeray's statement that a woman has "very little, except prejudice, on which to found an opinion."

Thackeray's essay on "The Fashionable Authoress" may seem at first an indictment of women writers, but a careful reading reveals that Thackeray is distinguishing between "fashionable authoresses" and women writers. For example, he wrote, "If [the fashionable authoress] did write well . . . she would not be praised by Timson and the critics, because she would be an honest woman and would not bribe them" (*Works* 5: 383–84). He scorns the word *authoress* as a fashionable folly and points out that Sappho was no "authoress," she was an *auctor,* or author. He concludes finally that, "The woman herself is not so blamable; it is the silly people who cringe at her feet that do the mischief" (*Works* 5: 389). It is a view that respects the potential abilities of women, even as it points out their errors as actual writers and readers.

Catherine is designed to demonstrate the realities of the criminal mind, the sordid, trivial ugliness Thackeray felt was obscured by the writers of criminal romances. And yet, since Catherine is a woman, she is more constrained and harmed by social attitudes than a male character would be, and she is motivated in large part by dependence on her lover and love for her son. Thackeray tells us at the end of *Catherine* that, "one of her last expressions to the executioner, as she was going from the sledge to the stake, being an inquiry whether he had hanged her dear child" (*Fraser's* 21: 208). Thackeray's illustrations reflect this mixture of pity and horror at her story (see figure 3).

During the course of writing *Catherine,* Thackeray's feelings were more engaged by the central character than he had expected: he wrote to his mother in March 1840 that it was "ingenious" of her to find beauties in *Catherine* and went on to acknowledge that "the author had a sneaking kindness for his heroine, and did not like to make her utterly worthless" (*Letters* 1: 432–33). As he constructed an imaginary character and history for his fictitious Catherine Hayes (whose historic original was executed by burning in 1726 for the murder of her husband), he por-

3. Initial letters from *Catherine* (*Works* 24: 47, 58, 146, 172, 186).

trayed a woman whom Robert Colby described aptly as "sinned against as well as sinning."[20]

One cause for Thackeray's "sneaking kindness" for Catherine is that her emotions are genuine, though misguided. She does love "Count" Galgenstein: she cooks and cleans for him, centers the whole of her fiery nature on him, and tries desperately to win some kindness from him. Thackeray's narrator, Ikey Solomon, informs us, "The woman loved him, that was the fact" (*Works* 24: 37). Her first attempt at murder, when she tries to poison Galgenstein, is motivated by jealousy and rage at his intended abandonment, passions more understandable than Galgenstein's cold-blooded opportunism. Catherine submits to Galgenstein's mistreatment, Thackeray makes clear, because she fears losing the first man she has ever loved.

As an illiterate orphan whose beauty her aunt Mrs. Score uses to further business at the inn, Catherine is extremely vulnerable. And so she is easily taken in by "Count" Galgenstein's superficial charm and deceptive displays of wealth, power, and luxury. She is as much duped as the naive country boys whom Galgenstein impresses into service in a corrupt army, only Catherine's service is more personal, her "induction" more internalized.

Juliet McMaster has pointed out that Thackeray is well aware of the subtle, irrational workings of masochism, especially in women.[21] For example, Galgenstein's philosophy is that "Women are like dogs, they like to be ill-treated" (*Works* 24: 36). One man in the story even jokes about it: "Mrs. Hall had a real affection for the gallant Count, and grew, as Mr. Brock was pleased to say, like a beefsteak, more tender as she was thumped" (*Works* 24: 38–39). However, McMaster does not explore the degree to which such masochism is, in Thackeray's rendering, caused by social and political forces. Thackeray recognizes that it is not women's "nature" but social attitudes that make people slavish. The phenomenon originates partly in power and wealth and has its parallel in English "Snobbery": as Yellowplush remarks in "Foring Parts," "[I]f you wish to be respected by English people, you must be insolent to them. . . . We *like* being insulted by noblemen. . . . I've known many and many a genlmn about town who'd rather be kicked by a lord than not noticed by him" (*Works* 5: 47–48).

After her unsuccessful attempt to poison Galgenstein, Catherine runs away. What follows is a double-edged portrait, in part comic, in part very dark indeed, of marriage and family life. Over it all hovers the voice of Ikey Solomon, obtusely declaring that "we have [our failings] from nature" (*Works* 24: 106). Finding herself alone and penniless, Catherine becomes "an honest woman again" by contracting a loveless marriage with Hayes. Marriage provides her with a home, respectability, and economic survival—indeed, a profession. Like a number of other Thackerayan characters (Helen Pendennis, Madame de Florac, Colonel Newcome, or Clive Newcome), Catherine makes this marriage of convenience only after the loss of the person who is actually desired (a pattern that follows Thackeray's mother's own history). But more than any of these characters, Catherine is forced to marry for economic survival; in this her case resembles Becky Sharp's.

The comic side of the story derives from Thackeray's satire of polite fictions: the loveless marriage that makes Catherine "an honest woman"; the blame that attaches to Hayes for neglecting his family when he begins to spend too much time in taverns to escape his miserable home; the patently false language that society uses to describe marriage and children—"Mrs. Hayes had now been for six years the adored wife of Mr. Hayes, and no offspring had arisen to bless their loves and perpetuate their name" (*Works* 24: 108). At the same time, Thackeray counterbalances the comic elements with a dark portrait of loveless marriage. Catherine's relations with the ever-present Brock, and with her son (a relationship that one critic termed incestuous, as indeed it seems to have been, as represented in the *Newgate Calendar*), form a complex but undeveloped undercurrent to the narrative—early examples of triangular love relations involving competition between husband, lover, and son.[22] As evil as Catherine's attempt to murder her husband is, the novel does drive home every reader's own "affinity with criminals" and society's culpability in producing such persons.[23] The emotional poverty of Catherine's life, her lack of education, and factors connected more specifically with being a woman, such as her psychological and economic dependence, all contribute to her destiny as murderess.

At times, it is possible to read Thackeray as the "snob" he claimed to be. For instance, he writes of Catherine and her clumsy rustic admirers, "O woman, lovely woman! what strong resolves canst thou twist round thy little finger!" (*Works* 24: 14) and follows the sentence with a series of gradually trivializing parallel phrases: what gunpowder passions can you kindle, what lies and nonsense can you make us listen to, what bad liquor can you make us swallow. Thackeray's tone seems to mock his lower-class characters' passions as shallow. Yet it is only Thackeray who can write, in the same work, "Love, like Death, plays havoc among the *pauperum tabernas,* and sports with rich and poor, wicked and virtuous alike" (*Works* 24: 22) and who can comment of a butcher, "that calm flesh-mountain—who can tell me that calmness itself is not DESPAIR?" (*Works* 24: 23).

It is not the characters Thackeray mocks; it is the falsely elevated sentiment of their "betters." This is his quarrel with the works *Catherine* parodies: in all his representations of human relations, whether historical, literary, or personal, Thackeray is engaged in distinguishing the real and honorable from the falsely elevated. Regarding women, this means distinguishing the reality from shams. "Catty Hall" or "Cattern" is no devil; rather, she has human weaknesses—she is vain, simple, easily taken in, and then caught in a web she cannot escape. Thackeray's is the language of intelligent perception, of clear-eyed justice.

Thackeray's portrait of Caroline Gann in *A Shabby Genteel Story,* also published in *Fraser's* (from June through October 1840), is as complex and shifting in its narrative stance as *Catherine.* Whereas Catherine had been intended to represent the ugliness of the criminal mentality and had soon evoked an unexpected "sneaking kindness" from her creator, Caroline seems at first a portrait of a good woman and turns out to be at least in part a parody of the middle-class feminine ideal.

Caroline Gann and Catherine Hayes demonstrate that, although their disadvantages vary according to class, women's troubles are essentially similar. Both are young, naive, and destined to be exploited (first by women—Catherine's aunt uses her niece's sexual attractions to draw in customers, whereas Caroline's mother uses her daughter as a boardinghouse servant). Later, both become "fallen women." It is to Thackeray's credit that he presents them as being more sympathetic than their predecessor Moll Flanders but less pathetic than Dickens's Nancy or Little Emily. Long before George Eliot's *Adam Bede,* Elizabeth Gaskell's *Ruth,* Thomas Hardy's *Tess,* or George Moore's *Esther Waters,*

Thackeray represented Caroline and Catherine as fallen women whose crime was not greed, ambition, or lust so much as blind devotion to men who had been taught by society to take advantage of their naïveté. In both works, Thackeray shows there is little difference between a "fallen woman" and a married—or "honest"—woman. Catherine is in fact more honest before her marriage to Hayes than after. And Caroline, though fallen, is more honest than anyone else in the story: "Not that there was any wickedness on *her* side, poor girl! or that she did anything but follow the natural impulses of an honest little female heart, that leads it to trust and love and worship a being of the other sex whom the eager fancy invests with all sorts of attributes of superiority" (*Works* 18: 92).

With these similarities as a starting point, Thackeray goes on to present Caroline Gann as quite different from Catherine Hayes. Because the "shabby genteel" is one of Thackeray's targets here, Caroline has many weaknesses of middle-class women. Although, unlike Catherine, she can read, she relies on romantic novels for all her knowledge of love and sex (*Works* 18: 93). In *A Shabby Genteel Story*, it becomes clear that a middle-class education teaches silly ideas rather than none, confinement and passivity rather than mobility and activity, and a fatal reliance on social forms and appearances (the sham marriage, romantic novels, shabby gentility itself).

Gordon Ray accounts for many of the differences between Catherine and Caroline when he attributes Thackeray's "tender and protective" attitude toward Caroline to her being "the first of a series of fictional portraits of Isabella."[24] As Ray also points out, the crime at the heart of this work is seduction rather than murder, and Caroline is not a criminal but a victim. It is unfortunate that, for some critics (among them Gordon Ray), the parallels between Thackeray's fictional "good women" and Isabella Thackeray obscure the penetrating social criticism that came of his personal tragedy. Isabella's final, irreversible mental breakdown caused Thackeray to hurry *A Shabby Genteel Story* through to an incomplete conclusion. By the time he resumed the story in *Philip* twenty years later, Thackeray had changed a great deal. It is difficult to say where Caroline Gann's story would have ended, originally. But there is enough satire of the genteel ideal of womanhood here to give intimations of Amelia Sedley, who was to appear in *Vanity Fair* seven years later.

IRONIC MALE NARRATIVE STANCES

Whereas Caroline Gann's personality reflects her middle-class, albeit shabby genteel, upbringing, it also reflects a middle-class idea of the good woman, which Thackeray had internalized, to some degree, but was already coming to reject. It is at this stage that Thackeray began to reveal his gift for self-parody. In order to show the power of convention over perception (including his own perception), Thackeray developed the ironic male narrative voice that is so characteristic of him. These ironic male narrators demonstrate the truth of what Ortega y Gasset was to write some hundred years later: "By means of ideas we see the world, but in a natural attitude of the mind we do not see the ideas—the same as the eye in seeing does not see itself."[25]

The view from behind George Savage Fitz-Boodle's ever-burning cigar provides an edifying perspective on women, a perspective not ostensibly Thackeray's, yet the persona Thackeray adopts here comes very close to Thackeray the man. Ray terms Fitz-Boodle his "alter ego."[26] In Fitz-Boodle's "Confessions" (first published in *Fraser's* 1842–1843), Thackeray presents his narrator as a rather shy man, awkward with women and hiding behind a mask of indifference. He pretends not to mind his bachelorhood, but the mask slips occasionally, in lines such as these from "Dorothea," where insecurity and selfishness merge seamlessly into hostile bravado:

> I don't know how it is, but I hate to see men evidently intimate with nice-looking women, and on good terms with themselves. There's something annoying in their cursed complacency—their evident sunshiny happiness. I've no woman to make sunshine for *me,* and yet, my heart tells me that not one, but several such suns would do good to my system.
>
> "Who are those pert-looking officers," says I, peevishly, to the guide, "talking to those vulgar-looking women?" (*Works* 24: 227)

Although lacking Thackeray's self-awareness and intelligence, the character developed through this ironic narrative comes very close in feeling to the Thackeray we can see in his letters, diaries, and works. Sensitive, self-conscious, disarmingly self-deprecating in his letters, Thackeray here projects onto the page the portrait of a likable but somewhat obtuse man—a self-conscious Thackeray parodying men of his own class and situation. Thackeray's irony does not distance the reader entirely from Fitz-Boodle: a subtle sympathy between narrator and reader gives poignancy to his loneliness and force to the insights provided, behind Fitz-Boodle's words, into something of Thackeray's own relations with women. In Ray's opinion, the second, third, and fourth "Confessions" may have "come so close to autobiography that Thackeray was unwilling to reprint them in his *Miscellanies* of 1857."[27]

At the age of thirty-one, Thackeray had already adopted the stance of a lonely old bachelor whom life was passing by (Fitz-Boodle claims to be thirty-eight, but his editor remarks that he must be at least forty-five), a precursor of William Dobbin and George Warrington, and even in some ways of Colonel Newcome and Major Pendennis. Thackeray's ironic narrative demonstrates how Fitz-Boodle's mask of conventional pieties allows him to deceive primarily himself. Fitz-Boodle blames his failure to find a suitable wife, for example, in one case on his cigar-smoking, in another, on his inability to dance. One need not be an expert in psychoanalysis to recognize the sexual connotations of cigars and dancing. Dancing, especially, takes on obvious sexual connotations: Fitz-Boodle's anxiety, the secret lessons taken under the name of Mr. Smith, the importance of the first performance, and the fall and subsequent rejection all confirm his initial fears and make another venture even more difficult.

His third attempt at love, however, is radically different, for here it is Fitz-Boodle and not the woman who breaks off the relationship. This lady, Ottilia, is a bluestocking "of the ultramarinest sort" (*Works* 24: 245) whose learning, passion, and wit are all shallow—but this is not what puts off Fitz-Boodle. In fact, being rather a simple fellow himself, he admires her. Fitz-Boodle's admiration changes to revulsion only when he sees her eating. Thackeray was aware of the traditional belief that oysters are an aphrodisiac; he uses them with just such connotations in "Dando the Oyster-Eater." But Fitz-Boodle, as he tells us, is not "much of an oyster-eater, nor can I relish them *in naturalibus* as some do, but require a quantity of sauces, lemons, cayenne peppers, bread and butter, and so forth, to render them palatable" (*Works* 24: 256). And so, to see Ottilia "gobbling" them, ignorant of the difference between fresh and spoiled, crushes all desire to marry her. The narrative does not provide an evaluation of this scene; it seems clear, however, that fear of female sexual appetite is one component of Fitz-

Boodle's psychic makeup. Fitz-Boodle is unable to explain his loneliness and his repeated disappointments in love; to him it is "as if some fatality pursued my desire to become a domestic character" (*Works* 24: 212). In Thackeray's texts, this "fatality" originates in the social construction of love. Fitz-Boodle's awkward eagerness toward women and his bravado in the face of repeated failures to establish a relationship suggest that much masculine arrogance has its roots in this combination of fear and desire. Such a man will recur in Joseph Sedley.

Thackeray makes it clear too that masculine self-confidence is supported by social structures such as men's clubs, which make it possible for single men to live quite well without families. In *Snobs*, Thackeray wrote that men ought to be barred from clubs until they marry. And of course the kind of social and financial independence available to men smooths the way for such club-bachelors. When he portrays the difficulties unmarried women face, on the other hand, Thackeray does not use the same humorous tone, for he fully understands that here is where very real difficulties lie. Fitz-Boodle resembles the club-loungers Caroline Norton satirizes in her 1839 *Letter to the Queen:*

> The club-loungers smile in scorn. "What is all this disturbance about? Woman's rights and woman's wrongs?—pooh, pooh; nonsense; Bloomerism, Americanism! we can't have that sort of thing in England. Women must submit; those who don't are bad women—depend upon it: all bad women. There are no bad men. Who ever heard of a bad man?"[28]

Thackeray's next novel is in fact about a "bad man" and about "Woman's rights and woman's wrongs." *The Luck of Barry Lyndon: A Romance of the Last Century,* first published in *Fraser's* in 1844 and "edited" by Fitz-Boodle, explicitly confronts the social conventions that Thackeray treats with gentle humor in Fitz-Boodle's "Confessions." *Barry Lyndon* represents an immense step forward for Thackeray in the development of the ironic first-person narrator. Wayne Booth cites *Barry Lyndon* as a novel in which the narrator is placed as far as possible from the author, "who carries the reader with him in judging the narrator." James Wheatley demonstrates that Thackeray's narrative technique in *Barry Lyndon* is a continuation and complication of his early parody: "What we have been examining in Thackeray is an exploration out through parody to the character of the narrator, and the further step to making the narrator himself display the state of society."[29]

Through Barry Lyndon's ironic dramatized first-person narrative, Thackeray opposes several kinds of conventional value systems. One is the "moral materialism" of writers who reward (and thus implicitly equate) goodness with prosperity. The second is the misrepresentation of fighting and killing as heroism. The third (and most important, though it has received almost no attention) is the sanctioning of women's subjection by social, legal, and even religious elements of Barry Lyndon's culture. Misogyny is in fact Thackeray's primary target in *Barry Lyndon*.

Redmond Barry, the Irish "autobiographer" who would later take his English wife's family name, is unconscious of the immorality of his values and assumes that his readers share them. Some readers may indeed share some of those values. Many of Thackeray's contemporaries, for example, failed to recognize his irony; and the original text consequently contains increasing numbers of editorial asides, which act as counterpoint to Barry Lyndon's point of view.[30] One such aside, which unmistakably states Thackeray's purpose, is the following comment by the "editor," Fitz-Boodle:

> From these curious confessions, it would appear that Mr. Lyndon maltreated his lady in every possible way; that he denied her society, bullied her into signing away her property, spent it in gambling and taverns, was openly unfaithful to her; and, when she complained, threatened to remove her children from her. Nor, indeed, is he the only husband who has done the like, and has passed for "nobody's enemy but his own"; a jovial, good-natured fellow. The world contains scores of such amiable people; and, indeed, it is because justice has not been done them that we have edited this autobiography.[31]

Further evidence of Thackeray's original intentions lies in material that was deleted some time before the second edition was published in 1856 under the new title *The Memoirs of Barry Lyndon, Esq.*[32] In 1844 Thackeray was still in his "literary apprenticeship," as Harold Gulliver appropriately named it, and was not yet able to maintain perfect control over the narrative. But it is clear from the deleted passages that Thackeray intended the relations between men and women to take a central place in the work. Gordon Ray sums up: "the preoccupations that led him to write the book are much clearer in the *Luck* [than in the *Memoirs*]."[33]

For example, some of the passages deleted from the *Luck* sound out of place coming from Redmond Barry, such as the observation that, while men expect women to bring "virgin hearts" to the marriage altar, they are not so squeamish about their own. It is not likely that Barry Lyndon would condemn the sexual double standard. Nor is it likely that he would complain that "the jealous, greedy, selfish sultan, Man, would . . . confine [women's] affections, if he could, nor allow them to think and feel until such time as he chooses to select them as objects of his favour" (1.1.62). Such passages express Thackeray's ideas, not Barry Lyndon's, and he did well to delete them and to limit the presentation of meaning to the indirection of irony. But these remarks certainly signal Thackeray's original preoccupations.

The first sentence of the novel remained untouched, however, for it reveals the cultural foundation on which Barry Lyndon's self-justifying misogyny rests: "Since the days of Adam, there has been hardly a mischief done in this world but a woman has been at the bottom of it." It is interesting that this very topic had been chosen for Thackeray's Cambridge debating club to discuss in 1829: "Has woman, since the Fall, been the cause of more good or evil to mankind?"[34] At the time, Thackeray took the position that woman had been the cause of more good; here he has Barry take the opposite position. Perhaps Thackeray was haunted by the insidiously familiar ring of his opponents' arguments, that women were cause of all human evil.[35] Barry Lyndon is, according to James Wheatley, "fundamentally identified with the society on which he preys," and his angry denunciation of women reflects a fundamental moral difficulty in our cultural tradition. As Rosemary Radford Reuther puts it in *Sexism and God-Talk*, the cosmology that "scapegoat[s] women as cause of mortality and sin is the real sin." It is the same woman-blaming that Lady Morgan tried to counteract in *Woman and Her Master* by demonstrating that woman has always benefited humanity.[36]

The novel's critique of misogyny is obscured by the fact that Lady Lyndon's motivations are unclear. Readers can be misled into thinking in Barry's terms: for example, that she chooses Barry because women like to be dominated. Barry Lyndon states that "I . . . witnessed with triumphant composure the mastery I was gaining over her. Terror, be sure of that, is not a bad ingredient of love" (1.16.280), and Lady Lyndon herself writes to friends that "the horrid look of his black serpent-like eyes fascinates and frightens me" (1.17.284). It is true that Barry Lyndon's relationship with Lady Lyndon is based on his desire for dominance, for when she sneers at her husband, Lord Lyndon, for associating with him, Barry determines "to bend this haughty lady" (1.14.245). Lord Lyndon even warns Barry against marrying her, after his death, as she is ungovernable. In a fine parody of traditional definitions of the "good woman," Lord Lyndon speaks longingly of the joys of marriage to a virtuous drudge. Such a wife, he tells Barry, provides a man with freedom, comfort, and untiring loyalty, while all the expense is on her side. "If he select the animal properly," Lord Lyndon tells Barry, "he will choose such a one as shall be no bar to his pleasure" (1.14.249).

However, Lady Lyndon is no masochist. Thackeray makes it clear that social pressures play a part in her capitulation. As a wealthy young heiress she had been pressured into marrying her guardian's son (1.14.242). After her husband's death, Barry starts rumors that she is in love with him by strenuously denying any interest in her. When Lady Lyndon flees London, he precedes her by a day (having bribed a servant to let him know her plans) so that she appears to be following him. Gradually she is shut out from society by the suspicions of the self-righteous, who in effect abandon her to fight him alone. Lady Lyndon's consequent social isolation helps explain why she finally is "captivated" by him, ironically fulfilling her husband's dictum regarding the virtuous drudge, that "if he is a brute, she will like him all the better for his ill-treatment of her" (1.14.249).

THE NOVEL AS "TRUE HISTORY"

Thackeray drew on both history and on contemporary life for the "originals" of Barry Lyndon, and the fact that the novel alludes to realities with which he and his audience were familiar gives greater weight to the work's critique of social beliefs and practices. Barry Lyndon is far more than an authorial mask or an unreliable narrator. His character is derived from a number of sources, real and fictive, and functions as a commentary on the society that produced such men. The novel even incorporates Caroline Norton and the infant custody debate.

One model for Barry Lyndon is Andrew Robinson Stoney-Bowes, an Irish adventurer. Born in Ireland in 1745, he first married the heiress of a coal fortune, whom he mistreated, even to the extent of pushing her down a flight of stairs at a public gathering. After this wife's death, Stoney ruthlessly pursued a wealthy young widow, Lady Strathmore (née Bowes), and succeeded in marrying her. Like Redmond Barry, he then added his wife's aristocratic family name to his own.[37] For a while, Stoney-Bowes seemed to settle down into his newfound prosperity; like Barry Lyndon, he even sat in Parliament for a term. Eventually, however, he returned to his old ways: he went deeply into debt, sold off what he could of his wife's estate, beat and starved her, and openly kept mistresses. When she challenged him in court, he abducted and tortured her. After eleven days, Lady Strathmore was rescued from her husband, and "For all of this Bowes was sentenced to only three years in prison."[38]

But Stoney-Bowes is not the only original for Barry Lyndon. Gordon Ray, Robert Colby, and Martin Anisman have put forward a number of other possible sources for the story, all of which demonstrate that a man might, if he wished, deprive his wife of children, property, safety, and sometimes even of her life.[39] The novel testifies to Thackeray's careful observation of British common law: it is quite specific about child custody, property, and inheritance laws. We learn, for example, that Barry Lyndon can take their son, Bryan, away from Lady Lyndon (this is his chief hold over her); that he pawns her diamonds; that at first he wants his wife alive because, if she died, her property would go to her first son, Lord Bullingdon; that after Bullingdon's disappearance, however, Barry's son Bryan becomes heir, and Lady Lyndon's death then becomes desirable; and finally, that Lady Lyndon's income is diverted to pay Barry Lyndon's debts, because "to secure an easy week with me she would *sign away* a thousand a year" (2.2.350; my italics).

Twentieth-century readers could easily miss such details in the narrative, but Thackeray's contemporaries were likely to understand them immediately, in terms of the ongoing debates over child custody and married women's property laws. *Barry Lyndon* was designed to parody the historical and criminal romances that Thackeray found so offensive, but it was also meant to question another text, English law. Thackeray's representations are detailed and accurate; they were written in opposition to laws that made such behavior possible. The law held, for example, that a husband had control over his wife's real property and any income derived from it but that he could not dispose of it without her consent. Hence Lady Lyndon had to "sign away a thousand a year." The law also held that the wife's personal property (Lady Lyndon's pawned diamonds, for example) belonged to the husband absolutely, and that when the wife died, her property went to her children—she could not will it away—but if a child was born of a later marriage, the widower enjoyed life interest. This is why Barry's concern for his wife's survival varied with the disappearance of Bullingdon and the birth (and later death) of Bryan. Finally, the husband had full custody rights over any children born of the marriage; this was Barry Lyndon's chief means of power over his wife.[40]

The death of little Bryan in a fall from a horse is another element of *Barry Lyndon* that is historically allusive. The accident would have reminded contemporary readers of Caroline Norton and her own son's death from a similar fall during the time her husband still had custody. The parallels are unmistakable: Norton's son was eight when he died in 1842; Bryan was nine at the time of his death in the novel (published in 1844—just two years later).

Barry Lyndon was published in *Fraser's,* the journal for which both Norton and Thackeray wrote. It is clearly based, at least in part, on Caroline Norton's life and dramatizes her ideas. Barry Lyndon resembles George Norton in several ways: both use their wives to promote their careers, both serve one term in Parliament, and both physically abuse their rebellious, intellectual wives. Acland's description of George Norton fits Redmond Barry equally well: "He was true to the spirit of his class and times in that money was more important to him than anything else—than honour, justice, or truth. Money was his obsession, and conditioned every thought and action."[41] Thackeray supports Caroline Norton's arguments for infant custody by demonstrating that Barry uses his wife's love for her son to bend her will to his. Norton had asked, in her 1839 *Plain Letter:*

> But the question is, on what principle the legislature should give a man this power to torment; this power to say to his wife, "You shall bear blows, you shall bear inconstancy, you shall give up property, you shall endure insults, and *yet* you shall continue to live under my

roof, *or else*, I will take your children, and you shall never see them more."[42]

Barry Lyndon lends imaginative life and power to Norton's argument for maternal infant custody and anticipates much of the debate that would surround the 1857 Divorce Act. Thackeray's purpose, he declares, is to do justice to the "amiable people" who so mistreat their wives, to whom the law has given absolute power, and the world thoughtless acceptance. The purpose of *Barry Lyndon* is to lay bare the unconscious assumptions that animate such men and to demonstrate how they operate in the larger world.

The pattern of male cruelty and violence toward women in the novel is not limited to Barry Lyndon. Thackeray shows it to be systemic through two apparently unimportant subplots. The first is the story of Miss Amelia Kiljoy, a wealthy young friend of Lady Lyndon, whom Barry Lyndon abducts and "gives" to his penniless cousin Ulick Brady. They force Runt, the minister, to perform a marriage ceremony that will give Ulick all conjugal and property rights over Amelia (1.17.284–92). The second story reflects two other Thackerayan preoccupations, seduction and the Bluebeard theme. In this embedded narrative, Princess Olivia is unhappy in her marriage to the stern and cold Prince Victor, and she takes a lover who, it turns out, regards her only as a conquest. When Prince Victor learns of the affair, he imprisons Olivia and tells the public she is ill with a brain fever. Finally she is beheaded, her "shrieking head" removed from "the miserable, sinful body" (1.13.216–35).

Thackeray adapted this story from a work by Baron de la Mothe-Langon, where it is told by Napoleon, but Thackeray chose to have it narrated by a woman, Rosina de Liliengarten, a wreck of a woman who was once mistress of Prince Victor's father.[43] By telling the tale from a woman's point of view rather than allowing Barry Lyndon to narrate it, Thackeray can introduce into the story a note of fellow feeling: Liliengarten is herself a victim of the same system of ruthless male power. Barry's role as Liliengarten's auditor adds to the irony of the presentation, for he does not comprehend the implications of the story: that the "disciplined obedience" he has achieved with Lady Lyndon leads to deceit and revolt. All forget, Fitz-Boodle tells us—husbands as well as schoolmasters and bullying sergeants—that "the very hypocrisy which forms a part of it (all timid people are liars in their hearts) may be exerted in a way that may be far from agreeable in order to deceive you" (2.19.376). And so Barry's dissolution includes as a major component the perversion and loss of family feeling. Barry himself must be included in the list of victims. As son, he regresses to infantile imbecility; as father, loving in his own way, he contributes indirectly to his child's death; as husband, he wastes and destroys all that home might have been, except for a highly neurotic remnant of Lady Lyndon's emotional attachment.

Through the narrative in *Barry Lyndon,* Thackeray has examined not only the subjectivity of the individual but the limitations and self-deception of an entire culture. It was through "legitimate authority" that Barry Lyndon brought his wife "into such a terror about me, that . . . if I beckoned to her, she would come fawning up to me like a dog" (2.19.376). Barry Lyndon does not deliberately choose evil; rather, his actions arise from a conscience that cannot perceive correctly. The significance of the work lies in its challenge to the unconscious assumptions that animate Barry Lyndon and that operate in the larger, "real" world. In *Barry Lyndon,* Thackeray shows that conscience is not merely self-justifying; it is limited by the criteria the mind has available for judging action. And as in *Barry Lyndon,* so in the world: misogyny, although evil, is not recognized as such, and like a materialistic value system or false sense of honor, it can flourish unrestrained and do inestimable harm. This is one of the major themes to which Barry Lyndon's narrative gives "unconscious testimony."

In recognizing the irony of the narrative, we are maneuvered into rejecting Barry Lyndon's point of view; and to the extent that his perspective is based on cultural discourse systems such as religion and law, we are asked to reexamine those also. Thus, the insidious power and ubiquity of antifeminist thought is exposed, at the very time that the women's movement was gathering strength and daily presenting the Victorian public with alternative visions (sometimes in the same journal, *Fraser's*). By presenting misogyny ironically, Thackeray helped to take apart the myth, and to unlock the conceptual prison, of women's inferiority.

Thackeray's early commitment to realism played a major role in shaping the novel as we know it today. He developed the use of the ironic first-person narrator to a new level of linguistic, psychological, and social awareness. Through realism, antiromance, and ironic narrative, he explored the conditions affecting women's lives and the culture that supported those conditions. His characters epitomize social laws and cultural belief systems. Thackeray demonstrates that their subjectivity is actually (in the words of Friedrich Engels) the "'driving forces of society and history operat[ing] in the brains of the actors.'" Thackeray's novels bring emotional and ethical dimensions to the representation of material reality. His truth is (to borrow Lukács's description of Tolstoy) the truth of the whole—of social systems and living relations. As in Tolstoy, so in Thackeray, "the destinies of his characters are inseparable from their 'psychology.' The characters develop on the basis of actions and events. . . . And the social environment, . . . as it is resolved into the actions of these concrete human beings, confronts them as an independent power."[44]

Thackeray's realism developed in part as a protest against the silver fork novel, which, as Bulwer-Lytton pointed out, feeds its readers' desires to rise in society while at the same time consoling them with a sense of their superiority to the more fortunate.[45] Such novels encourage both envy and emulation without providing an analysis of the larger social system or an understanding of true merit: the silver fork novel, in other words, is essentially an expression of the "Snobbery" that Thackeray defined so brilliantly in *The Book of Snobs*. The criminal romance, on the other hand, impelled Thackeray to repudiate its characteristically improbable events and idealized characterizations—most egregiously idealized in the case of "otto-of-rose murderers" but also in sentimentalized women such as Jack Sheppard's mother and Dickens's "Bis Dadsy." The sentimentality that warmed the criminal romance, Thackeray saw, created a steamy mist of sympathy that obscured the true criminal colors and, as Reynolds pointed out in his review of Ainsworth's romances, absolved readers and society as a whole of responsibility, even the minimal responsibility of a clear understanding of ethics, history, and the law. By simplifying and distorting complex social reality, the criminal romance employs emotion not for enlightenment but for a pleasurable, but false, sense of one's own goodness, based on warm, benevolent feelings.

Thackeray's realism engages emotion in service of understanding; this is why he came to see the novelist's task as being as important as the preacher's. In his novels, intellect and emotion are both engaged in shaping an ethical vision that challenges false forms of consciousness, whether they be romance, sentiment, or snobbery. Although he began as a parodist, and his early characters are sketchy, one can see in the early works the makings of a realist as Lukács defines the term. As Thackeray's artistry developed, he became more skilled at portraying individuals in complex, dynamic social relations with society. His characters are individuals (not illustrations of a thesis) with a private (and later increasingly complex) psychological life, but they are not limited to that. These characters also interact with and are shaped by society's structures and values, and the two are constantly acting upon one another. In Thackeray's early works, the effects of social structures upon women are foregrounded: economic and educational practices create a dependence that is both legal and psychological, leading to loveless marriages and feelings of unworthiness. That Thackeray did all this through style, while claiming to have "no head above the eyebrows," is reason more than sufficient for Carlyle to have called him the great stylist of his age.[46] In *Barry Lyndon,* style is more than a brilliant fictional technique: it is also Thackeray's means, as he put it in "French Fashionable Novels," of providing the "true character under false names" (*Works* 22: 99) of an entire civilization.

3/ *Vanity Fair*
Backgrounds

> The [ladies of the Seraglio] poor devils are allowed to
> come out, half-a-dozen times in the year, to spend their
> little wretched allowance of pocket-money in purchasing
> trinkets and tobacco; all the rest of the time they pursue
> the beautiful duties of their existence in the walls of the
> sacred harem.
>
> —*Cornhill to Cairo* (*Works* 6: 309)

Thackeray was admired by major feminist writers of the age, including George Eliot, Barbara Bodichon, Charlotte Brontë, and George Meredith. And *Vanity Fair* is one of the most significant works of Thackeray's career, indeed of the century. So it is a puzzle why *Vanity Fair* is not more studied and appreciated by feminist critics today. One explanation for this anomaly is that Thackeray's complex, highly allusive, and ironic narrative voice is rather perplexing, and so *Vanity Fair* is not taught nor read nearly so often as it deserves.

Another reason for the sparse and sporadic quality of feminist criticism of this novel is that its central characters, Amelia Sedley and Becky Sharp, elicit such a variety of responses from readers. Thackeray's "Amelia doll," for example, is sometimes discussed as a vindication of the Victorian feminine ideal, sometimes as an indictment of that same ideal, and sometimes as a denial of the possibility of any ideals (or values) at all in a civilization as corrupt as that found in *Vanity Fair*. [1] Even the friendliest of Thackeray's early reviewers, Robert Bell, asked in *Fraser's* in September 1848 for "more fresh air." John Loofbourow sums up critical responses to the novel as a whole in terms that exactly describe why Amelia is so puzzling: "The significance of his work has been obscured by its apparently conventional elements; whereas many of Thackeray's conventions were used for unprecedented artistic purposes, for instance, when he adopts the mannerisms of popular fiction to represent the compulsive emotional drives that animate his characters."[2]

In these chapters on *Vanity Fair,* I plan to address the novel's complex multiplicity of perspectives and to show how this complexity coexists with a fundamentally unifying, overarching perspective on women's issues, that is, to demonstrate that Thackeray is both "deconstructionist" and moralist. Roland Barthes wrote in *S/Z* that "the Fool, dressed in motley, a divided costume, was once the purveyor of the *double understanding*"; this double understanding offers the reader a "most precious nourishment . . . countercommunication"; and thus "the discourse, and not one or another of its characters, is the only *positive* hero of the story."[3] Thackeray's sketch for the yellow monthly covers of *Vanity Fair* shows the narrator as a fool addressing a crowd of fools from a barrel (see figure 4), and it is this image to which the narrator refers when he says: "And while the moralist, who is holding forth on the cover (an accurate portrait of your humble servant), professes to wear neither gown nor bands, but only the very same long-eared livery in which his congregation is arrayed: yet, look you, one is bound to speak the truth as far as one knows it."[4]

The present chapter will begin by presenting materials deemed "background" to the novel: Thackeray's travels, and the broadening of his perspective; his life, and the effect of experience on his understanding of gender issues; his fusion of several kinds of parody and satire into something very close to an obscure, ancient genre—Menippean satire; and his reception by critics and his place in the discourse of the day regarding women's education and the profession of governessing. The next chapter will resume the subject of nineteenth-century views of women and turn to the novel for evidence of *Vanity Fair*'s political topicality regarding the education, employment, and socialization of women. From there, I will expand the discussion to broader issues of gender as they play themselves out in the characterizations and conflicts of *Vanity Fair:* Dobbin's problematic love for Amelia, Lady Jane's confrontation with Becky and Pitt, and Amelia's determination to be free of the suffocating fictions and sham values that enclose her.

Biographical Foundations for *Vanity Fair*

By the time he began to write *Vanity Fair,* Thackeray had started taking the profession of novel writing very seriously. Indeed, he

VANITY FAIR:

PEN AND PENCIL SKETCHES OF ENGLISH SOCIETY.

BY W. M. THACKERAY,

Author of " The Irish Sketch Book :" " Journey from Cornhill to Grand Cairo " of " Jeames's Diary "
and the "Snob Papers" in " Punch :" &c. &c.

LONDON:
PUBLISHED AT THE PUNCH OFFICE, 85, FLEET STREET.
J. MENZIES, EDINBURGH; J. M'LEOD, GLASGOW; J. M'GLASHAN, DUBLIN.
1847.

4. Thackeray's sketch for the covers of the monthly *Vanity Fair,* showing himself as
"A Fool Addressing Other Fools" (*Works* 1: lvii).

was taking life more seriously. "I get painfully moral every day and find myself talking too much and practising so little" (*Letters* 2: 234). But he was also angered by people like his mother who set up narrow definitions of morality and condemned those who disagreed: "And it seems to me hence almost blasphemous: that any blind prejudiced sinful mortal being should dare to be unhappy about the belief of another; should dare to say Lo I am right and my brothers must go to damnation—I Know God and my brother doesn't" (*Letters* 2: 206–7). In *Vanity Fair,* Thackeray set out to write a "sermon"—a sermon that would do justice to the complexity of ethical issues involved in living in society, but that would preach without self-righteousness and remain intellectually open without moral relativism or skepticism.

The broadening of Thackeray's moral perspective may be attributed in part to his travels outside of the West. In the late summer of 1844, Thackeray impulsively accepted an offer of free passage on a cruise around the shores of the Mediterranean. He hoped to write a travel book as successful as Kinglake's *Eothen* (*Letters* 2: 152). Between bouts of seasickness, he sent the concluding sections of *Barry Lyndon* to *Fraser's* and "Fat Contributor" dispatches to *Punch.* The travel narrative *Notes of a Journey from Cornhill to Grand Cairo* gave Thackeray scope for reflecting on history and human behavior on a grand scale, covering three continents and three centuries.

During his travels, Thackeray saw that no matter how varied the forms it took, women's subordination was universal. Rather than conclude the phenomenon was "natural," Thackeray became ever more convinced of its injustice. His travels reinforced his early tendency to compare the subordination of women in European cultures with more obvious forms (such as foot-binding and harems) practiced in other cultures. Deborah Thomas's interesting recent work *Thackeray and Slavery* provides extensive discussion of Thackeray's use of slavery as a metaphor for the situation of women, and although Thomas concludes that Thackeray, "like most men of his day, . . . was in favor of . . . 'the subjection of women,'" the evidence points to the opposite conclusion.[5] In *Vanity Fair,* he wrote, "We are Turks with the affections of our women; their bodies may be allowed to move freely in the world, but their souls are to be possessed by only one man—and they obey" (169). Thackeray drew such comparisons, not to condemn non-Western cultures but to point out that, regarding women, Western cultures fall short of the superior ideals they profess.

By 1847, painful experience had made Thackeray more serious about his writing and more nuanced in his criticism, and he felt a responsibility to convey some of his understanding through his writings. Travel taught Thackeray to define more sharply the way in which culture shapes character. *Vanity Fair* is at once an analysis of a universal tendency to devalue women and an indictment of Western culture. It is also, finally, a private reflection on his own life. A letter Thackeray wrote to Mark Lemon in 1847 regarding *Snobs* is also appropriate for *Vanity Fair:*

> What I mean applies to my own case & that of all of us—who set up as Satirical-Moralists—and having such a vast multitude of readers whom we not only amuse but teach. And indeed, a solemn prayer to God Almighty was in my thoughts that we may never forget truth & Justice and kindness as the great ends of our profession. There's something of the same strain in Vanity Fair. And our profession seems to me to be as serious as the Parson's own. (*Letters* 2: 282)

Humbled and chastened by his wife's insanity, Thackeray wrote in his diary, "Oh Lord God—there is not one of the sorrows or disappointments of my life, that as I fancy I cannot trace to some error crime or weakness of my disposition" (*Letters* 2: 30–31). Thackeray not only wrote his sorrows into *Vanity Fair,* he also wrote in his own errors—and revealed them as Vanity Fair's errors too. A letter to Robert Bell, a friend who had published a favorable review in *Fraser's* (September 1848), confirms that the novel is simultaneously satirical and confessional:

> My dear Bell
>   [Your] I hope . . . excellent article . . . seems to me very just. . . . If I had put in more fresh air as you call it my object would have been defeated—It is to indicate, in cheerful terms, that we are for the most part an abominably foolish and selfish people. . . . Everybody is you see in that book, —for instance if I had made Amelia a higher order of woman there would have been no vanity in Dobbins falling in love with her, whereas the impression at present is that he is a fool for his pains that he had married a silly little thing and in fact has found out his error rather a sweet and tender one however, *quia multum amavit* I want to leave everybody dissatisfied

and unhappy at the end of the story—we ought all to be with our own and all other stories. Good God dont I see (in that may-be cracked and warped looking glass in which I am always looking) my own weaknesses wickednesses lusts follies shortcomings? in company let us hope with better qualities. (*Letters* 2: 423–24)

By the time Thackeray brought out the first number of *Vanity Fair* in January 1847, Isabella Thackeray's condition had become hopeless. Thackeray placed her in a home near London where he and the children could visit her, and he sometimes took her on outings, but her brief intervals of improvement were followed by an inevitable return to vacuity, or to the mysterious "nasty pranks" Thackeray alludes to, and so there was little hope that they could ever live together. Thackeray feared to excite her emotions in any way. His diary continues to record visits and outings dutifully maintained, but providing little hope or enjoyment. He had brought his two daughters to London and rented a double town-house at 13 Young Street, in peaceful, then still half-rural Kensington, to make a home for them and for himself. At this time he was also earnestly in love with Jane Brookfield and perhaps half-in-love with Caroline Norton.

The same diary entry that records Thackeray's sense of self-blame (cited above) also expresses his prayerful resolution to overcome the faults "of character which have borne such bitter fruit already" and to "be kept in a mood for seriously considering & trying to act up to my duty." Part of this duty was to take a greater interest in the domestic routines of his new home, and part, it seems, consisted of writing in a kinder and more humble spirit. Thackeray's mood at the time may be summed up in the words of John Robertson:

> Critics of all living men ought to cultivate the most generous and genial sympathies. It is their work to appreciate truth and beauty. The pleasures, such as they are, of writing and reading slashing articles, are bought very dearly by dulling the taste for new kinds of excellence, and deadening the sympathies, without which it is impossible to obtain even the slightest understanding, either of adverse or of novel truths.[6]

Thackeray was relinquishing his "slashing articles" and cultivating an understanding of the adverse truths of his own life, especially in regard to Isabella and the factors that had led to their mutual sorrow.

I have said that Thackeray's extraordinary sympathy for women has been obscured by critical controversy over whether Amelia was meant to be an example of goodness and whether Thackeray actually admired the fascinating Becky. Some of these problems of interpretation begin with Thackeray himself and his own ambivalence about certain women in his life. Concerning Amelia, the ambivalence is twofold: first, Thackeray seems uncertain about who his sources for Amelia are; and then, when he acknowledges that his wife was at least part of Amelia, he is faced with the unsettling recognition that Amelia's character is based on a woman who is tending toward a complete mental breakdown. Thus, his own love for his wife is, like Dobbin's for Amelia, both "sweet and tender" and also an "error," if not downright "folly," and society's role in forming such women may come under the heading "wickedness."

Thackeray introduces the issue of Becky's popularity and Amelia's lack of it in his preface, and he continually challenges the inscribed reader (Jones in his club sneering at Amelia's sentimentality, for example, or women inclined to criticize Becky for husband hunting) not to leap to conclusions about either woman. Such narrative ploys operate as a reminder of the limitations of both Becky and Amelia and link them with all women in opposition to the power and relative freedom of the male characters.

Thackeray's own comments confirm his ambivalence. When his mother objected that Amelia was selfish, he replied, "my object is not to make a perfect character, or anything like it" (*Works* 1: xliv). On 30 June 1848, Thackeray wrote to Jane Brookfield to apologize for what he calls a "bad joke"—he had given Amelia's maid the name of Mrs. Brookfield's maid, Payne, and then attempted to allay her anticipated anger by writing, "You know you are only a piece of Amelia—My Mother is another half: my poor little wife *y est pour beaucoup*" (*Letters* 2: 394). A month later, Thackeray referred jokingly to Amelia as "always an overrated woman I thought" (*Letters* 2: 407), and in October he wrote again to Jane Brookfield to say, "after all I see on reading over my books, that the woman I have been perpetually describing is not you nor my mother but that poor little wife of mine, who now does not care 2d. for anything but her dinner and her glass of porter" (*Letters* 2: 440). Behind similar suggestive lines to be gleaned from letters must lie years of painful introspection, as Thackeray watched

Isabella's personality degenerate into exaggerated manifestations of once-loved characteristics.

Jane Brookfield provided Thackeray with another model for the ideal Victorian woman, and he was at the same time socializing with highly independent, unconventional women such as Lady Ashburton—formerly Lady Harriet Mary Montagu, a friend of John Stuart Mill, and a woman of great intelligence and strength of character (*Letters* 1: lxxxv)—Lady Morgan, Lady Blessington, and Caroline Norton, all of whom had characters and lives that resembled Becky Sharp's. Others Thackeray was socializing with at this time—Harriet Martineau, John Stuart Mill, George Lewes, and (beginning probably in 1849) Lady Eddisbury, who worked for women's education—all provided, by their writings and conversation, analyses of the institutions affecting women's lives that are consistent with Thackeray's novel.

Thackeray seems torn at this time between witty, worldly women like Norton and more respectable women like Jane Brookfield and his mother, to whom he wrote on 6 March 1846:

> I don't like or trust the new acquaintances, and shabby fashionable people. The women are abominably free and easy, and inspire one with involuntary doubts, that it is not all talk with them. Mrs. Brookfield is my beau-ideal. I have been in love with her these four years—not so as to endanger peace or appetite but she always seems to me to speak and do and think as a woman should. (*Letters* 2: 231)

Lest this letter be read as a remarkable confession, or a complete statement, of Thackeray's views, it should be noted that his defending Brookfield's respectability and contrasting her with other friends was probably meant in part to allay his mother's jealous suspicions about their relationship. He was probably exaggerating, but there is some truth in his self-description. It represents one side of his ambivalence, the side that preferred "milk-and-water women" (*Letters* 1: 460).

Among the "free and easy" women of whom Becky Sharp is a composite were Caroline Norton and Sidney Owenson, Lady Morgan. Lionel Stevenson's essay "*Vanity Fair* and Lady Morgan" suggests a convincing number of parallels between Becky Sharp and Sidney Owenson. Like Becky Sharp, Owenson rose "entirely by her own wit and shrewdness from a childhood of Bohemianism and poverty through the stages of governess and lady-companion to rank and social prestige through a judicious marriage and a sound business sense."[7] The fact that Lady Morgan was a feminist would add to the resonance of her portrait for Thackeray's contemporary readers.

The other "original," Caroline Norton, seems to have had a greater influence on Thackeray, however, for her character and life run through his works as a sustained and insistent theme. Some of the similarities between Caroline and Becky have already been outlined. Both women are witty and unconventional, both know how to deal with the law, and according to the title of *Vanity Fair's* chapter 36, both know "How to Live Well On Nothing A-Year." Becky is even complimented by her creditors' lawyers "upon the brilliant way in which she did business, and [they] declared that there was no professional man who could beat her" (*Vanity Fair* 357). Norton, too, engaged the legal system of her day with considerable success.

Thackeray's descriptions of Becky often recall Norton: "Becky loved society, and, indeed, could no more exist without it than an opium-eater without his dram" (623). Becky's relationship with Lord Steyne resembles Norton's with Melbourne in significant ways. Both men are considerably older than the women, both are powerful and wealthy, and both have had previous scandalous love affairs. Melbourne had been sued before for "criminal conversation" and had been found guilty. And Steyne, Thackeray tells us, "whose carriage was always at [Becky's] door, who passed hours daily in her company, and whose constant presence made the world talk about her. . . . Lord Steyne, though a nobleman of the greatest station and talents, was a man whose attentions would compromise any woman" (508). These words were as true of Melbourne as of Steyne.

Although Becky may exemplify Norton's intelligence, wit, and humor, and elements of her life seem to allude to Norton's, there are also significant differences. Thackeray's greatest indictment of Becky is that she cares little for her son or her dull but generous and loyal husband, Rawdon. Neither of these charges fits Caroline, for she loved her children—they were the true motivating passion of her work—and George did not deserve her love, for he was abusive and violent. These alterations make Becky Sharp a less sympathetic character than her counterpart Norton.

Why would Thackeray make such changes? The good woman–bad woman dualism that runs through *Vanity Fair,* ironic though it may be, makes some simplification necessary. But the significance of Becky's story as a reflection of Caroline's history remains: both represent women's powerlessness—good women and bad are equally liable to lose their children. By making Becky's character even less conventional than Norton's, Thackeray made possible a more thorough critique of respectable society: Becky's defiant "wickedness" simultaneously contests and exploits Vanity Fair values, while Norton never rejected them altogether. Becky may represent also Thackeray's "involuntary doubts, that it is not all talk" about Norton and her relationship with Melbourne. And yet, perhaps because of the mystery and fascination surrounding Norton, Becky calls forth some of Thackeray's best writing. He even seems to delight in the uncertainty surrounding her, in that Becky represents a greater truth—that none of us knows our neighbor's heart, and certainly no one has the right to judge: "Her history was after all a mystery. Parties were divided about her. Some . . . said that she was a criminal; whilst others vowed that she was as innocent as a lamb, and that her odious husband was in fault. She won over a good many by bursting into tears about her boy" (621).

Thackeray's loves and friendships entered into *Vanity Fair* at the deepest levels. They generated a harvest that includes a complex emotional and ethical discernment regarding "good" women and "bad," a distrust of any single system of ethics, and a nuanced and yet remarkably comprehensive portrayal of the larger social and cultural patterns of nineteenth-century England. As Barbara Hardy wrote, "His brilliant understanding of the surface, and his abstention from systematic criticism and voiced social ethic, allow society to show itself, astounding, mad, hollow, frightening."[8]

VANITY FAIR AS MODIFIED MENIPPEAN SATIRE

Although traces of Thackeray's private ambivalences remain, *Vanity Fair* is neither sentimental nor cynical. It begins by parodying both those stances—the sentimental, in Amelia's twelve dearest friends, and the cynical, in Jones's reading about them at his club—and moves out from parody to set up a discourse that reflects the debates of the day regarding men and women. Thackeray's dedication to truth in all its complexity led him to construct a novel that is both as timeless as the Bible or myth and an integral part of its century. In that it reproduces the debates and brilliantly captures the varied voices of its participants, *Vanity Fair* is very much a product of the nineteenth-century women's movement. But in order to capture the complexity of this (to him) "modern" debate, Thackeray employed the techniques of a classical genre, Menippean satire.

F. Anne Payne's description of Menippean satire provides a paradigm for the intellectual dynamics of *Vanity Fair,* and a brief digression into this genre promises to be useful to this study, especially in light of Thackeray's ability to absorb and employ the tropes of classical literature.[9] Just as Peggy O'Dowd's revels conjure up Juvenal's Messalina leaving the brothels, "wearied but not yet satisfied" (418), and just as Becky, after her break with Rawdon, is "as restless as Ulysses" (625), so are the structure and philosophy of *Vanity Fair* informed by Menippus.

The first shared characteristic is Thackeray's extensive use of parody, which is, according to Payne, "a common device in [Menippean] satires, . . . as important as the dialogic structure. The parody causes us to sense continually the presence of another genre, another story, another mind."[10] Loofbourow links *Vanity Fair* to two other parodies of chivalric romance that Thackeray wrote at about the same time, *A Legend of the Rhine* (1845) and *Rebecca and Rowena* (1849). The structure of the novel itself expresses a twofold parodic intent: sentimental romance is his target in Amelia's story, and criminal romance in Becky's.[11]

Another characteristic of Menippean satire is the use of the carnival or fair as a structuring and thematic foundation. Thackeray's prefatory "Before the Curtain" address, and his self-characterizations as quack, clown, moralist, man and brother, Fool addressing other fools, and Fool looking into a cracked looking-glass (see figure 5), all reflect the Menippean carnival of multiple perspectives. Society—even life itself—is represented as a fair throughout the novel. The sale of the Sedley home after the father's bankruptcy is one instance:

> If there is any exhibition in all Vanity Fair which Satire and Sentiment can visit arm in arm together; where you will light on the strangest contrasts laughable and tearful: where you may be gentle and pathetic, or savage and cynical with perfect propriety; it is at one of those public assemblies. (*Vanity Fair* 158–59)

The narrator's comment on Miss Crawley's death is another:

O brother wearers of motley! Are there not moments when one grows sick of grinning and tumbling, and the jingling of cap and bells? This, dear friends and companions, is my amiable object—to walk with you through the Fair, to examine the shops and the shows there; and that we should all come home after the flare, and the noise, and the gaiety, and be perfectly miserable in private. (180–81)

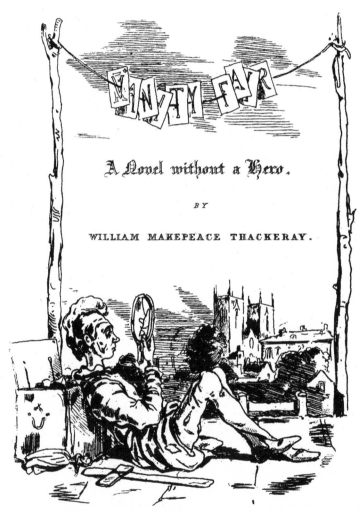

5. Frontispiece to *Vanity Fair,* showing the self-reflecting author (*Works* 1: iii).

Another Menippean characteristic found in *Vanity Fair* is the deployment of parody to define not characters so much as mental attitudes. Wheatley discusses Thackeray's bewildering "air . . . of constantly shifting evaluations," in the scene in which Becky uses dolls to caricature the two Misses Pinkerton, and concludes that the point of such passages is "primarily stylistic," to focus "on the variety of perspectives available to the mind."[12] The scene in which old Mr. Osborne crosses George's name out of the family Bible does not evade the father's culpability and yet evokes pity for his pain, which is after all caused by his love for George and by his limitations, which are not entirely his fault—they are the limitations of Vanity Fair: "What humiliation and fury: what pangs of sickening rage, balked ambition and love; what wounds of outraged vanity, tenderness even, had this old worldling now to suffer under!" (224). The frontispiece to the family Bible represents Abraham sacrificing Isaac and is another example of Thackeray's joining a specifically realized character portrait with allegory and broad cultural allusion: Mr. Osborne is both the representative of an abstract idea and a realistically historicized individual.[13]

Vanity Fair, like all Menippean satire, is deeply paradoxical. Rather than contrasting his characters against some unstated ideal, Thackeray allows a multiplicity of antitheses to stand unresolved. When poor Lady Steyne speaks to Becky (whom everyone else is condemning and avoiding as Steyne's mistress), a startling and moving scene follows:

> [Becky] sang religious songs of Mozart, which had been early favourites of Lady Steyne, and with such sweetness and tenderness that the lady lingering round the piano, sate down by its side, and listened until the tears rolled down her eyes. . . . She was a girl once more, and the brief period of her happiness bloomed out again for an hour—she started when the jarring doors were flung open and with a loud laugh from Lord Steyne, the men of the party entered full of gaiety. (474–75)

Perhaps it does not matter that Mozart's ethereal music is being played by Steyne's reputed mistress, or more likely, it is profoundly appropriate that Becky join with Steyne's wife in a poignant moment of fellow feeling—united by the sacred music that surpasses all differences and rivalry and that contrasts them to the loud, laughing, powerful men. Becky may not be Steyne's mistress after all and, Clytemnestra-like, may well be Lady Steyne's avenger: Steyne will carry the scar of Rawdon's diamond pin on his forehead for the rest of his life.

Thackeray's complicated intelligence finds brilliant expression here in the interplay of positive and negative valuations of Becky and Amelia, valuations that are themselves unstable and reversible. Amelia's greatest quality, her ability to love, changes its aspect continually, sometimes to trivial sentimentality, sometimes to foolishly indulgent maternal affection, sometimes to blind worship of an unworthy husband. Amelia is good because she loves. But she lives in a society in which good can be subverted by cultural forces: woman's work, performed perhaps for love, results in economic powerlessness and psychological dependency, and altruism too often sours into feelings of worthlessness. Love can either be cloying or be transformed into servitude and self-hatred, which is what Thackeray may have observed in Isabella.

Becky lives in the same system, but she is neither angel nor amiable slave. Maria DiBattista's "The Triumph of Clytemnestra" provides a fine analysis of Thackeray's allusive linking of Amelia as Iphigenia and Becky as Clytemnestra, one representing female victimization and the other vengeance. Questions of who is the "good" woman become irrelevant as the issues become more finely delineated. Through such contradictions and ambiguities, Thackeray questions the possibility of any permanent standards other than truth, kindness, and laughter at fools and quacks— "other quacks, plague take them!" (*Vanity Fair* 5). In Thackeray, as in Chaucer, satire opens all intellectual positions to questioning and allows the socially marginal points of view to compete with the most powerfully entrenched ideas.

Vanity Fair is an adaptation of the *Menippia Satura* to the requirements of the modern novel, as it was then evolving—and certainly Thackeray helped shape it. Like other Menippean satires, *Vanity Fair* cannot be understood unless, as Payne puts it, "we master the necessary art of reading [it]." It is a genre she describes as "profoundly thoughtful," which "requires that we accept as necessary the presentation of simultaneous unresolved points of view." And in a sentence that recalls *Vanity Fair*'s concluding paragraph, "*Vanitas Vanitatum!* Which of us is happy in this world? Which of us has his desire? or having it, is satisfied?—Come children, let us shut up the box and the puppets, for our play is played out," Payne wrote:

The air of hope, the courtesy, and the sense of intellectual freedom that we find in these satires are the happy by-products of the satirist's projecting a world without dead ends, without the destructive (if somewhat comforting) dictum, the one or the other. . . . The dialogue, which is composed of the interactions of a series of stereotyped characters, is probably the most frequent device in Menippean satire for portraying the multiplicity of the universe and the impossibility of finding the ultimate answer to any mortal question.

Payne's description of Menippean satire may be applied to *Vanity Fair* to explain its unique quality of being both historically specific and timeless:

> In times of historical crisis . . . times of clashing philosophical, political, economic, or religious systems—Menippean satire affords a constructive method of containing ideological disagreements, a method of broadening the base upon which we must stand in order to investigate the conflicting evidence that creates the spiritual dilemma of man. . . .
>
> The great evil Menippean satire perceives is the propensity human beings have for creating faulty systems and institutions that drag them into the abuse and limited understanding of even such ideals as they have managed to build into those systems and institutions.[14]

Thus it is that the Menippean structure of *Vanity Fair* allows Thackeray to preach his "sermon" with humor, fellow feeling, and intellectual play of the highest order.

EASTLAKE'S REVIEW RECLAIMED

One reason for feminist scholars' neglect of *Vanity Fair* seems to be that one of its most prominent reviewers, Lady Eastlake (previously Elizabeth Rigby), has been misread as attacking *Jane Eyre* for its "feminism" and thus (it is inferred) praising *Vanity Fair* for its conservatism. The review in question, entitled "Review: *Vanity Fair, Jane Eyre,* and *The Governesses' Benevolent Institution—Report for 1847,*" appeared in the *Quarterly Review* in 1848. Among the critics who dismiss Eastlake's review are Sandra M. Gilbert and Susan Gubar, who cite the review as a condemnation of valid feminist anger. In *Literary Women*, Ellen Moers cites the review as an example of the harsh treatment that Victorian women writers had to endure from women reviewers. These characterizations of Eastlake's review, however, are partial in both senses of the word. In actuality, Eastlake acknowledged *Jane Eyre*'s "high power, intense feeling, and fine religious instinct."[15] It should also be noted that her remarks on weaknesses in Brontë's novel anticipate Virginia Woolf's discussion in *A Room of One's Own* of the artistically destructive power of Brontë's (and of most early women writers') anger.

One of the more regrettable attacks on Eastlake's review occurs in the otherwise excellent three-volume study of the women's rights movement, Bell and Offen's *Women, the Family, and Freedom*, in which an *ad feminam* attack betrays the fair-mindedness that feminist criticism should represent:

> Shortly after this review appeared in print, Rigby married for the first time, at the age of forty, the much-admired painter Sir Charles Eastlake, whose position as president of the Royal Academy did nothing to hinder her future as an art critic. . . .
>
> Rigby's rage against *Jane Eyre* and Jane's passion for Rochester, on the eve of Rigby's own belated marriage, probably betrayed her unrequited passion for her editor John Lockhart.[16]

Unfortunately, some critics have concluded that Eastlake's criticism of *Jane Eyre* implies approval of prejudice against women in *Vanity Fair*. In reality, Lady Eastlake regrets that *Jane Eyre* will not help the governesses "whose cause it affects to advocate," although no cause more "deserves and demands . . . befriending." Eastlake's analysis is, like Thackeray's, a broad social analysis. In a sentence that applies to both Amelia's and Becky's fathers, Eastlake reminds her readers:

> We need the imprudencies, extravagencies, mistakes, or crimes of a certain number of fathers, to sow that seed from which we reap the harvest of governesses. There is no other class of labourers for hire who are thus systematically supplied by the misfortunes of our fellow creatures. There is no other class which so cruelly requires its members to be, in birth, mind, and manners, above their station, in order to fit them for their station.[17]

Perhaps the most compelling evidence for ridding feminist criticism of the notion that Lady Eastlake (and by implication, Thackeray) is hostile to reform is that, in the same essay, she proceeds to advocate the professionalization of governessing by means of training, examinations, and certification (a revolutionary idea at the time) in order to provide governesses greater prestige, a just wage, higher educational standards, and retirement security. Whereas Brontë concludes *Jane Eyre* with the sentimental, romantic solution of a private and reclusive marriage, Thackeray and Eastlake reject such easy and false answers.

Lady Eastlake recognized the remarkable quality of Thackeray's realism: *Vanity Fair,* she wrote, is "a literal photograph of the manners and habits of the nineteenth century, thrown on to paper by the light of a powerful mind" ("Review" 161). In it, "Thanks to Mr. Thackeray, [in Becky] the world is now provided with an *idea,* which if we mistake not, will be the skeleton in every ball-room and boudoir for a long time to come" (161). Perhaps because she knew Thackeray socially and suspected that Amelia might be based on Thackeray's wife, Amelia is mentioned briefly, only to be dismissed for her "philoprogenitive idolatries" (160). The one quarrel Eastlake allows herself is with Thackeray's hints that Becky is a murderess, which she finds unrealistic, because Becky is too clever to have to resort to crime, and she advises readers to take up scissors and cut out "Becky's Second Appearance as Clytemnestra" (see figure 1). On the whole, she finds *Vanity Fair* "one of the most amusing, but also one of the most distressing books we have read for many a long year . . . [for it] weighs down our hearts, not for the Amelias and Georges of the story, but for poor kindred human nature" (155–56).

Eastlake's appreciation of Thackeray's novel, combined with her denunciation of the treatment of governesses, is far more socially aware than is usually acknowledged. She does recommend a certain degree of Christian resignation and gratitude to the Jane Eyres of the world, and she finds Jane Eyre's general resentfulness and her readiness to listen to her employer's sexual exploits disturbing and the author a bit ingenuous. But in her sympathy for governesses and in her linking of their status to the social and economic evils of her society, Eastlake provides the groundwork for an analysis of women's simultaneous dependence on men and exploitation of other women that supports feminist readings of Victorian society and even of *Jane Eyre.*[18] In so doing, she illuminates the central thesis of Thackeray's novel.

Robert Colby's discussion of the governess heroine in *Fiction*

with a Purpose reveals that Becky has evolved from a long line of fictive governesses that includes Maria Edgeworth's "The Good
French Governess," published in *Moral Tales* (1801), Lady Blessington's *The Governess,* and novels by Jane Austen, Elizabeth
Sewell, and Harriet Martineau. In this context, both Becky Sharp
and Jane Eyre belong to a tradition of social protest. Mary
Poovey's chapter on the governess and *Jane Eyre* in *Uneven Developments* reviews the extraordinary amount of discussion in the peri-
odical press of the "plight" of the governess and suggests that this
interest, which is disproportionate to the magnitude of the problem, stems from "the place [governesses] occupied in the middle-
class ideology . . . as bulwarks against [the] erosion" of middle-
class values.[19]

Thackeray and Brontë both seem to have chosen the governess
figure to redefine those values. Thackeray had read Brontë's *Jane
Eyre* in 1847 with delight and admiration. Indeed, he accorded it
more recognition than his own novel generally receives from feminists today:

> I wish you had not sent me Jane Eyre. It interested me so much that
> I have lost (or won if you like) a whole day in reading it. . . . I have
> been exceedingly moved & pleased by Jane Eyre. It is a womans
> writing, but whose? Give my respects and thanks to the author—
> whose novel is the first English one . . . that I've been able to read
> for many a day. (*Letters* 2: 319)

And in a brief essay that is part eulogy, part introduction to an unfinished fragment of Brontë's last novel, *Emma,* Thackeray calls
Jane Eyre the "masterwork of a great genius."[20]

THE ECONOMICS OF CHARACTER

Eastlake recognized that both *Vanity Fair* and the *Report of the
Governesses' Benevolent Institution* indicted the economic and educational limitations placed on Victorian women. *Vanity Fair* began
publication at about the same time that the first attempt at higher
education for women was undertaken by the Governesses' Benevolent Institution, under the title of "Lectures for Ladies."

Thackeray was aware of what was at stake in women's education;
his satire on Miss Pinkerton's Academy was based in part on problems he had encountered in educating his own daughters, espe-

cially the more thoughtful, less placid Annie. Regarding one governess, he wrote to his mother: "Alexander is another bore: but admirable in many points keeping the children to their work unceasingly always kind & gd-humoured with all their factiousness and bent on doing her duty—only she is no more a fit match for Anny's brains than John [Thackeray's servant] is for mine" (*Letters* 2: 373). At another time, he wrote: "The governess is very good very honest very eager to do her duty very gawky not by any means wise, or fit to guide Anny's mind. But she can teach her geography and music and what they call history and hemming . . . and my dear old Nan goes on thinking for herself" (*Letters* 2: 335).

In an 1864 *Cornhill* article entitled "Middle-Class Education in England: Girls," Harriet Martineau appraised the relationship between girls' education and social and economic conditions in terms that exactly fit Thackeray's analysis, provided some seventeen years earlier in *Vanity Fair:*

> Within half a century the girlhood of the upper middle class has gone through an experience of permanent historical importance. At the beginning of that time, it was assumed . . . that every woman is maintained by her father or her husband, or other male relative. . . . When the war was over . . . the lot of increasing numbers of middle-class women became appalling. After the suspense and crash of 1825–6, there seemed to be nothing between them and despair. Their fathers or husbands ruined, . . . what was to become of the hundreds of thousands of women who had always been told, and had always believed, that they would be taken care of as long as they lived? . . . [W]omen did anything that they could devise to escape the workhouse. The greater number, perhaps, could do nothing but accept charity in the form of dependence, with its carking cares and intolerable humiliations; but there was such a rush into governessing as was never seen before. . . . Something must come out of such a state of things. . . . But the grand step was the familiarizing the mind of society with the idea of women becoming self-dependent.[21]

In Amelia's world, "self-dependence" was little thought of for women: sweet and amiable, she will try to sell hand-painted cards in a vain effort to keep her son. But Thackeray had emphasized Becky's need to look out for her own interests from the beginning.

Thackeray differed from most of his predecessors and many of his contemporaries in that he did not view women's education as primarily a training for marriage and child-rearing. In this he goes further than Maria Edgeworth, whose interest in the moral and intellectual improvement of women is somewhat reformist:

> Sentiment and ridicule have conspired to represent reason, knowledge, and science, as unsuitable or dangerous to women; yet at the same time wit, and superficial acquirements in literature, have been the object of admiration in society; so that this dangerous inference has been drawn almost without our perceiving its fallacy, that superficial knowledge is more desirable in women than accurate knowledge. This principle must lead to innumerable errors; . . . instead of making women more reasonable, and less presuming, it will render them at once arrogant and ignorant; full of pretensions, incapable of application, and unfit to hear themselves convinced.

And yet resigned:

> We wish to educate women so that they may be happy in the situations in which they are most likely to be placed . . . girls should be more inured to restraint than boys because they are likely to meet with more restraint in society.[22]

Unlike Edgeworth, Thackeray emphasized the harmful effects of restraint. In chapter 4 of *The Book of Snobs,* he drew an analogy between the bound feet of a Chinese girl and the "pinched and distorted" brains of many English women. There is no hint that girls should be "inured to restraint" in an 1836 letter to his wife:

> When I said you were frivolous I meant no harm, all women are so I think from their education, and I want my wife to be better than all women: and then comes the definition of the word, a woman who occupies herself all day with her house and servants is frivolous, ditto she who does nothing but poonah-painting and piano forte, also the woman who piddles about prayer-meetings and teaches Sunday schools; into which 3 classes, I think, the race of women are divided. But I want my Puss to be a little paragon, and so it is that I am always belabouring her with advice. (*Letters* 1: 317)

Two days earlier he had written a few lines that make his meaning more clear: "For I want you to be not a thoughtless and frivolous girl, but a wise and affectionate woman, as you will be, dearest Puss, if you will but *love* enough" (*Letters* 1: 316). For Thackeray, as for domestic realists in general, education meant primarily the education of the heart. Thackeray sometimes found Isabella to be cold and unemotional; his ideas about how to educate the heart in courage and passion are implicit in the Pumpernickel section of *Vanity Fair* (as we shall see in the next chapter).

But that will be Amelia's second education; her first takes place at Miss Pinkerton's school, and Thackeray uses Barbara Pinkerton's letter to satirize the kind of education many girls were receiving in the first half of the nineteenth century. The reader will recall that the letter reintroduces Miss Amelia to her home as a young lady whose accomplishments and character are suitable for "the young English gentlewoman":

> "Those virtues which characterise the young English gentlewoman . . . will not be found wanting in the amiable Miss Sedley, whose *industry* and *obedience* have endeared her to her instructors, and whose delightful sweetness of temper has charmed her . . . companions. In music, in dancing, in orthography, in every variety of embroidery and needle-work, she will be found to have realised her friends' *fondest wishes.*" (*Vanity Fair* 12)

Years later, one of the members of the Schools' Enquiry Commission was to complain of the general state of girls' education, for reasons that Thackeray had anticipated. It is again Lady Eastlake who, in an 1878 *Quarterly Review* article on "The Englishwoman at School," states that the Commission found:

> [A] small amount of professional skill, an inferior set of school books, a vast deal of dry uninteresting taskwork . . . a very false estimate of the relative value of the several kinds of acquirement; a reference to effect, rather than to solid worth; a tendency to fill or adorn, rather than to strengthen the mind.[23]

That intelligence and learning are not the real criteria of a governess's desirability is made absurdly clear by another letter of Miss Pinkerton's, this one to Mrs. Bute Crawley. The real purpose of the letter is to dissect Becky's character, but its ostensible purpose is to recommend a governess. Miss Pinkerton's first candidate is the daughter of a deceased Cambridge Fellow and is a scholar of Greek, Latin, Hebrew, French, Spanish, Italian, and Syriac who can teach Constitutional law, mathematics, history, geography, music, and the natural sciences. But, Miss Pinkerton concludes, this woman would probably be "objectionable in Sir Huddleston Fuddleston's family" because she is young and attractive. Instead, she recommends an older woman—whose only qualification seems to be that she is unattractive—and concludes, "Their terms, of

6. Becky Sharp on female education: leaving Miss Pinkerton's Academy
(*Works* 1: [facing] 9).

course, are such as their accomplishments merit" (96–97).

When Becky flings the Johnson Dictionary out the carriage window (see figure 6), she is partially justified by Thackeray's implicit disdain for such schools; this is one of the places where Becky's attitude parallels Thackeray's.[24] That the book is Samuel Johnson's is a fine touch; he is after all the man who said, "Sir, a woman's preaching is like a dog's walking on his hinder legs. It is not done well; but you are surprized to find it done at all."[25] Becky's livid look of hatred and her motive (vengeance) will be repeated when she plays the part of Clytemnestra; the similarity points to a concern that goes beyond the problem of girls' academic education, for it is part of the larger pattern that Thackeray addresses in *Vanity Fair*. This pattern includes not only the negative "feminine" characteristics such as superficiality, idleness, and dependency that are fostered by girls' education but also passivity and passionlessness.

Becky's performance as governess provides another commentary on girls' education. When Becky goes to Queen's Crawley, the two girls under her negligent charge read racy French novels, and Miss Violet climbs trees, robs birds' nests, and is generally "rude and boisterous" (*Vanity Fair* 90). Thackeray's illustration of the scene, "Miss Sharp in Her School Room" (see figure 7), is not only a parody of Richard Redgrave's painting "The Poor Teacher" (1843), it is also a comic example of Thackeray's advice to parents, to "leave children to themselves":

> [I]f teachers would cease to bully them; if parents would not insist upon directing their thoughts, and dominating their feelings—those feelings and thoughts which are a mystery to all (for . . . how far more beautiful and sacred are the thoughts of the poor lad or girl whom you govern likely to be, than those of the dull and world-corrupted person who rules him?) . . . small harm would accrue. (47)

Becky "fails" in part because she does not train the girls in the proper Missish virtues. Her pose also conveys boredom, another accompaniment of education, worse for girls than for boys. In true Menippean fashion, Thackeray parodies both the sentimental representation and his own parody of female education. Becky, crying "I'm no angel" (19), is a brilliant vehicle.

7. Miss Sharp in her schoolroom (*Works* 1: 106).

To his credit, Thackeray never merely attacks women; he always provides reasons for their failings and conveys a sense of fellow feeling with them, which is notably absent in the writings of many contemporaries. Edward Bulwer-Lytton, for example, in "The Spirit of Society in England and France," blamed the corruption of public life on women, whom he saw as deficient in principles of public virtue and political integrity. If women were better educated, he wrote, they would perform their social duties better; that is, without neglecting a single domestic obligation, they would exert a calm, felicitous influence on the men whom they sent out into the world each day.[26] Although Thackeray also recognized the deficiencies of women's education, he never adopted such a tone of denunciation.

Thackeray makes another point against the Miss Pinkerton theory of education: that it does not prepare women for any kind of useful work, or for self-support. Lady Eastlake wrote, in "The Englishwoman at School," that Englishwomen were not only withering on the vine but starving on it too, and their plight was due to a combination of "false authority and false indulgence."[27] Like Maria Edgeworth, Thackeray recognized not only that women's education was generally inadequate but also that education, economic independence, and mental and spiritual stature are all interconnected. In 1798, Edgeworth—whose *Parents' Assistant* Amelia Sedley purchased (*Vanity Fair* 449)—wrote that governesses should be given greater respect and financial recompense, because

> [t]here is no employment, at present, by which a gentlewoman can maintain herself without losing something of that respect, something of that rank in society, which neither female fortitude nor male philosophy willingly undergoes. The liberal professions are open to men of small fortune; by presenting one similar resource to women, we should give a strong motive for their moral and intellectual improvement.[28]

After her father's death, Rebecca Sharp "determined . . . to get free from the prison in which she found herself [Miss Pinkerton's], and now began to act for herself, and for the first time to make connected plans for the future" (*Vanity Fair* 22). Her plans, of course, revolve around marriage; governessing is but a stopgap. There are no alternatives, as Edgeworth pointed out. Thackeray's treatment of marriage in *Vanity Fair* provides further analysis of women's economic helplessness and of the harm it does.

4/ *Vanity Fair*
Dynamics of the Text

An exquisite slave is what we want for the most part; a
humble, flattering, smiling, child-loving being. . . . What
are these but lies that we exact from our slaves? lies, the
dextrous performance of which we announce to be the
female virtues. . . . In the bargain we make with them I
don't think they get their rights. And . . . I doubt
whether we get the most out of our women by enslaving
them as we do by law and custom.
                              —*Mr. Brown's Letters:* "On Love" (*Works* 9: 305–8)

"The more I read Thackeray's works the more certain I
am that he stands alone—alone in his sagacity, alone in
his truth, alone in his feeling. . . . Thackeray is a Titan . . .;
there is the charm and majesty of repose in his greatest efforts; . . . his energy is sane energy, deliberate energy,
thoughtful energy. . . . [T]here are parts of *[Vanity Fair]*
that sound as solemn as an oracle. . . . His genius obeys
him. . . . Thackeray is unique. I *can* say no more, I *will* say
no less."

                                                    —Charlotte Brontë

When Charlotte Brontë wrote the passage above[1] in praise of
Thackeray's truthfulness, she must have recognized the deep similarities between *Vanity Fair* and her own *Jane Eyre:* in the 1849 *Mr.
Brown's Letters* that followed *Vanity Fair,* Thackeray declared openly
that "the female virtues" were no more than "lies that we exact
from our slaves" by means of "law and custom." Rather than pitting
Jane Eyre against *Vanity Fair* any longer, it is time for us to recognize,
as Brontë did, that both novels affirm the same values: financial independence, freedom, and equality for women. Thackeray's meth-

ods of conveying these values in *Vanity Fair* are less direct than Brontë's, but even a preliminary examination of the text will show that Thackeray understood the ambitions of women who wished to "get their rights."

Vanity Fair opens with a "Before the Curtain" address that emphasizes the allegorical intentions implicit in the title; it asks the reader to conjoin the surface texture of domestic realism with an allusive undercurrent of myth, folk literature, classical theater, and opera, which extends the implications of the book far beyond nineteenth-century England. The Bluebeard and Scheherazade motifs from *Arabian Nights,* both narratives about murderous husbands, are linked (in a chapter entitled "Rebecca is in Presence of the Enemy") to Becky's dreams of marriage to Jos: "She had a vivid imagination; she had, besides, read the 'Arabian Nights' and . . . she had arrayed herself in an infinity of shawls, turbans, and diamond necklaces, and had mounted upon an elephant to the sound of the march in Bluebeard, in order to pay a visit of ceremony to the Grand Mogul" (*Vanity Fair* 28).

Thackeray's allusions extend even to his own earlier works, for *Vanity Fair* is in many ways a deepening and an extension of ideas and qualities found there. Becky is a reworking of Catherine Hayes, for example: both are orphans, exploited by their female guardians; both marry gullible men for economic security and respectability; and in the end Catherine definitely and Becky possibly resort to murder. In a similar way, Amelia is an extension of Caroline Gann; both are gentle, sensitive, romantic, easily led, and infatuated with unworthy men.

The portrayal of male dominance is another recurring element; in *Vanity Fair* this dominance is more sophisticated than it is in *Barry Lyndon,* and Thackeray explores with greater subtlety why women seem to accept their own subordination. George Savage Fitz-Boodle reappears in *Vanity Fair* in the character of Jos Sedley: timid, yet vain and pompous, afraid of women, but provided with the trappings of male authority to provide a "cover"—cigars, male clubs, and a military (or pseudomilitary) persona. Both George and Jos, men whom intelligent women must placate to survive, represent, in Van Ghent's phrase, the "sickness of a culture."[2] In every instance, *Vanity Fair* provides analysis that is more instructive than the earlier rendition, more carefully developed, and more sympathetic to women.

The marriage market is a favorite target for Thackeray. It is a measure of the difference between Amelia and Becky that Amelia will never consciously marry for security, no matter how miserable she is, whereas Becky sets out without a qualm to catch a husband. Thackeray's portrayal of the man she pursues indicates how desperate a woman in her position can be. Jos Sedley—pompous, vain, insensitive, greedy—is Becky's only alternative to governessing. Thackeray reminds us that she is only doing what women do every day, forming the respectable attachments of well-bred young women with well-regulated minds. But the deeper consequences of such a system are also made clear. When Sir Pitt's wife dies, the narrator remarks, "Her heart was dead long before her body. She had sold it to become Sir Pitt Crawley's wife. Mothers and daughters are making the same bargain every day in Vanity Fair" (140).

Economically, Amelia begins as counterpoint to Becky. Her family is well off; her father will pay Miss Pinkerton's substantial bill; and, in Thackeray's sketch, she even looks well fed in contrast to Becky. But she is no more secure. Her father, who controlled the family money, "never talked of money before women and so they had no idea when troubles approached" (448). Money is power, both within the family and beyond it, but the Sedley women know nothing about it; in this way they are less secure than Becky, for she has great talent in the financial line and manages her own affairs. Amelia, on the other hand, will always be dependent on men: she is supported in turn by her father, her husband George, Dobbin's gifts after George's death (which Amelia assumes were left by George), Jos's allowance, old Osborne's "reward" money for giving up her son, then the bequest in his will, and finally, Dobbin's support as her husband.

Amelia does make some pathetic attempts to help her parents and keep her son; she sells the shawl Dobbin gave her, tries to sell hand-painted card-racks, and advertises as a tutor, all with no success. "She finds that women are working hard, and better than she can, for two-pence a day" (476). Finally, seeing ahead only "misery for all, want and degradation for her parents, injustice for the boy" (477), she lets Georgy go to live with his grandfather. Amelia is caught between the two fathers. Mr. Sedley had brought his family to ruin, and "She had to bear the blame for all his misdoings"

(576), and Mr. Osborne relentlessly pursues full control over Georgy, motivated by the desire for an heir and by implacable hatred for the Sedley family. Amelia's education and her economic helplessness, interrelated as they are, have weakened her character and contribute to the tyranny of the fathers.

Even Amelia's virtues are negations. In the original manuscript, Thackeray first described her as the "best and dearest creature that ever lived," but in a later edition, that passage was changed to "dear little creature" and one page later he is already describing her as "the silly thing" (14–15). Later, Thackeray clarifies the link between weakness and feminine charm: "I think it was her weakness which was her principal charm: —a kind of sweet submission and softness, which seemed to appeal to each man she met for his sympathy and protection" (376). Then follow three full pages of examples of how men admire Amelia, until finally Mr. Binny's sister declares that, in truth, Amelia has nothing to say, and is "a poor lackadaisical creature" with no heart and nothing but a pretty face (379). The narrator suggests that Miss Binny is jealous; but the novel shows how complex a phenomenon female jealousy is, arising from economic competition and (as in Amelia's case) from men's preference for weak women. The reason that Amelia—who was so beloved at Miss Pinkerton's—is spurned by women after leaving school is that "there were no men at Miss Pinkerton's establishment" (109).

Thackeray consistently contrasts the sentimental ideal represented by Amelia with the economic realities of the marriage market, represented by Becky. Despite the fact that she was always an "eagle. . . . never had been a girl" (21), Becky must be, with Joseph Sedley, "the picture of youth, unprotected innocence, and humble virgin simplicity. 'I must be very quiet, . . . and very much interested about India'" (30). She had to do her own matchmaking, for she lacked a mother, "a dear tender mother—who would have managed the business in ten minutes, and . . . would have extracted the interesting avowal from the bashful lips of the young man!" (56). Because she is really neither artless nor simple, Becky's career is one of hypocrisy, whereas Amelia's is a career of delusions, tears, helplessness, and (ironically) repeated rejection, even by the men she loves—her father, George, and finally Dobbin, who must cease to love her before he can marry her.

Through most of the novel, women seem to have only three

options. First there is the spinster's life, which can be bleak and poor. The novel is filled with lonely unmarried women: Miss Crawley and her "companion" Briggs, the Dobbin sisters, Miss Jane Osborne, Miss Wirt the governess, Firkins, the Bute Crawley daughters, the Huddleston Fuddleston daughters, and Miss Glorvinia O'Dowd. Their presence helps explain the constant jealousy and competitiveness among women, and the narrator's remark, "Of what else have young ladies to think, but husbands?" (88). The second option is the sentimental marriage, fraught with dependency and false idealizations, and demanding an "amiable slavishness" on the part of the woman. Amelia exemplifies all too well the "tenacious and all-pervasive" ideal of the Victorian lady, who is educated to be submissive, affectionate but not passionate, and who must choose between marriage or emotional and financial bankruptcy.[3] Before her marriage, Thackeray tells us, Amelia knows that George is her inferior, but her heart is imprisoned, as women's hearts often are. In describing Amelia, Thackeray points out that women's very kindness may be a kind of sickness:

> I know few things more affecting than that timorous debasement and self-humiliation of a woman. How she owns that it is she and not the man who is guilty: how she takes all the faults on her side: how she courts in a manner punishment for the wrongs which she has not committed, and persists in shielding the real culprit! It is those who injure women who get the most kindness from them— they are born timid and tyrants, and maltreat those who are humblest before them. (481)

Occurring just as Amelia is taking leave of Georgy, this passage implies that Amelia's relationship with her son is becoming like her marriage, that her attitude contributes to the moral deterioration of the men she loves. Thackeray also implies here that women's gentleness originates in fear and is far from genuine. (He will develop this idea further in later works, when he explores the "Christian humility" of Rachel Castlewood and Helen Pendennis, or the ingenuous sweetness of Rosey Newcome.) The passage also accounts for Amelia's almost inexplicable devotion to her husband George: his mistreatment confirms her sense of unworthiness whereas Dobbin's worship makes her uncomfortable. (We should recall that Amelia's sense of unworthiness reflects Isabella Shawe's attitude toward Thackeray, both before and after her insanity.)

Three paragraphs later, the reader is again reminded of the social forces at work in forming masculine and feminine character: noticing that Georgy is becoming rather imperious now that he lives with his wealthy grandfather, Amelia thinks to herself, "he was born to command, . . . as his father was before him." Clearly, neither father nor son was born with innate qualities of command, any more than women are born timid, for Georgy has changed after being placed in his grandfather's care. Thus the ideal of romantic love imposes a full spectrum of false values—weakness and debasement on women, pride and conquest on men—and Amelia and George, who might have been happy otherwise, find themselves trapped in a marriage in which neither ideas nor genuine feelings can be expressed.

The third alternative for a woman, mercenary marriage, is represented by Becky Sharp. Becky represents, in part, a parody of the feminine ideal that adheres to the figure of the governess. In Becky's career, although the outer forms of sentimental attachment and feminine weakness must be observed, all relations are at bottom a business venture. Frederick Bullock's engagement to Maria Osborne is another such attachment; his threats to withdraw from the engagement when it becomes apparent that Georgy is going to be made one of Osborne's heirs are edifying. But Maria too is marrying for a position in society. Here, too, there is a terrible loneliness, for money cannot replace human relationships or self-respect, and the children of such unions are harmed by the lack of love and morals in the home. Little Rawdon is saved by being taken into Lady Jane's family, as Sir Pitt Crawley's girls—neglected by their parents and by Becky too—get "a little wholesome society and instruction" in the lodge of the Scotch gardener and his good wife (83). As Thackeray says of the Osborne family portrait, "what bitter satire there is in those flaunting childish family portraits, with their farce of sentiment and smiling lies" (233).

In contrast to the admonitory lectures on women's moral responsibility to family and society indulged in by writers such as Bulwer-Lytton, Ruskin, and (indirectly) Dickens, Thackeray presents a powerful and valid insight into the moral bankruptcy that undermines so many marriages and families. With so few alternatives, it is no wonder that, as Thackeray says of Becky, the "good housewife is of necessity a humbug," and "goodness" in women may be in fact antagonistic to genuine ethics:

> The best of women (I have heard my grandmother say) are hyp-
> ocrites. We don't know how much they hide from us: how watchful
> they are when they seem most artless and confidential: how often
> those frank smiles which they wear so easily, are traps to cajole or
> elude or disarm—I don't mean in your mere coquettes, but your
> domestic models, and paragons of female virtue. Who has not seen
> a woman hide the dulness of a stupid husband, or coax the fury of
> a savage one? We accept this amiable slavishness, and praise a
> woman for it: we call this pretty treachery truth. (165)[4]

BENEATH THE WAVES

Sexuality itself is affected by the mercenary nature of relations
in *Vanity Fair*, and the dark underside of sentimental romance is
the suppression or the manipulation of sexual desire. Becky's
function as barometer of sexual mores is clear, but Amelia too
plays a significant role in Thackeray's delineation of the relationship between sexual desire and culture.

Becky is Thackeray's instrument of discovery; wherever she
goes, the novel unveils duplicitous sexual standards. George Osborne, who on the eve of Waterloo asks Becky to run away with
him, does not mind admitting that he is rather free about women,
and Stubble and Spooney respect him for this, for "conquering in
love has been a source of pride, time out of mind, amongst men
in Vanity Fair, or how should . . . Don Juan be popular?" (275).
Later Thackeray alludes to Rawdon's friendships as a young man:
"The times are such that one scarcely dares to allude to that kind
of company which thousands of our young men in Vanity Fair are
frequenting every day . . . but which the most squeamish if not the
most moral of societies is determined to ignore" (472–73). Although Becky's reputation had been salvaged by her presentation
in King George's court ("Ah, what a high and noble appreciation
of Gentlewomanhood there must have been in *Vanity Fair*, when
that revered and august being was invested . . . with the title of Pre-
mier Gentilhomme of his kingdom" [459]), the reader knows that
she is wearing diamonds given her by both Pitt Crawley and Lord
Steyne.

The ruthless economics of power and desire become more explicit toward the end of *Vanity Fair*. Thackeray's sketch of "The Triumph of Clytemnestra" shows Becky curtseying to the king with a
deadly looking dagger held in her left hand (see figure 8). In

Rome, Becky hides behind some shrubbery as Lord Steyne's magnificent carriage comes "whirling along the avenue, borne by the almost priceless horses, and bearing Madame de Belladonna lolling on the cushions, dark, sulky and blooming, a King Charles in her lap . . . and old Steyne stretched at her side with a livid face and ghastly eyes" (629). This scene, following Steyne's threat to kill Becky if she attempts to see him, is his last in the book, and it hints at the kind of world Becky was moving into when she entered Steyne's society.

8. Becky's first appearance as Clytemnestra (*Works* 2: [facing] 198).

Thackeray is reticent about how much of Becky's charm is simply skill in raising hopes, how much is based on real sexual activity. Whether innocent or not, Becky attracts many admirers, and Thackeray shows for how many men the desire for, if not the actuality of, a liaison is present. Sir Pitt the elder, after his wife's death and Becky's refusal of marriage, takes up with his butler's daughter, Miss Horrocks, who dresses up and amuses the old man in his wife's old clothes, in doubly parodic "imitations of genteel life" (389). His son, "the most exemplary and correct of gentlemen," is horrified—but again it is his diamond that Becky wears to Court (389).

It is to communicate such truths that Thackeray refuses to conclude his novel with a happy marriage: his purpose is rather to show what happens after the hero and heroine marry. And the picture, so far, is a bleak one. Many have felt that the novel is hopelessly cynical, that no solutions are possible in this Thackerayan universe, but Thackeray does in fact provide some strong indications of where the antidotes to this social sickness lie.

AMELIA'S EDUCATION AT THE OPERA

One source of hope lies in what a Victorian would describe as the convergence of love, desire, and marriage—which union is, after all, one of our own enduring "Victorian" ideals. The ideal requires relations between men and women to be characterized by feelings more deep and genuine than those conventional sentiments that form the boundaries of a proper Englishwoman's emotional repertoire. It also requires that sexual desire be removed from the dark underside of life and merge with affection and marriage. This ideal union eludes the characters in *Vanity Fair,* but the novel diagnoses subtle reasons for their disappointment. Toward the end of the novel, Dobbin and Amelia tour the Continent, chaperoned by Georgy and Jos. Until now, the narrator tells us, Amelia "has not . . . fallen in the way of means to educate her tastes or her intelligence. She has been domineered over hitherto by vulgar intellects. It is the lot of many a woman" (601).

Amelia's education at the opera is an education in passion as well as in appreciation of fine dramatic music, as John Mathison points out.[5] The excitement Amelia feels at the opera seems to be partly sexual: the first opera Thackeray mentions is *Don Juan,* which "awakened in her raptures so exquisite that she would ask herself when she went to say her prayers of a night, whether it was not wicked to feel so much delight as that with which 'Vedrai Carino' and 'Batti Batti' filled her gentle little bosom?" (601). Both of the songs Thackeray mentions are sung by Zerlina, a peasant woman who has been seduced away from her own wedding party by Don Juan. In the first song, Zerlina tries to comfort her husband after Don Juan's servants have beaten him; in the second song, she asks him to punish her so that he can forgive and love her again. Both songs express enormous and complicated love, sorrow, and pain in an opera that explores the power of sexual love, both for good and evil. In contrast, the love relationships of *Vanity Fair* are relatively unfeeling.

Amelia's guilty response to Mozart's sublime music denotes this contrasting sterility (recall that Lady Steyne wept when Becky played Mozart for her). When Dobbin responds to Amelia's scruples by saying that every beauty of art or nature is to be appreciated, he is expressing the values inherent in the narrative: that both the opera (art) and its content (sexual love, or nature) are a part of "educated taste" and could be objectionable only to the "vulgar minds" who had educated Amelia heretofore. We should note, however, that Thackeray is silent about Dobbin's own responses to the opera, which allows the reader to assume that Dobbin is capable of appreciating its beauty and passion. But then a crucial argument between Dobbin and Amelia, possibly precipitated by emotions raised at the opera, casts some doubt on his awareness of his own feelings and motives.

The next opera Amelia sees is *Fidelio,* which Beethoven revived to celebrate Napoleon's defeat at Waterloo. In this opera Leonora, disguised as a man, becomes her husband's jailer and, at the crucial moment before his execution, saves his life. The work celebrates freedom, reintroduces the motif of imprisonment (which Thackeray has used in connection with Becky and Rawdon and will use again in reference to Amelia), and provides an example of active courage in a woman. During this opera, Amelia is in such a state of joy that one "blasé attaché . . . drawled out, as he fixed his glass upon her, 'Gayd, it really does one good to see a woman caypable of that stayt of excaytement'" (603). Mathison points out that Amelia here is "framed" by male eyes—the narrator's and Dobbin's, as well as the attaché's, whose comment reminds us of the disparity between the ideals of womanhood being represented on stage and the actual middle-class Englishwoman, timid and unresponsive.

Amelia's emotional awakening at the opera is a first step—indeed a prerequisite—toward a realignment of her relationship with Dobbin. The resolution of their emotional impasse requires that Amelia give up a lifetime of passivity and victimization and take on some authority, even if the change means that Dobbin's adulation ceases, and his love dies, for he cannot love where he does not worship.

Two Amazing Displays of Vigor

The complex issues surrounding romance, sexuality, and marriage are replayed in varying combinations in the careers of Becky and Amelia. Thackeray joins these issues at the end of the novel in a series of confrontations in which neither Becky nor Amelia serves as the normative figure, but each serves the other as counterpoint, and both are contrasted to a figure who has been until now relatively minor—Lady Jane Sheepshanks, wife of Sir Pitt Crawley. Lady Jane's moral stance in the confrontation with her husband aligns her with the values of the novel as a whole, and the scene deserves more attention than it has hitherto received.

The setting is the mansion of Sir Pitt Crawley on a Sunday morning. Rawdon, haggard and sleepless, has discovered his wife, Becky, alone with Lord Steyne the previous night and awaits his brother's appearance, as Jane hears her children's prayers upstairs. Thackeray describes Pitt in a lyrical passage reminiscent of Edwin Arlington Robinson's "Richard Corey":

> Punctually, as the shrill-toned bell of the black marble study clock began to chime nine, Sir Pitt made his appearance fresh, neat, smugly shaved, with a waxy clean face, and stiff shirt collar, his scanty hair combed and oiled, trimming his nails as he descended the stairs majestically, in a starched cravat and a gray flannel dressing gown,—a real old English gentleman, in a word,—a model of neatness and every propriety. (520)

A distraught Rawdon tells Pitt the story of his break with Becky, and leaves. At four o'clock Becky arrives. Jane is praying again, this time at church. Becky surprises Pitt in the study, and "with perfect frankness" tells him her side of the story, that she had led Steyne on only for the sake of her husband's promotion.

> And as she spoke she flung herself down on her knees, and bursting into tears, seized hold of Pitt's hand, which she kissed passionately.
>
> It was in this very attitude that Lady Jane . . . found the Baronet and his sister-in-law.
>
> "I am surprised that woman has the audacity to enter this house," Lady Jane said. . . .
>
> Sir Pitt started back, amazed at his wife's display of vigour.

Sir Pitt attempts to defend Becky, but Lady Jane interrupts:

> "I have been a true and faithful wife to you, Sir Pitt," Lady Jane continued, intrepidly; "I have kept my marriage vow as I made it to God, and have been obedient and gentle as a wife should. But righteous obedience has its limits, and I declare that I will not bear that—that woman again under my roof. . . . You—must choose, sir, between her and me. . . ."
>
> As for Becky, she was not hurt. . . . "It was the diamond-clasp you gave me." (531)

This scene, like Rawdon's discovery scene in the previous chapter, releases a great deal of pent-up emotional energy. Its significance may easily be overlooked because the narrative style is comic and no marriage is ended here. But the many parallels with Rawdon's discovery scene show that it holds a similarly important place in the novel. Rawdon and Jane are both absent when their spouses' seducers, Steyne and Sharp, arrive: Rawdon is detained at a bailiff's house, Jane at church. Both find Becky holding hands with someone, an ambiguous kind of position, and both flare up for the first time after much trust and tolerance. Both scenes follow the one in which Lady Jane bailed Rawdon out of jail (a brief period of intense closeness for them), during which Rawdon, deeply moved, stammers out how much he has changed since he has known her and little Rawdy. The honest intimacy between Rawdon and Jane contrasts sharply with the devious conduct of Becky and Sir Pitt, and the two innocent partners draw strength from their largely unspoken alliance. Thackeray also frames both scenes with the image of Jane at prayer.

Although Rawdon's discovery of Becky has received the lion's share of critical attention, Lady Jane's denunciation of Becky is more deeply connected to the themes of *Vanity Fair*. First of all, Rawdon is forced to recognize Becky's duplicity: when Mr. Moss locks him up, Becky fails to release him, and when Lady Jane comes to his rescue, he emerges to find Becky with Steyne, wearing Steyne's jewelry and with a secret hoard of money in her desk. (Note that Becky's refusal to help Rawdon contrasts with both *Fidelio* and with Fielding's *Amelia*, in which the heroine visits her husband in jail and is mistaken for a prostitute.) Rawdon cannot possibly overlook Becky's questionable behavior (even if there is no more to it than leaving him in jail for the night), but until then he has played the role of indifferent or naive husband. Lady Jane, on the other hand, could have accepted that Sir Pitt's interview with Becky was only the benevolent action of a brother arbitrating a family quarrel. She is not forced to interfere and risk the loss of her home, reputation, and children. But she does interfere, for a number of reasons. Her motives probably include jealousy and indignation on behalf of Rawdon and his son. But her interference also represents a rejection of the system of masculine authority and power that dominates the lives of women. The fact that Pitt Crawley is so pointedly typical of the respectable Victorian gentleman makes this scene more significant than Becky's exposure.

Thackeray seems not to have anticipated this scene and, unfortunately, has not prepared the reader for this kind of behavior from Lady Jane. She moves too quickly from being a minor character, a passive young wife anxious about her babies and dominated by her mother (although Miss Crawley likes and respects her), to becoming a figure of courage and fierce indignation. However, Lady Jane's earlier obscurity may prove the importance of her rebellion; she emerges here to provide a pattern against which to measure the other characters, and her behavior in this scene affects the plot by altering Becky's course and affirming the value of a woman's integrity over a husband's power, distinguishing it from "righteous" authority. Lady Jane comes, late in the book, as Thackeray's first attempt to portray the intelligent "good woman." (Recall that another Jane, Jane Brookfield, was Thackeray's "beau-ideal" at the time.) Her presence provides a conceptual antidote to the negative portraits of women otherwise provided in *Vanity Fair,* and this scene establishes her as the moral center of the book.

The second scene in which a woman challenges masculine authority takes place when Amelia quarrels with Dobbin and thereby brings a number of latent tensions in their relationship into the clear light of day. As a result, Amelia's supposed naïveté regarding Becky and her adored George is cast into doubt; Dobbin's love for Amelia is shown to be oppressive in its overvaluation; and as the mutually sustained illusion of Amelia's innocence breaks down, an element of contempt surfaces in Dobbin's attitude toward her that explains why both have found it necessary for so long to keep a certain psychic distance between them.

Early in the novel, Dobbin has an argument with his sisters regarding his obvious attachment for Amelia, which suggests the theme of Dobbin's excessive susceptibility. Dobbin, roaring like an "uproused British lion," declares Amelia to be "the sweetest, the purest, the tenderest, the most angelical of young women," to which Miss Jane replies, "La, William, don't be so highty-tighty with *us.* We're not men. We can't fight you." Miss Ann suggests that now Amelia is free, perhaps Dobbin should propose to her himself, which makes William blush and talk fast and return to his defense of "that angel." Ann remarks that they are not at present in a barracks, at which William cries out that "men don't talk this way . . . it's only women, who get together and hiss, and shriek, and cackle" (173).

It is, as Iser would point out, the gaps in this scene that provide its meaning. Ann's remark that they were not then in a barracks implies, incongruously, that Amelia's sexual character was being attacked, not defended. Ann's reference to barracks reminds the reader how George had boasted of his conquests to Stubble and Spooney and that it had been Dobbin who blurted out Amelia's name there, incurring George's anger (116). (In 1858, in an ironically similar incident, Thackeray defended Dickens against charges that he was involved with his sister-in-law, by impulsively blurting out that Dickens was involved with an actress.)[6] Dobbin's confusion and embarrassment at the mention of marriage to Amelia is suggestive. He idealizes Amelia, as his list of feminine superlatives indicates. But then follows the reverse side of the coin, the underlying hostility to women that is glossed over by idealization: Dobbin says it is only women who hiss and shriek and cackle.

He means geese, but the words carry other connotations—of snakes, demons, and witches. Dobbin does not want a wife, he wants an idol, as we shall see.

Thackeray understood, long before Freud formulated the concept, that love like Dobbin's includes a large measure of overvaluation. According to Freud, the interrelated phenomena of overvaluation and debasement of women are present, to some degree, in all but a few men: "The whole sphere of love in [civilized] people remains divided in the two directions personified in art as sacred and profane (or animal) love. Where they love they do not desire and where they desire they cannot love."[7] Thackeray presents the same insights here: sacred (angel) and profane (geese) are both components of Dobbin's attitude toward women. But, however apropos Freud's analysis, it describes only a portion of the relationship between Dobbin and Amelia. Thackeray goes further, exploring Amelia's responses to Dobbin, the roles Becky and George play in their relationship, and ultimately, the conjunction of private emotion and public or social life.

George Osborne did not want to marry Amelia. His boyish liking for her had not developed into love. The arrangement was essentially a business deal, and when the firm of Sedley fell through, the senior Osborne member was anxious to cancel the merger. But Amelia's emotional collapse (recall that she would weep over a dead bird) convinces Dobbin that she will die if she does not have George, even though by now it must be apparent even to Amelia that George does not care for her. Becky says with a smile, "I daresay she'll recover [from the loss of George]" (166). Whether the remark reveals Becky's heartlessness or her perceptiveness is not clear. But she is probably right; Amelia is not as weak as she appears.

But now comes Dobbin, to send the gift of the piano to Amelia, which she takes to be from George, and to carry her farewell letter to George, with the information that she is dying, all of which serves to "reconcile" the young couple and to pressure them into a marriage that would have been a disaster had George lived—that was in fact a disaster within weeks. It is Dobbin, not George, who is in love with Amelia. He presses his friends into an illusory love match, and after George's death, Dobbin continues to maintain the fiction of George's love. Shortly before his final quarrel with

Amelia, as she sits upstairs listening to Becky's lies, he sits downstairs and recalls George's "understanding" with Becky. The Battle of Waterloo had prevented George from running off with Becky, but on that morning, facing possible death, George had expressed regret and had hoped that "Emmy will never know of that business." Thackeray tells us, "William was pleased to think, and had more than once soothed poor George's widow with the narrative, that Osborne, after quitting his wife, . . . spoke gravely and affectionately to his comrade of his father and his wife" (640). Dobbin has transformed the casual, vernacular remark of a guilty man into a soothing narrative couched in hollow terms of solemn formality.

Readers often express impatience with Amelia's refusal to accept reality and her tendency to worship the dead George Osborne. It is true her perception is limited, especially when compared to Becky's. But to some extent Amelia's continued hero worship represents the valid favoritism of a loving heart. Loyalty is one of the keys to character in the novel: vide Rawdon, Raggles, Georgy, and Dobbin. But other motives also help explain Amelia's excessive loyalty: with her father a wreck of a man, and Jos either off in India or sitting about in his dressing gown, Amelia may have felt the need to create some kind of male image for her boy to internalize. She might have wished to choose Dobbin (and the boy's farewell to "Old Dob" provides one of the most moving scenes in *Vanity Fair*) but their relationship would not permit it. Finally, pretending that she and George had been a happy loving couple saves her pride and makes of Amelia a good wife (read hypocrite) and a good widow and serves to keep Dobbin at arm's length.

The most important reason for Amelia's hero worship, however, is Dobbin's insistence on the triple fiction that George had loved Amelia, that he had been a good and faithful husband, and that Amelia is too pure and innocent to know otherwise. These fictions satisfy Dobbin's need to idealize Amelia as an angelic, nonsexual being. To admit to an erotic component in her nature or in their relationship would render her unworthy of his love. It could be said in George's favor that, despite the pain his neglect and indifference caused, he at least did not demand that Amelia satisfy his longing for an ideal woman.

Most women would have been happy to marry Dobbin; Becky declares that she might have been a good woman had she married him. Part of Amelia's reluctance stems from her sense of inferiority before Dobbin. The causes include a real inferiority of education, which puts her in the relation of pupil to Dobbin; financial dependence, of course; and her habit of feeling worthless before men, which Thackeray explicitly described as a component of her relationship with George. Finally, there is the discomfort of feeling patronized by Dobbin, a feeling that is also expressed by George and Jos and that is intensified for Amelia by her inability to live up to Dobbin's image of her. George is the first to express the common resentment of Dobbin's manner: "Seems be hanged, Dobbin, . . . I am under obligations to you, I know it, a d—d deal too well too; but I won't be always sermonised by you. . . . I'm hanged if I'll stand your airs of superiority and infernal pity and patronage" (116). Jos feels much the same thing:

> The Civilian was not a little jealous of the airs of superiority which the Major constantly exhibited towards him, as he fancied . . . and he began a blustering speech about his competency to defend his own honour, his desire not to have his affairs meddled with, his intention, in fine, to rebel against the Major. (643)

Thackeray placed these speeches deliberately: they foreshadow Amelia's crucial rebellion against Dobbin's "airs of superiority."

There is never any question of Dobbin's attractiveness as a husband. Yet when a fiction becomes the basis of their relationship, and when for eighteen years that fiction keeps Dobbin and Amelia apart rather than bringing them together, something is wrong. Thackeray makes it clear that Dobbin's weaknesses, wickednesses, and so on are not intentional; he acts according to the best of his knowledge and abilities. The problems lie on a deeper level than Dobbin's self-knowledge can penetrate and are affected by the equally irrational signals he receives from Amelia, and by a society that dictates many of the elements of sexual relations.

The relationship between Dobbin and Amelia depends on several kinds of idealization. Dobbin had, from the first, created a fictional George, loving and faithful, and an image of Amelia—pure, angelic, innocent—that she accepted and attempted to live up to. (Becky is not the only actress in *Vanity Fair,* nor the only one who is no angel.) But when Amelia carries this "innocence" too far, to the point of inviting Becky to live with her, she precipitates a quarrel that finally forces both Dobbin and Becky to admit the truth. When she no longer has to pretend that George was a wonderful husband, she is relieved of the attendant feelings of unworthiness and duty toward George's memory that have haunted her for so long. Only then is she free to marry Dobbin. But now Dobbin, too, has lost his illusions and makes it clear that he knows she is not the woman he had pretended to think her.

It is Amelia's *presumed* innocence that causes the conflict with Dobbin, as she resolves to take the fallen Becky into her home, "in the most innocent way in the world" (642). Amelia is not innocent where Becky is concerned: when Jos visits Becky's room, learns from her that she is the most innocent and persecuted of women, and returns to tell Amelia that Becky's sorrows have driven her to taking laudanum, Amelia only "smiled a little" (636) for she is less gullible than her brother. Later, when in anger Dobbin blurts out, "She was not always your friend, Amelia," Amelia leaves the room. She needs no explanation of Dobbin's allusion to Becky's flirtation with George, but in the next paragraph Thackeray shows her thoughts moving, characteristically, from recognition to denial:

> "To allude to *that!*" she said, when the door was closed. "Oh, it was cruel of him to remind me. . . . If I had forgiven it, ought he to have spoken? No. And it is from his own lips that I know how wicked and groundless my jealousy was; and that you were pure—oh yes, you were pure, my saint in heaven!" (642)

Amelia begins her overwrought soliloquy by referring to George's infidelity as fact ("*that!*"). But gradually it is transformed into something forgotten, something forgiven, and finally, a "wicked and groundless" delusion about a pure saint in heaven, heresy against a faith taught her by Dobbin ("from his own lips that I know").

Thackeray concludes a paragraph of sympathetic, slightly ironic commentary on "poor old Dobbin" with an image of hunting and entrapment: "And away flew the bird [Amelia] which he had been trying all his life to lure" (642). Thackeray had used the same bird imagery for Becky, when he asked, "O why did Miss Pinkerton let such a dangerous bird into her cage?" (21). Becky, previously, had "determined to get free from the prison in which she found herself" (22), and Amelia now "determined to be free" (645). The similarities in language correlate confinement in a girl's school with marriage to Dobbin. Both are part of the system Lady Eastlake described as "false authority and false indulgence."[8]

Thackeray has already shown that Dobbin has a negative effect on those nearest him. As the quarrel between Dobbin and Amelia begins, certain elements parallel the points made by George and Jos. When the Major says, "If I have any authority in this house—" Amelia breaks out, "Authority, none! . . . Rebecca, you stay with me" (646). And when Dobbin modifies the word "authority" to "claims to be heard," Amelia answers, "It is generous to remind me of our obligations to you" (647). And now that the bird has escaped, Dobbin goes on to express the contempt he has always felt: "No, you are not worthy of the love which I have devoted to you. I knew all along that the prize I had set my life on was not worth the winning; that I was a fool, with fond fancies, too, bartering away my all of truth and ardour against your little feeble remnant of love" (647).

When the crisis between Dobbin and Amelia finally arrives, he falls back first on authority, then on obligation (implying dependence), and finally on expressions of superiority. What Dobbin asks of Amelia is ignorance and obedience. Not long before, he had congratulated himself on the way he had hidden George's relationship with Becky from Amelia. Now that Amelia decides to act on that ignorance, he asks that she treat Becky as an enemy. When Dobbin recognizes that Amelia will no longer play the roles he asks of her, despite the lack of logic in his position, he repudiates her, and the pattern of simultaneous overvaluation and contempt is broken. Only after Dobbin's kneeling posture of angel worship has been challenged and discredited, can they marry. The marriage is a disappointment to Dobbin, as are all things in Vanity Fair, but if Amelia had not resisted him, there would have been no marriage at all. Amelia is not entirely content, either, as she reflects that Dobbin is fonder of their daughter Janey (another Jane), and perhaps even of his "History of the Punjab," than he is of her, but the central tension in the book has been resolved.

When read against Lady Jane's confrontation with Sir Pitt and Amelia's confrontation with Dobbin, it becomes clear that Rawdon's discovery of Becky alone with Steyne is composed of some of the same elements. Becky, Lady Jane, and Amelia all live in the same world of male authority and female dependence, of respectable surfaces concealing dangerous struggles for power, money, and desire. All three have to make their way in a world circumscribed for women by ideals of "feminine" attractiveness, submissiveness, and innocence. All three are shown resisting in some way.

Becky, who we know has to make her own way and later Rawdon's way, has few opportunities to support herself legitimately. She could live humbly on Rawdon's small salary, but Becky is ambitious. She finally exploits the exploiters and takes revenge on the Bluebeards, Sultan Schahriahs, and Don Juans of legend as represented by Rawdon and Pitt Crawley, Lord Steyne, and Jos Sedley. Lady Jane's confrontation with her husband represents a rejection of the system of mutual exploitation, but the confrontation requires that she defy the religious and legal traditions that give husbands almost complete power over their wives.

Most importantly, Amelia emerges, after all, as Thackeray's heroine as she ends her long, confused struggle against fictions of which she was only imperfectly aware, fictions of her happy marriage to George, of the supposed purity and innocence that permit her no knowledge of the truth, and of her great good fortune in being the object of Dobbin's confining love. It is Mozart's great opera that awakens her slumbering spirit and Beethoven's that provides her with the courage to act on behalf of her own freedom.

The remarkable quality of Thackeray's sympathetic perception is best summed up in his own words:

> O you poor women! O you poor secret martyrs and victims, whose life is a torture, who are stretched on racks in your bedrooms, and who lay your heads down on the block daily at the drawing-room table; every man who watches your pains, or peers into those dark places where the torture is administered to you, must pity you—and—and thank God that he has a beard. (552)

5/ *Henry Esmond* and Eighteenth-Century Feminism

> We have but to change the point of view, and the greatest action looks mean; as we turn the perspective-glass, and a giant appears a pigmy.
>
> —*Henry Esmond*

> "Thackeray used all his powers; their grand, serious force yielded a profound satisfaction. 'At last he puts forth his strength,' I could not help saying to myself. No character in the book strikes me as more masterly than that of Beatrix. . . . Beatrix is not, in herself, all bad. So much does she sometimes reveal of what is good and great."
>
> —Charlotte Brontë

Henry Esmond is Thackeray's most "careful book," the only full-length novel to be completed before publication. Thackeray himself judged it "the very best I can do," and added, "I stand by this book and am willing to leave it, when I go, as my card."[1] Charlotte Brontë, quoted above, also recognized *Esmond* as the fulfillment of Thackeray's powers.[2] It is also the most introspective of his works, filled with a "cutthroat melancholy" (*Letters* 2: 807), and according to George Eliot the most uncomfortable.[3] In it, Thackeray exorcised some of his own demons, particularly the pain and disillusionment he felt following his break with Mrs. Brookfield. He wrote to his mother on 20 December 1852, "I can contemplate that grief now, and put it into a book" (*Letters* 3: 149).

The events of this period deepened Thackeray's understanding, not only of his own needs, failings, and motives, but of the psychological and cultural dynamics of love. Here, in fulfillment of what had been begun in *Vanity Fair*, love becomes one of the vanities, for it is part of our mortal nature and will be over "as everything else is over in life; as flowers and fury, and griefs and pleasures are over."[4] Gordon Ray wrote, "In *Esmond* he has written *finis* to the Brookfield affair. . . . He sees its whole meaning clearly, without ceasing to feel it deeply. The result is a narrative marked equally by detachment and penetration."[5]

Eve Sedgwick concludes that *Esmond* is a "radical and *a*historical critique of patriarchy." However, I would argue that the novel is both radical, in that it examines the psychological elements of gender relations, *and* historical, in that it traces the effects of public, historical change on those relations. Beneath the surface of Esmond's narrative lies a subtext that simultaneously explores his unacknowledged feelings and historicizes them. Thackeray demonstrates the truth of René Girard's statement that "The great writers apprehend intuitively and concretely, through the medium of their art, if not formally, the system in which they were first imprisoned together with their contemporaries."[6]

HENRY ESMOND AND THE "BROOKFIELD AFFAIR"

Ann Monsarrat has examined the complex relations between William Thackeray and the two Brookfields with clarity and insight. Their relationship need be summarized only briefly here to give an idea of this new aspect of Thackeray's experience of the "system in which they were . . . imprisoned." The most eloquent statement of the influence upon *Esmond* of Thackeray's love for Jane Brookfield is Monsarrat's, who wrote, "At last, *Esmond* became the repository for his wounds and rages, a charting of his own passions, a text-book of desire. And every book that followed bore traces not only of his own scars, but pity for all women locked by convention within the prison of a loveless marriage."[7]

Thackeray's relationship with Jane Brookfield began as a friendship with her husband William. They had been undergraduates together at Cambridge, where Brookfield's wit and gentlemanly bearing made him popular despite his family's lack of money and social status. That same wit struck many as irreverent, however, when he became a clergyman, and he never achieved the success that his abilities had seemed to promise. Jane Elton met him when she was sixteen and he was twenty-eight, and she admired the handsome, clever, young man. They married and settled in London in 1842 where Thackeray, by now well into his "married bachelorhood," renewed his old friendship with William. At first Jane Brookfield did not wish her husband to socialize with Thackeray, who was living a rather Bohemian existence with friends such as Caroline Norton. But with the success of *Vanity Fair,* Thackeray suddenly became socially acceptable.

Jane Brookfield's feelings for Thackeray will never be fully known. In the end, she broke off their friendship at her husband's request. Thackeray angrily claimed that she had never cared for him. The reality, as Thackeray's fiction testifies, was more complex. Each of the three was served in some way by the triangular relationship. William was gratified that other men admired his wife; as Thackeray put it, "a part of poor Brookfield's pride of possession was that we should envy him and admire her" (*Letters* 4: 431). But Jane became increasingly unhappy: the man she had once worshiped was treating her unkindly, she suffered at least one miscarriage, and at one time they were so poor that William lived in the vaults beneath his parish church while Jane traveled about "visiting" her friends but, in reality, was homeless.

Thackeray's admiration met Jane Brookfield's emotional needs just as Henry Esmond's devotion fulfilled similar needs in Rachel Castlewood, but it is unclear whether the analogy can be extended, whether Brookfield came to feel the same kind of suppressed passion for Thackeray as Rachel feels for Henry. Perhaps Thackeray's love was gratifying for its own sake, or perhaps Jane was hoping that Thackeray's admiration would raise her in her husband's estimation. Thackeray knew well that love has its selfish and irrational components. Therefore, Rachel Castlewood's concealed and suppressed sexual desire may originate in Thackeray's imagination, or it may reflect his perception of Jane Brookfield's emotions. A poem Thackeray wrote in his diary in 1846 indicates that he (then) believed his love was reciprocated. It concludes:

> Though we may not say it
> And the secret rests
> In two sad breasts
> In silence folded
> Yet we both obey it
> And it throbs and smarts
> And tears our hearts
> But we never told it.
>
> Though my lips are mute
> And the signal flies
> In a flash from my eyes

When your own behold it
And reply unto it
With a glance of light
O so beaming bright
Yet we never told it.[8]

Thackeray probably benefited from Jane Brookfield's reserve (although he was to interpret it later as indifference) in that it made this relationship "safe." Although he was to describe it later as "playing with edged tools" (*Letters* 4: 431), Jane provided him with the perfect kind of love affair. He did not have to overcome sexual or ethical inhibitions; he risked losing neither children nor reputation; and since he knew he could not respect his partner in an illicit liaison, he avoided what would soon have developed into a painfully embarrassing relationship. For such a man the perfect love affair was one that excluded sex. Like William Dobbin, William Thackeray desired an idealized lover; such idealization, and its underlying motives, became an important component of Thackeray's thought and writing. This is one reason why Thackeray wrote once that "it is the unwritten part of books that would be the most interesting" (*Letters* 3: 391).

As Jane came to replace Isabella as Thackeray's model of what a woman should be, she provided him with an ideal that was more articulate, witty, and socially adept than Isabella had ever been. As she complained privately to Thackeray about her marriage, Thackeray's attraction carried with it an undercurrent of anger at his friend and her husband, William Brookfield, and that anger led Thackeray to some of his feminist insights into sexual relations. Brookfield himself was hostile to Jane's feminist friends, commanding her in one letter to give her friend Mrs. Fanshawe "either a stupid stare of unapprehension or box on the ear" whenever she uttered "an incoherent abstraction against the male persuasion."[9] But Thackeray, under no such injunction, came to feel that men were sometimes responsible for their wives' unhappiness and ill health and wrote to his mother on 15–16 May 1848:

> It is a pity to see how [James Carmichael's] wife has changed in a year from being a pretty young woman to being a fatigued middle-aged person.
>   I am afraid my dear Mrs. Brookfield will die. . . . She sinks and sinks and gets gradually worse. . . . I know the cause of a great part

of her malady well enough—a husband whom she has loved with
the most fanatical fondness and who—and who is my friend too—
a good fellow upright generous kind to all the world except her.
(*Letters* 2: 380)

Thackeray's passion for Jane Brookfield lasted for about five years,
occupying a major portion of his mental and emotional energies
during the writing of *Vanity Fair, Pendennis,* and *Henry Esmond.* It is
a part of that "secret history," which is not written in books but
shapes them. In *Esmond,* it animated Thackeray's insights into the
relations between men and women. Eve Sedgwick wrote: "Of
course Thackeray was no . . . feminist . . . but[,] like George Eliot,
was an inspired specialist in the analysis of gender roles as forms
of power, and for that reason it behooves feminists to situate our
theoretical formulations in some intelligible relation to their find-
ings."[10]

THACKERAY'S ANTIQUARIANISM

Before any discussion of the feminist elements in *Esmond* can
begin, we must address Thackeray's narrative strategy, for it is possible (and was once common) to read Esmond as a hero whose
judgment represents wisdom and to miss the author's ironic un-
dercutting of his perspective. *Henry Esmond* "has taken me as much
trouble as 10 volumes, and for no particular good for most of my
care and antiquarianism is labor thrown away" (*Letters* 3: 27). Biographical and historical evidence shows that Thackeray well knew
the ideas of eighteenth-century feminists and that indirectly,
through ironic narrative, he incorporated them into his text.
Henry Esmond contains in its double narrative not one, but several,
centuries of feminist discourse.

The novel consists of Esmond's memoirs, ranging from the year
1690, when he is a boy of twelve, to King George's ascension to the
throne and the marriage of Rachel and Henry Esmond and their
emigration to America, some time after 1718. The first part of the
book describes the deterioration of the marriage between Francis,
Lord Castlewood, and Rachel, Lady Castlewood, and the incorpo-
ration of Esmond into the family, with his becoming both foster
son and companion to Rachel, as it becomes clear that her husband has little in common with her. At the same time, Esmond
takes on the role of older brother to Rachel's children, Frank and

Beatrix. These "familial" relations are important. They will later add to the novel's delineation of love an incestuous component that accounts for much of the discomfort many readers, including George Eliot, have felt with this novel.

In the novel's early sections, Esmond expresses a concern for the position of women that is driven largely by gratitude toward his unhappy foster mother and by an unconscious competition with her husband Francis. However, Esmond's early insights disappear later in the novel. The change can be explained as part of the larger pattern of suppression of emotion and blindness to his own motives that dominates Esmond's narrative. But the idea of women's "dispossession," as Auerbach terms it, will still inform the novel.[11] Hereafter, it will be conveyed indirectly.

Thackeray provides many "clues" to ensure that the complexities of the narrative point of view are not lost.[12] The obvious subjectivity of Esmond's vision in other areas such as religion or politics is one indication that his viewpoint is not reliable. The frequent shifting of the narrative from third-person to first-person warns the reader that Esmond's "objectivity" is unreliable. The preface written by Esmond's daughter, Rachel, provides a counterpoint to his perspective, and her editorial comments as well as those of Rachel Castlewood sometimes undermine Esmond's narrative. Despite all Rachel Warrington's praise, the only concrete instance of Esmond's supposed greatness that she provides leaves the reader with the impression of an unpleasant man who mocks his wife and daughter, saying that, "All women [are] alike; that there was never one so beautiful as [Beatrix]; and . . . we [Esmond's wife and daughter] could forgive her everything but her beauty" (*Esmond* 41).

Sutherland in *Thackeray at Work* provides another indication of the subjectivity of Esmond's point of view. Apparently Thackeray attached a footnote (later deleted) to the manuscript of *Esmond* in which Rachel—then Esmond's wife—remarks, "My husband was ever in the habit of sneering at women."[13] It was Rachel's last desperate complaint against a male writer, this time her husband, and whatever the reason for its later deletion, this remark indicates the complexity of the author's perspective, a perspective that clearly excels Esmond's on the subject of women.[14]

George Brimley, whose review was Thackeray's favorite, noted the discrepancy between Esmond's limited self-knowledge and the reader's broader perspective:

> The record of Colonel Esmond's life is throughout a record of his attachment to one woman, towards whom his childish gratitude for protection grows with his growth into a complex feeling, in which filial affection and an unconscious passion are curiously blended. So unconscious, indeed, is the passion, that, though the reader has no difficulty in interpreting it, Esmond himself is for years the avowed and persevering, though hopeless lover of this very lady's daughter.[15]

Elaine Scarry's essay "The Rookery at Castlewood" provides a fine analysis of the novel's irony. Her final sentence, recalling Thackeray's image of Jervas's portrait of Esmond "smiling upon a bombshell," sums up the relationship between Esmond's narrative and the novel's subtext: "Esmond's surface narrative is dominated by the tone of serene conviction; but immediately beneath this glacine surface is the restless energy of Thackeray, ever threatening to explode in the smiling face of the self-assured narrator."[16]

Wolfgang Iser's reader response analysis in *The Implied Reader,* by demonstrating how much of the narrative must be "filled in" by the reader, provides another method of demonstrating how irony operates in the novel. He demonstrates that in *Esmond,* "The road to the self is a continual overcoming of the self, the success of which may be measured by the self's awareness that the manifestations of the past were limited and contingent." Thus, *Esmond*'s subject is "subjectivity itself."[17] Lionel Stevenson points out that Thackeray had used the untrustworthy first-person narrator many times before he wrote *Esmond:* Ikey Solomons, Michael Angelo Titmarsh, George Fitz-Boodle, and Barry Lyndon are a few examples. By the time he wrote *Esmond,* Thackeray had so refined the use of ironic narrative that his meaning was in danger of being lost; the irony is so subtle that many "generations of readers and critics have accepted [Esmond's narrative] at face value."[18] Indeed, part of the problem is that our culture still encloses us in a subjectivity similar to that of Thackeray's original readers, a subjectivity that prevents us from recognizing Thackeray's critique. John Sutherland, in his introduction to the Penguin edition of *Esmond,* best sums up Thackeray's achievement in terms of Western cultural history: "It is quite feasible to see in *Henry Esmond* the nineteenth-century mind tracing the genealogy of its civilization in the eighteenth century . . . [and at the same time providing twentieth-century insights] astonishing in fiction of this period."[19]

EIGHTEENTH-CENTURY ORIGINS

Thackeray's knowledge of the eighteenth century was both deep and broad.[20] His readings and reflections brought him remarkable understanding of the age, which included insights into the early stages of feminist theory. It is certain that Thackeray's reading included some early feminist texts, and it is possible to speculate on others, based on indirect evidence. One idea, purely speculative, is that the title and some of the plot of *Esmond* may echo Charlotte Smith's 1792 novel *Desmond,* which has an outspoken feminist introduction to the story of a married woman's love affair. (In Smith's work, however, the feminist ideas expressed in the introduction seem to be missing from the novel itself. Thackeray, I intend to show, incorporated them into his novel.)

Another work of interest (although we can only infer that Thackeray actually read it) is Judith Drake's *An Essay in Defence of the Female Sex, By a Lady.* The work, long thought to have been written by Mary Astell, was found in Thackeray's library at the time of his death. Joseph Grego cites it as a possible model for *Vanity Fair,* because Drake uses puppet characters to satirize various forms of vanity. However, Grego does not mention the remarkable and essential feminist purpose of the major portion of the work. Dated 1697, the *Essay* argues that it is custom, not nature, that keeps women from developing their full potential, and that women's disadvantages then reinforce the myth of male superiority and result in a great deal of masculine vanity.[21]

Other eighteenth-century feminist works can be cited with more certainty. For example, Thackeray refers often to Lady Mary Wortley Montagu. In *Barry Lyndon,* Lady Lyndon is Lady Mary's goddaughter (1.14.243). And in *Notes of a Journey from Cornhill to Grand Cairo* he mentions Lady Mary's description of a Turkish bath as the last good one (*Works* 6: 297). In *English Humourists,* Lady Mary's *Letters and Works* are cited at least seven times, and (although some of the notes to *Humourists* were written by James Hannay) the numerous allusions do indicate that Lady Mary's writings formed a part of the "long-sustained personal reading in the period" that gave Thackeray his sense of the age.[22] Further evidence of Thackeray's familiarity with Lady Mary's writings is his statement concerning Fielding's realism, that "I know Amelia [Fielding's heroine] just as well as Lady Wortley Montagu" (*Works* 11: 306). If Thackeray "knew" Lady Mary, presumably he would be familiar with her feminist writings, such as *The Nonsense of Commonsense* (1737–1738), *Woman not Inferior to Man* (1739), and *Woman's Superior Excellence Over Man* (1740).

However, because of the way Thackeray absorbed historical information, a too exact reliance on citations could be misleading, for he did not rely so much on facts as on general impressions: "*[Esmond]* takes as much trouble as Macaulay's History almost and he has the vast advantage of remembering everything he has read, whilst everything but impressions I mean facts dates & so forth slip out of my head" (*Letters* 3: 38). It is clear that in *English Humourists* Thackeray has drawn some of his "impressions" from Lady Mary's work. In his discussion of Pope, for example, concerning Pope's letters to women, he wrote:

> [T]here is a tone of not pleasant gallantry, and, amidst a profusion of compliments and politenesses, a something which makes one distrust the little pert, prurient bard. . . . He wrote flames and raptures and elaborate verse and prose for Lady Wortley Montagu; but that passion probably came to a climax in an impertinence and was extinguished by a box on the ear. (*Works* 11: 252)

Thackeray echoes here Lady Mary's condemnation of one of Pope's satires as "ribaldry" and "scandal," and her declaration that "Horace can laugh, is delicate, is clear, / You only coarsely rail, or darkly sneer." And, when Pope proposed marriage to Lady Mary, she is said to have fallen into "an immoderate fit of laughter." Thackeray's high esteem for Richard Steele is also, according to Edgar Harden, based on her appreciations.[23]

These echoes of eighteenth-century feminist writers suggest the value of reading *Esmond* with an ear attuned to its feminist voice. But the novel is more than a sampler of feminist ideas. It is a deeply felt, finely nuanced fictional representation of the issues, both personal and public, addressed by feminism. The greatness of *Henry Esmond* is due in large part to Thackeray's ability to portray history in all its psychological and cultural complexity.

Seventeenth- and eighteenth-century feminists were as divided as their twentieth-century counterparts regarding essentialism and cultural construction of gender. Most early feminists accepted that women's roles in society will differ from men's. Some argued that women ought to withdraw from public life where, they felt, women's activities were frivolous and designed only to please men. These feminists were critical of the abuses of marriage but generally did not attack the institution itself; they felt that the devaluation of women was an evil, but many proposed that women could live in separate spheres and yet be equal to men.

Mary Wollstonecraft, Mary Astell, and other seventeenth-century feminists urged that wives and mothers be accorded respect and honor and that women take up the responsibilities inherent in their particular gifts as women. Drake urged women to avoid hiding their intelligence and to write and publish their views: as an act of self-definition, as self-assertion in the face of society's undervaluation, and to improve men, whose follies went unchecked by those best qualified to point them out. In sum, seventeenth- and eighteenth-century feminists often saw women as differing from men in social and emotional attributes, but they considered their souls and rational faculties to be identical and therefore recognized no claims of superiority. Other seventeenth- and eighteenth-century feminists argued that education, to be effective, required goals beyond marriage, motherhood, and conversation and that women should be allowed to participate in the world. Ironically, the "feminine mystique" (or "domestic feminism") that the majority of twentieth-century feminists have rejected was to some degree the accomplishment of seventeenth- and eighteenth-century feminists who succeeded all too well in valorizing maternal domesticity as a component of woman's nature.[24]

Both essentialist and social constructionist viewpoints are represented in *Esmond,* in addition to the antifeminism that is being undercut by the narrative irony. Rachel, for example, embodies domestic virtues sometimes considered "natural" to women, whereas Beatrix, with her longing for a more active role in the world of power and politics, represents the beginnings of a later stage of feminism. Both are conscious of feminist issues, in different ways, but both are warped and defeated too by their environment—which includes Esmond himself.

Certain ideas of the early feminists are given strong expression in *Esmond.* The first is that history and literature present an account of men and women that is not a true and objective account, but one colored by the subjectivity of male writers (Esmond's autobiography constitutes a case in point). The second is that women are intellectually as capable as men, but that they will not achieve or even aspire to accomplishment as long as their lives depend on pleasing men who envy, fear, and attempt to thwart their intellectual powers. The third feminist idea is that sexual attraction is not a fit basis for marriage. Like Wollstonecraft, Thackeray seems here to advocate marriage based on mutual esteem, for he shows that if the sexual attraction fades, as it does with Rachel and Francis, the marriage will die, whereas if the passion remains, as happens with Rachel and Henry, the couple will be excessively devoted to one another, even to the jealous exclusion of their own children. The fourth feminist idea is that because the only career for women is marriage, they are barred from direct and open participation in public life regardless of abilities or interest and from the education that could develop abilities and character. Thus, like other people out of power, they resort to stratagems: to selling themselves on the marriage market and to attempting to influence history through their one avenue to influence—sex. In either case—whether as "good" wives or as the "bad" mistresses of powerful men, or, in other words, whether as Rachel or as Beatrix—women's "power" depends on their ability to "manage" men.

Thackeray was aware that literature and history contain a misogynistic bias. In *English Humourists,* he surveys the attitudes of a number of eighteenth-century writers and concludes that Steele was the only man of the eighteenth century who respected women: "All women especially are bound to be grateful to Steele, as he was the first of our writers who really seemed to admire and respect them" (*Works* 11: 216). Esmond states the same idea in the novel: "There's not a writer of my time of any note, with the exception of poor Dick Steele, that does not speak of a woman as a slave, and scorn and use her as such" (*Esmond* 154). Thackeray also remarks in *English Humourists* that Congreve, although aware of the problem of prejudice against women in Shakespeare's time, still viewed women only as "mere instruments of gallantry, and destined, like the most consummate fortifications, to fall"; Swift addressed women in a tone of "insolent patronage and vulgar protection"; Addison laughed at women; only Steele respected them (*Works* 11: 216). Thackeray credits Steele with the "finest compliment to a woman that perhaps was ever offered" (217), and it is significant that the woman complimented—Lady Elizabeth Hastings—was, like Lady Mary Wortley Montagu, a friend of Mary

Astell and a feminist. The compliment was that "to have loved her was a liberal education."[25]

In Thackeray's time, Drake's *Essay in Defence of the Female Sex* was mistakenly attributed to Mary Astell, and Thackeray, thinking that he was reading Astell's ideas, may have based his portrait of Rachel Castlewood on Astell's life; there are some striking parallels. Astell was born in 1668 into a royalist Anglican family and was educated by an uncle who was a clergyman. Her circle consisted mostly of Anglican divines, and she was known as a powerful advocate of Anglicanism and an acute controversialist whose writing sometimes, Dean Atterbury wrote, "attacks me very home."[26] To show the similarities: Rachel Castlewood would have been born in about 1671, her father was Dean Armstrong, and her confessor was Dean Atterbury. And although not a polemicist like Mary Astell, Rachel is a staunch Anglican, and it is she who converts Henry Esmond to Anglicanism:

> Under her ladyship's kind eyes (my lord's being sealed in sleep pretty generally), Esmond read many volumes of the works of the famous divines of the last age, and was familiar with Wake and Sherlock, with Stillingfleet and Patrick. His mistress never tired to listen or to read, to pursue the text with fond comments, to urge those points which her fancy dwelt on most, or her reason deemed most important. (*Esmond* 136)

Not only does Rachel resemble Astell in background, education, and religion, she also expresses ideas that Astell had advocated. Lady Castlewood's attacks on male subjectivity as a dominant cultural force provide a point of comparison. Astell wrote on the subject a number of times: in *Christian Religion* she argues that the reason women do not often appear in history is not that they are inferior but that history is written by men. And in *Some Reflections Upon Marriage,* she derides the poor education women receive because "according to the Tradition of our Fathers, (who, having had *Possession* of the Pen, thought they had also the best *Right* to it) Womens Understanding is but Small."[27]

Drake's *Essay,* the book found in Thackeray's library, also addresses male subjectivity. While discussing the fact that historians invariably defend and justify laws that keep women out of power, she remarks that, if any historians were women, time and the malice of men would have suppressed their work.[28] In a prefatory note dedicating the *Essay* to Princess Anne, later to become the Queen Anne who appears in *Esmond,* Drake wrote: "Our sex are by Nature tender of their own Off-spring, and may be allow'd to have more fondness for those of the Brain, than any other; because they are so few, and meet with so many Enemies at their first appearance in the World." Rachel expresses the same anger at the male bias written into literature and the law when she tells Henry:

> "The men who wrote your books, your Horaces, and Ovids, and Virgils, as far as I know of them, all thought ill of us, as all the heroes they wrote about used us basely. We were bred to be slaves always; and even of our own times, as you are still the only law-givers, I think our sermons seem to say that the best woman is she who bears her master's chains most gracefully." (*Esmond* 134)

Drake had resolved to avoid the question of whether men or women are more intelligent, because that point could not be settled as long as men had so many advantages "by their Education, Freedom of Converse, and Variety of Business and Company" (*Essay* 6). She does point out, however, that in other species no differences in intelligence can be shown between males and females. And she notes that in the poorer classes, where males are not provided the benefits of superior education and freedom, women are generally quicker and more polite than men. She concludes that a comparison of bodies and minds seems to show that it is women who are designed for thought and men for action. And yet, she notes, the myth persists that women are less intelligent: "Men call our quickness 'Flash' and their own Dulness and Stupidity, Judgment and Solidity" (*Essay* 19). In a passage reminiscent of Thackeray's words on male jealousy, "Why is it that one does not like women to be too smart?—jealousy I suppose" (*Letters* 1: 447), she concludes:

> This is our Case; for men being sensible as well of the Abilities of Mind in our Sex, as of the strength of Body in their own, began to grow Jealous, that we [might] become their Superiours; and therefore began in good time to make use of Force (the Origine of Power) to compel us to a Subjection, Nature never meant. (*Essay* 20)

In *Henry Esmond,* Lord Castlewood envies his wife's learning: "She made herself a good scholar . . . hiding these gifts from her husband . . . for my lord . . . would have been angry that his wife could construe out of a Latin book of which he could scarce understand two words" (*Esmond* 131). The fiction that women are mentally inferior to men legitimizes male power, and when reality asserts itself (despite such attempts to hide it as noted above), the response is anger:

> Much of the quarrels and hatred which arise between married people come in my mind from the husband's rage and revolt at discovering that his slave and bedfellow, who is to minister to all his wishes, and is church-sworn to honour and obey him—is his superior; and that he, and not she, ought to be the subordinate of the twain. (*Esmond* 154)

And so, Esmond states, using a metaphor of revolution, the husband will crush "the outbreak" of his wife's abilities.

Another similarity between eighteenth-century feminism and *Henry Esmond* concerns the idea that sexual attraction does not provide a solid foundation for marriage. Marriage, Wollstonecraft wrote, should be based on friendship, for passion usually does not last, nor should it: "[a] master and mistress of a family ought not to continue to love each other with passion," for then they will neglect their duties in society and to their children.[29] In *Esmond*, one of the reasons Rachel's marriage fails is that she loses her beauty to smallpox. (Smallpox inoculation had been introduced to England from Turkey by Lady Mary Wortley Montagu.)[30] Esmond states: "'tis certain that a man who marries for mere *beaux yeux*, as my lord did, considers his part of the contract at end when the woman ceases to fulfil hers, and his love does not survive her beauty" (*Esmond* 129). Rachel too mourns the loss of her beauty, for she knows that it means the loss of her power. And, also in fulfillment of Wollstonecraft's warning, Rachel's excessive attachment to Esmond after marriage causes her to neglect her children and to be jealous of Esmond's love for them. In the preface, their daughter writes of "a devotion so passionate and exclusive as to prevent her, I think, from loving any other person except with an inferior regard. . . . before her, [Esmond] did not show the love which he had for his daughter" (*Esmond* 39).

Through Beatrix, Thackeray represents women's frustration at being excluded from direct participation in the world, and he demonstrates how this exclusion harms women's characters. Drake's *Essay* points out that Dutch women are trained to run businesses, whereas English women are prevented by prejudice from learning how to understand merchants' accounts. This, she says, wastes the talents of men, who could be freed to do other work while the women kept the accounts, and is a source of hardship for women and children, for when a man dies, his wife frequently loses the family's income through her ignorance (*Essay* 14–17).

Thackeray was familiar with the writings of Sarah, Duchess of Marlborough, whose correspondence he reviewed in 1838 (*Works* 25: 87–96), and whom he described as Marlborough's "fiery spouse." Like Beatrix, she was a close personal advisor to Queen Anne, signing her letters to the Queen with the nickname "Freeman" (88). Foreshadowing Beatrix's dealings with royalty in Thackeray's novel, Sarah wrote: "Women signify nothing unless they are the mistress of a first minister."[31] To some degree, Beatrix's flirtation with James reflects Sarah's views. Beatrix has only a few choices: she may marry Esmond and play Joan to his Darby, as she puts it; or she may sell herself on the marriage market, which she mocks: "My face is my fortune. Who'll come?—buy, buy, buy!" (*Esmond* 386). Or she may seek the position of king's mistress. The final alternative—spinsterhood—brings disgrace: "The most beautiful woman in England . . . a lady of high birth, and . . . with a thousand fascinations of wit and manners. . . . The young beauties were beginning to look down on Beatrix as an old maid, and sneer, and call her one of Charles II's ladies" (*Esmond* 395).

Before he turns to the mother, Esmond courts the daughter, and Rachel repeatedly accuses Beatrix of worldliness because she will not marry Esmond. But Beatrix's answer shows that her refusal is based on more than money: it has to do with character and ambition. Not only is Esmond "too poor to keep a cat" after his man has been paid, she says, but his wife would have to sit home and play cribbage with him for the rest of her life. Beatrix has too much spirit for such a life of dependency:

> Shall I be Castlewood's upper servant? . . . Why am I not a man? I have ten times [Frank's] brains, and had I worn the—well, don't let your ladyship be frightened—had I worn the sword and periwig in-

stead of this mantle and commode, to which nature has condemned me . . . I would have made our name talked about. (*Esmond* 385–86)

Priscilla Wakefield had written in her 1798 *Reflections on the Present Condition of the Female Sex,* "If it be really honourable in a man, to exert the utmost of his abilities, whether mental or corporal, in the acquisition of a competent support for himself, . . . it must be equally so for a woman." Wakefield is echoed by Beatrix, who tells Henry: "Why should I not own that I am ambitious . . . if it be no sin in a man to covet honour, why should a woman too not desire it?" (*Esmond* 407–8). Charlotte Smith had also protested the exclusion of women from politics and government in *Desmond:* "But women it is said have no business with politics—Why not?—Have they no interest in the scenes that are acting around them, in which they have fathers, brothers, husbands, sons or friends engaged?"[32]

Beatrix's failure provides a haunting note of sadness to a conclusion that Esmond attempts to portray as happy, for her intelligence and spirit deserve better than to be condemned by the self-righteous, jealous, and unforgiving Henry and Rachel. After her expulsion from Castlewood, Beatrix's descent into the life of a courtesan is a painful reminder of the waste of talented women's lives caused by their exclusion from most of the legitimate work of the world. In *A Serious Proposal to the Ladies* (1701), Mary Astell had argued for a college and religious retirement house for unmarried women, who would otherwise have no other means of improving their minds and doing useful work. And in *Esmond,* Beatrix and Rachel both speak of a longing to go to such a place (*Esmond* 255; 444).

In her *Reflections Upon Marriage,* Astell attacks the system of education then current for women in terms that fit Beatrix—her restlessness, her faults, and her final ruin:

> But according to the rate that young Women are Educated, according to the Way their Time is spent, they are destin'd to Folly and Impertinence, to say no worse, and, which is yet more inhuman, they are blam'd for . . . those Faults they are in a Manner forc'd into. . . .
>
> Even men themselves improve no otherwise than according to the Aim they take, and the End they propose; and he whose Designs

are but little and mean, will be the same himself. . . .

But alas! what poor Woman is ever taught that she should have a higher Design than to get her a Husband?[33]

TWENTIETH-CENTURY INSIGHTS

At issue in *Esmond* as in *Vanity Fair* is an ideology that simultaneously demeans women and overvalues them. Eighteenth-century feminists recognized the phenomenon and termed it "gallantry"; Thackeray has commented on it in other works; and Freud provided a vocabulary that describes the phenomenon in terms of psychological dynamics. A number of early feminists distrusted courtly behavior; Mary Astell provides an example:

> We were not made to Idolize one another, yet the whole Strain of Courtship is little less than rank Idolatry; . . . and if the Lover is so condescending as to set a Pattern in the Time of his Addresses, he is so just as to expect his Wife should strictly Copy after it all the rest of her Life.[34]

Thackeray had already expressed similar ideas elsewhere: in *English Humourists,* his recognition of overvaluation appears in a discussion of Steele: "In his comedies the heroes do not rant and rave about the divine beauties of Gloriana or Statira, as the characters were made to do in the chivalry romances and the high-flown dramas just going out of vogue. . . . It is this which makes his comedies so pleasant and their heroes such fine gentlemen" (*Works* 11: 216–17). Of Swift, Thackeray wrote: "He had a sort of worship for her while he wounded her [Stella]. . . . he falls down on his knees . . . before the angel whose life he had embittered . . . and adores her with cries of remorse and love" (*Works* 11: 156–57). And the reader will recall Dobbin's rejection of Amelia, which reflects not a change but a surfacing of attitudes always present, when he tells her, "I knew all along that the prize . . . was not worth the winning" (*Vanity Fair* 647). Excessive esteem and contempt for women, Thackeray makes clear, are two sides of the same coin; that is why "Men serve women kneeling; when they get on their feet they go away" (*Pendennis* 326).

In *Henry Esmond,* Thackeray depicts the overvaluation of women from the point of view of a man who unconsciously represents its complexity and harmfulness. Thackeray's portrait of Esmond not only anticipates the revolt against chivalry, and Freudian insights into the "family romance" that twentieth-century readers are familiar with, but also encompasses the dilemma of nineteenth-century feminists who, having succeeded in winning respect for women as wives and mothers, found that they then had to contend with an excess of respect—women were now being "enshrined" in their homes by writers like Comte, Dickens, Ellis, and Ruskin who reified them as goddesses and angels.

In *Esmond,* both Rachel and Beatrix are affected by Esmond's unconscious needs and fears, by his tendency (like Swift) to worship them and embitter their lives at the same time, and by his need to deny his own desires and to punish theirs. Esmond's relationship with Rachel is marked from the beginning by a sense of sin or debasement, for it begins while Francis, Lord Castlewood, is still alive, and it is sexual guilt that Rachel has to wash away with tears, confession, and years of self-discipline and penance. Sexual guilt also attaches to Esmond's mother: after being abandoned by his father, she had entered a convent and taken the name Sister Mary Magdalene. It is an ironic reflection on the status of women in the eighteenth century that Esmond's search for a father brings him a title, wealth, and power, while his search for a mother brings him to the grave of a nun named Magdalene.

However, Esmond never acknowledges the adulterous aspect of his relationship with Rachel. His complacency will not allow such self-reflection, for he is, as Thackeray once remarked, "a little bilious fellow."[35] Esmond is also restrained from acknowledging his love for Rachel, even to himself, by the dread of incest. He seems unconscious of anything untoward in his feelings, but there is evidence in the narrative that he suppresses such knowledge. Nineteenth-century readers like George Brimley immediately recognized the problematic nature of Esmond's feeling, "in which filial affection and an unconscious passion are curiously blended" (166). In fact, the incestuous aspect of the work has disturbed critics from the first, and *Esmond* has been called depraved and disgusting.[36] But Thackeray was aware of the complexity of family relationships. He wrote once of his own mother's "jealousy and disappointed yearning to . . . be . . . mother sister wife everything" to him (*Letters* 3: 12). This incestuous element exists as much in Esmond's love for Beatrix as in his love for Rachel and causes him to vacillate between them—in fact, to tease and torture them much as Swift had tortured Stella and Vanessa. According to Freud, a boy's early attachment to his mother, because associated with incestuous feelings, leads to a psychic separation (common to most civilized men) between his feelings of affection and esteem for women and his sexual feelings. Because the sexual components of his love for mother and sister figures have to be denied, Esmond seems, as Tilford remarks, "rather dully oblivious."[37] The situation recalls Freud's words, "Anyone who is to be really free and happy in love must have surmounted his respect for women and have come to terms with the idea of incest with his mother or sister."[38]

Esmond's posture toward Rachel as gallant knight kneeling before his mistress is clearly an emblem of overvaluation; he cannot acknowledge a sensuous component to this love, for such a love would be virtually incestuous, as well as adulterous. Rachel receives what Freud would call the "affectionate" component of Esmond's love, esteem. Rachel ultimately settles for this. Yet she becomes a fanatically jealous wife, as her daughter's introduction has hinted, because she knows she has only a part of Esmond's love. The erotic current is directed forever toward Beatrix, and Freud's description of civilized men fits Esmond as well as Dobbin: "Where they love they do not desire and where they desire they cannot love."[39]

These tensions explain Esmond's evasions in the narrative. For example, when he returns to Castlewood after a year's absence, he greets "his beloved mistress, who had been sister, mother, goddess to him during his youth—goddess now no more, for he knew of her weaknesses" (*Esmond* 250–51). Rachel tells Henry that there is no sin in her love for him now, for her tears and prayers have washed away her sin. When Henry asks her to go to America with him, in terms that imply (but do not specify) a marriage proposal, she answers only "You never loved me dear Henry." His answer reflects a continuing pattern of emotional avoidance disguised as devotion: "I think the angels are not all in heaven" (256).

Soon afterwards, Esmond sees Beatrix, now sixteen, and finds her beauty dangerous; she is his Eve as (Esmond tells us) he looks at her "with such rapture as the first lover is described as having by Milton" (258). Esmond decides to make "a brisk retreat out of this temptation," lies to Rachel that he has been summoned by his "new Mistress" (his elderly aunt), and listens once again to Rachel's warnings that Beatrix has too many faults to make any man happy. Then, in the clearest example of Esmond's capacity for self-deception, he decides on the road away from Castlewood that:

> His mistress, from whom he had been a year separated, was his dearest mistress again. . . . If Beatrix's beauty shone upon him, it was with a friendly lustre, and he could regard it with such delight as he brought away after seeing the beautiful pictures of the smiling Madonnas in the convent at Cadiz . . . : and as for his mistress, 'twas difficult to say with what a feeling he regarded her. 'Twas happiness to have seen her: 'twas no great pang to part; a filial tenderness, a love that was at once respect and protection, filled his mind as he thought of her. (272–73)

This despite the proposal to Rachel and the need to flee Beatrix's beauty as if it were the temptation in the Garden! Clearly, Thackeray is depicting a narrator whose capacity for self-deception is great, whose passions are habitually watered down to bland pieties, and who particularly evades acknowledging sexual desire. Even the ambiguities in Esmond's use of the term "mistress" are a part of his evasiveness.

Throughout the novel, Rachel and Beatrix are locked into opposing roles, partly by Esmond's influence. Rachel assumes the part (assigned by Esmond) of domestic angel and Beatrix that of siren or demon. One of the most telling aspects of this domestic triangle is Rachel's relentless criticism of Beatrix. And Beatrix at one time tells Esmond that she might have been better if Rachel were not so good (400). However, if she must choose between being worshiped or being reviled, Beatrix (like Amelia) prefers the latter. It is her refusal to allow Esmond to idealize her that prevents him from loving her, not his lack of wealth and title, as he believes, or pretends. Just before the final series of events, Beatrix tells Esmond:

> "[I]f you had not been down on your knees, and so humble, you might have fared better with me. . . . All the time you are worshipping and singing hymns to me, I know very well I am no goddess, and grow weary of the incense. . . . You never fall into a passion; but you never forgive, I think." (408)

Esmond cannot forgive Beatrix for arousing passions he cannot control; he responds to her with a sensual attraction that he feels to be morally debasing—he calls it "degrading" (402)—and he fears her power over him. It is significant that Beatrix calls Esmond a "black-dyed Othello" (408), for he is indeed motivated by a powerful and dangerous sexual jealousy. Beatrix fears Esmond because she knows that the alternative to being worshiped as a goddess is contempt, and punishment as a devil. And that is exactly what happens when she is expelled from Castlewood by Rachel and Esmond. It is their anticipation of Beatrix's *possible* sin (becoming the Pretender's mistress) that impels them to drive her out of the family, thereby exorcising their own demons, and bringing about the very event they had supposedly wished to avert. No resolution between the idealized and the erotic elements of sexual love is possible, in part because Esmond views the erotic as degrading and in part because the idealization is fundamentally hostile to women.

Before Beatrix leaves, an incident occurs that demonstrates the complexities of the narrative point of view: when Rachel reminds Beatrix that she has forgotten her portrait of the man who almost became her husband, Esmond remarks of Rachel: "There are some moments when the tenderest women are cruel, and some triumphs which the angels can't forego." Esmond's daughter, "editing" his memoirs years later, appends the following: "This remark shows how unjustly and contemptuously even the best of men will sometimes judge of our sex" (483). The comment echoes Esmond's in its structure and reminds the reader once again that Esmond's ideas are to be read as subjective—especially regarding women.

The entire structure and meaning of the novel turn on the question of Esmond's relationships with the two women, for he switches religious and political allegiances to conform with his emotional realignments. Esmond could be describing himself when he remarks: "Not one of the great personages about the Queen had a defined scheme of policy, independent of that private and selfish interest which each was bent on pursuing" (469). After Esmond sends her away from London, Beatrix writes a note secretly inviting James to visit her, and when Anne dies and the crisis is at hand, the would-be king is at Castlewood, pursuing Beatrix rather than the crown; again, private motives supersede public. Were it not for the Othello-like jealousy that caused Esmond to drive Beatrix out of London, James might have been king.

One effect of his attitudes toward women is that Esmond is unable to love freely anywhere. There are important differences, however, between his love for Rachel, who accepts the role of domestic angel, and his love for Beatrix, who rejects all of Esmond's attempts to reify her: Rachel wins Esmond by being a good woman and by conspiring to force Beatrix into the correlative role of the bad woman. The role Rachel chooses represents, in one sense, the eighteenth-century feminist ideal: knowing her intellectual and spiritual equality, she nevertheless accepts a way of life that is "womanly" and restricted. She is home-loving, husband- and child-centered, reclusive, and spiritually disciplined. Beatrix, on the other hand, anticipates a later strain of feminism: she rejects the domestic ideal and seeks action, power, freedom, and a relationship with Esmond that is not constrained by his style of devotion, an overvaluation that makes love impossible.

Thus, when Esmond and Rachel drive Beatrix out of the family, their relationship survives as a combination of the eighteenth-century feminist vision of how a woman can achieve an honorably fulfilling life as wife and mother, and the conservative Victorian attitude that a woman must be the Angel in the House that Nature designed her to be, or she is nothing. On the surface, the two attitudes seem to agree, yet their underlying assumptions are incompatible, because (as Beatrix makes clear) women want equality, not glorification, even in the domestic role. And so Rachel and Esmond marry—in what strikes many readers as a remarkably passionless marriage, described by Esmond in rather ambiguous terms: "We had been so accustomed to an extreme intimacy and confidence, and had lived so long and tenderly together, that we might have gone on to the end without thinking of a closer tie" (512).

Esmond's perspective is not the means to an end; it is, as Iser states, the subject of the work. Esmond's self-deluding vision is a paradigm for the distorted lens through which society views women. Esmond's relationships with Rachel and Beatrix reveal both the individual and the public psychologies operating in their culture. It is a mark of Thackeray's skill that the reader can see, beneath the narrator's words, Esmond's unconscious suppression of the disturbing sexual elements of his inner life and, at the same time, can recognize the identities of the two women, Beatrix in particular, as something beyond Esmond's comprehension. *Esmond* is a brilliant reconceptualization of *Vanity Fair;* as George Eliot recognized, Rachel is Amelia, Beatrix is Becky, and Esmond is Dobbin:

> H[arriet] M[artineau] extols "Esmond" but thinks "Vanity Fair" a raking up of dirt and rotten eggs, a miserably mistaken criticism *selon moi.* The distinction . . . [is] quite unfounded. There is the same spirit—there are the same characters in both—Lady C is Amelia, Esmond is Dobbin, and Trix is Becky—pure egoism. . . . There is not a pin to choose between them morally—and yet they are as good as the mass of women—only a little more clever and beautiful.[40]

Thackeray recognized the similarities himself: in 1852 he wrote to Mrs. Gore, "I have got into the confounded old character in spite of the change of costume—it's the same woman over again who has bored you all so" (*Letters* 3: 27).

The disillusionment that Thackeray had experienced in his relationships with his wife and Mrs. Brookfield, and the "care and antiquarianism" he had exercised in writing the novel, are translated here in *Esmond* into an exquisitely subtle narrative stance: that of a narrator who describes his passions without recognizing his motives and who is so imprisoned in the cultural systems of his age that he cannot comprehend them. Thackeray knew that all people are so imprisoned, which is why he wrote, in *English Humourists,* "I doubt all autobiographies I ever read" (*Works* 11: 199). In *Esmond* Thackeray re-creates, both on and beneath the surface of this complex narrative, the multiplicity of perspectives that informs our culture.

6/ The Emergence of the Thackerayan Heroine

> Living as he had done amongst the outcasts, his ideal of
> domestic virtue was high and pure. He chose to believe
> that good women were entirely good. . . . Their nature
> was to love their families; to obey their parents; to cher-
> ish their children. Ethel's laugh woke him up from one
> of these simple reveries very likely.
>
> —*The Newcomes* (*Works* 12: 440)

> Oh, to think of a generous nature, and the world, and
> nothing but the world, to occupy it!—of a brave intel-
> lect, and the milliner's bandboxes, and the scandal of
> the coteries, and the fiddle-faddle etiquette of the Court
> for its sole exercise!
>
> —*The Newcomes* (*Works* 13: 96)

In this chapter I break slightly with chronology, by bringing the earlier work *Pendennis* (1848–1850) forward, past *Henry Esmond* (1852), to pair it with *The Newcomes* (1853–1855). Not only is *The Newcomes* a sequel to *Pendennis*, but also—unlike *Vanity Fair* and *Henry Esmond*—*The Newcomes* and *Pendennis* realistically mirror and comment on mid-century Victorian England, sometimes in pointedly specific allusions that Thackeray's contemporaries would have recognized immediately, as twentieth-century readers often do not. Even as these two novels engage in contemporary public discourse on broad social and legal issues, many of the incidents and characters in *Pendennis* and *The Newcomes* derive from Thackeray's personal life. The public and the personal are not incompatible: the search for truth in the public arena and the search for wisdom in one's own life are complementary activities in Thackeray's art. The most remarkable and significant of Thackeray's public allusions refer to events and debates that directly concern us here because they introduce aspects of the Woman Question into the novels: allusions to Caroline Norton's divorce, for example, or to the Marital Causes Act, to midwifery, puerperal fever, and the use of chloroform in childbirth.

In both novels, the central consciousness is that of a young man much like Thackeray himself; Arthur Pendennis is most definitely an autobiographical figure. Thackeray's mother (who was "mighty angry" about it) is reassessed in the figure of Helen Pendennis; Isabella haunts *The Newcomes* as Rosey; and Jane Brookfield, who provides a model for Laura Bell in *Pendennis,* is later displaced as heroine in *The Newcomes* by a character based in part on Sally Baxter—Ethel Newcome. *Pendennis* and *The Newcomes* both invite new readings of what constitutes the feminine or the masculine and together constitute a major development in Victorian literary representations of women.

BIOGRAPHICAL SOURCES

On 24 November 1848, Thackeray wrote to Arthur Hugh Clough that "Mrs. Pendennis is living with me" (*Letters* 2: 457). Mrs. Carmichael-Smyth, unlike some twentieth-century critics, labored under no delusions that Helen Pendennis was an idealized portrait of herself: when Anne said to Thackeray, "O how like Granny is to Mrs. Pendennis, Papa," he replied, "Granny is mighty angry that I should think no better of her than that" (*Letters* 3: 13). It is only partially true—if at all—that Thackeray's ideal of womanhood was fixed by childhood memories of his mother, as Gordon Ray claims.[1] Thackeray himself soon learned how faulty that ideal was, and *Pendennis* reflects a profound ambivalence, culminating in his renunciation of his mother's emotional and ethical standards. Thackeray frequently disagreed with Mrs. Carmichael-Smyth's Evangelical doctrines. One source of disagreement was her insistence on strict religious observances; she banned card playing in her home, for example. A more general source of controversy was the question of the literal truth of the Bible; she believed in it, whereas he thought it a fallible document, a relic of an ancient culture.

When Helen Pendennis finds Fanny Bolton installed as a nurse in her son's chambers, the discovery sets off a crisis that exposes the self-will lurking just beneath the surface of Helen's religiosity.

Based on an incident in his own life, the scene represents Thackeray's mature understanding of his relationship with his mother. During the last three months of 1849, while writing *Pendennis*, Thackeray became seriously ill, and among the friends who cared for him was Jane Brookfield.[2] At his request, she did not notify Mrs. Carmichael-Smyth of Thackeray's illness until he had begun to recover. Thackeray's mother was angry at being kept in ignorance and suspicious about his relationship with Mrs. Brookfield. In a letter to Brookfield dated Christmas Day 1849, Thackeray wrote, probably in reference to his mother's suspicions and anger:

> I think that cushion-thumpers and high & Low Church extatics have often carried what they call their love for ___ to what seems Impertinence to me.
>
> . . . Who says that we are to sacrifice the human affections as disrespectful to God?—the Liars?—the wretched canting Fakeers of Christianism the Convent & conventicle dervishes. . . . they say "Shut your ears and dont hear music close your eyes and dont see nature and beauty. Steel your hearts and be ashamed of your love for your neighbor"—and timid fond souls scared by their curses and bending before their unending arrogance & dullness, consent to be miserable. (*Letters* 2: 615–16)

Not only does the relationship between Thackeray and his mother inform the fictional relationship between Pen and Helen; but Thackeray's illness becomes Pen's, and Jane Brookfield becomes, at least in one sense, Fanny Bolton—and is treated with the cruel injustice Thackeray felt his mother was exercising toward Brookfield. The novel expresses Thackeray's own anger at his mother's behavior through Pen's words to Helen:

> "It is you who are cruel," cried Pen, more exasperated and more savage, because his own heart, naturally soft and weak, revolted indignantly at the injustice of the very suffering which was laid at his door. "It is you who are cruel, who attribute all this pain to me: it is you who are cruel with your wicked reproaches, your wicked doubts of me, your wicked persecutions of those who love me." (*Pendennis* 593)

Thackeray did indeed put his mother into his book and found her lacking in compassion. As Laura and Helen stand in Pen's doorway, "there was no more expression in the latter's face than if it had been a mass of stone. Hard-heartedness and gloom dwelt on the figures of both the newcomers; neither showed any faintest gleam of mercy or sympathy for Fanny" (539). And that there be no doubt about Helen's tyranny, Thackeray has her go so far as to read and conceal Fanny's letter—a small example of the kind of "religious persecution" Pen had argued against in his discussion with Warrington: "Make a faith or a dogma absolute and persecution becomes a logical consequence" (646). Reading and concealing Fanny's letter is significant enough in the book, but to Mrs. Carmichael-Smyth this scene must have been doubly painful; her own first love—similar to Helen's for Francis Bell—had been disrupted by her grandmother's interception of young Carmichael-Smyth's letters to her.

The faults in Helen's character reflect more than Thackeray's anger over a single incident, however. They appear in parts of the novel written before his illness, in her pride, and in her intense need for Laura to marry Pen. Thackeray describes Helen's possessiveness as a "sexual jealousy" (264), and the phrase echoes his view of his own mother's feelings toward him:

> It gives the keenest tortures of jealousy and disappointed yearning to my dearest old mother . . . that she can't be all in all to me, mother sister wife everything but it mayn't be—There's hardly a subject on which we don't differ. . . . a jealousy after me tears & rends her. Eh! who is happy? When I was a boy at Larkbeare, I thought her an Angel and worshipped her. I see but a woman now, O so tender so loving so cruel. (*Letters* 3: 12–13).

Helen's cruelty to Fanny is foreshadowed in her cruelty to Laura; when Laura refuses Pen's first offer of marriage, the "poor girl" is made to shed "bitter tears" (*Pendennis* 304). Pen's fever is linked to real events in Thackeray's life, but also represents a completion or fulfillment of what the early sections of the novel had promised: that Helen's "jealousy and disappointed yearning" would themselves reach fever pitch. Helen Pendennis's behavior toward Fanny is not only unkind, it is mean-spirited snobbery. Bows tells Pen:

> "[Fanny] has been very ill, sir, ever since the day when Mrs. Pendennis turned her out of doors—kind of a lady, wasn't it? . . . Why, a countess couldn't have behaved better; and for an apothecary's lady, as I'm given to understand Mrs. Pendennis was—I'm sure her behavior is most uncommon aristocratic and genteel." (578)

So, interspersed with the narrator's praise of this perfect lady—possessed of "that adorable purity which never seems to do or to think wrong" (49)—are quite a few instances of imperfection.

Robert Bledsoe has argued that when Pendennis marries Laura, he is reaffirming Helen's sentimental ideals.[3] I would argue rather that Pen's marriage to Laura *displaces* the system of values that Helen represents. That is, the marriage represents both a rejection of the clinging, dependent image of women represented by Helen and her predecessor Amelia and also an affirmation of a more complicated but ultimately self-reliant type of woman. In the larger pattern of all Thackeray's novels, Pen's marriage reflects a stage in Thackeray's increasing commitment to feminist views of marriage and female character. For example, one important distinction between Laura and Helen is that Laura definitely does not worship men. Helen makes idols of them. She speaks of her dead husband as if he had been "the Pope of Rome on his throne" (50). The Major to her is "a Bayard among Majors" (50), and regarding her feelings for Pen, Thackeray comments: "This unfortunate superstition and idol-worship was the cause of a great deal of the misfortune which befell the young gentleman who is the hero of this history" (50). Laura's judgments, on the other hand, are unclouded by either sentiment or selfishness: "Now, Miss Laura, since she had learned to think for herself (and in the past two years her mind and her person had both developed themselves considerably), had only been half pleased with Pen's general conduct and bearing" (228).

Thackeray has noted the damaging effects of this kind of idol-worship before, in Mrs. Redmond Barry and Amelia Sedley. Now he suggests ironically that a female "slave revolt" would be a good thing:

> The women had spoiled him, as we like them and as they like to do. They had cloyed him with obedience, and surfeited him with sweet respect and submission, until he grew weary of the slaves who waited upon him. . . . Does this . . . run a chance of being misinterpreted, and does any one dare to suppose that the writer would incite the women to revolt? Never. . . . He wears a beard, and he likes his women to be slaves. (552)

Although Laura takes part in the spoiling at first, she learns gradually to judge for herself and comes increasingly to see both Pen and the Major more clearly than Helen can. She even learns to value Helen's love over Pen's: "If Pen had loved me as you wished, I should have gained him, but I should have lost you, Mama, I know I should; and I like you to love me best. Men do not know what it is to love as we do, I think" (582). Here Thackeray's control flounders as the narrator agrees with Laura, that woman knows how to love best, and then goes on to praise her parasitical nature—despite the fact that Laura has just refused Pen's offer of marriage.

Out of this confusing body of occasionally conflicting narrative tones emerges finally, as the dominant tone, the perception that women should be emotionally self-reliant: "The girl's spirit would brook a husband under no such conditions: she was not minded to run forward because Pen chose to hold out the handkerchief, and her tone, in reply to Arthur, showed her determination to be independent" (302). (The reader will recall that, in *Vanity Fair*, Becky had "determined to get free" of Miss Pinkerton [22], and Amelia, before the quarrel with Dobbin, had, in the narrator's words, "determined to be free" [645].) It might be argued that, in holding out for a more loving proposal from Pen, Laura is acting conventionally, but the narrative makes it clear that she is acting courageously and honorably. Laura loves Pen, and she would rather make Helen happy than provoke her formidable anger, but she refuses to demean herself by marrying a man who proposes primarily because his mother wishes it and who assumes that Laura will fall gratefully at his feet. Laura's refusal is a reversal of the spoiling that had created "Sultan Pen," and the first sign of Pen's improvement comes when he acknowledges he "is not fit for such a mate as that" (305). Until Pen matures, there can be no love. The implicit ideal is an equal relationship, mutually loving and free of either dominance or subservience. Helen is incapable of such a relationship; Laura is impelling Pen toward it.

Laura is not a static character, however. Like Amelia, she must undergo an education of the heart before she attains maturity. In this, Laura resembles Thackeray: her experience of "longing passion unfulfilled"[4] approximates Thackeray's own. Perhaps this experience of desire helps explain what is otherwise inexplicable, Laura Bell's very name. Can it be a coincidence that Laura Bell was the name of a well-known, high-priced London prostitute?

According to Catherine Peters, the actual Laura Bell was a "courtesan who had a liaison with a Nepalese prince, Jung Bahadoor, who figures in Thackeray's comic poem 'Mr. Molony's Account of the Ball.'" And she "was the subject of some of the bawdy songs sung, after midnight . . . at Evans's supper Rooms, one of Thackeray's regular haunts."[5] Known as "the Queen of London Whoredom," Laura Bell accumulated considerable wealth, fame, and perhaps some political influence through her lovers. Then she married, reformed her ways, and—very much like Becky running her charity booth at the bazaar—became an Evangelical preacher. Also like Becky, Laura Bell's husband died a mysterious death: in 1874, he "fell" out of bed onto his revolver and killed himself. Thackeray it seems had a gift for discerning character that allowed him to write occasionally prophetic narratives.

But did he predict Laura Bell's arrival in London? According to Ronald Pearsall, Laura Bell did not come to London until 1851, three years after Thackeray began publishing *Pendennis*. It is possible, however, that Thackeray had met Laura Bell during his travels in Ireland, or she may have visited London before 1851, or her fame may have preceded her there. Further research may prove one of these hypotheses; until then, we can only tentatively assume that Thackeray expected his male readers to recognize the name. And for those readers, Laura Bell would never be the pure English Miss represented in the text. For those readers Laura was, to some extent, "demystified" from the start. When, in *Vanity Fair,* Thackeray gave Amelia's maid the name of Jane Brookfield's maid, he claimed he had intended the choice only as a joke—but the point had been made, as he well knew. Here, the "joke" is the apparent disparity between the character and her name. With a possible irony that he managed to sustain through three novels, Thackeray conveys to some readers a subtle reminder of female sexuality every time he names this woman for whom "there has been no fall" (737), as Pendennis describes her.[6] Laura's name suggests a variety of extratextual resonances, but we must recall that Thackeray had more sympathy than most of his contemporaries for the demimondaine (vide Becky Sharp and Beatrix) and accepted female sexuality more than most—Rachel's passion lies at the heart of *Henry Esmond,* and Ethel Newcome's frank fascination with handsome young men forms an important component of her character.

Unfulfilled love is an important theme in Thackeray's work, and forbidden sexual desire is a component of that love, for women as often as for men. Catherine Hayes kills her husband so that she can renew her old love affair with Galgenstein; Dobbin loves Amelia while Amelia pines for George (who pursues Becky); and Helen Pendennis goes to her grave still longing for her first love, Francis Bell. In *Esmond,* Rachel loves Henry, despite her position as his foster mother; in *The Newcomes,* Clive loves Ethel and she him, despite his marriage to Rosey; and Clara leaves Barnes Newcome for Jack Belsize, her first love. Colonel Newcome dies calling out for Leonore. It is apparent that Laura Bell's feeling of love for Warrington is important in the larger pattern of the novels, and her name, while not a key to her character, is a clue to the complexity of Thackeray's intentions.

Laura's struggle with desire reflects Thackeray's own. On 28 March 1857, he wrote to his daughters, "The frontispiece of Pendennis is verily always going on in my mind" (*Letters* 4: 28). That frontispiece (see figure 9) shows Pendennis being pulled in two directions: on his right, a siren and two imps; on his left, a clinging Victorian woman and two children. The illustration alludes to a long tradition of pictorial representations of "The Choice of Hercules" between Virtue and Pleasure, which is just one aspect of Thackeray's complex intertextuality.

Martin Meisel's interesting *Realizations* reminds us that the choice of Hercules between Virtue and Pleasure became in the Christian tradition a choice between Virtue and Vice; that is, Pleasure came to be identified with Vice. Thackeray's most notable divergence from traditional representations of Virtue, Meisel points out, is his "shift from a strenuous Virtue to clinging domesticity and dependence." Meisel pointedly sums up Thackeray's frontispiece and much of his work in general: "Virtue . . . will have to be looked for within, since the figure who should embody it is no longer upright and monitory, but passive and dependent."[7] Thackeray's letters express the same ambivalence about virtue and domesticity represented in the frontispiece. In a letter to Mrs. Brookfield dated 18 December 1848, he wrote:

> You see what I was thinking about—about you always, whose attachment I assume as awarded to me: and that dear old woman with the solemn eyes at home, God bless the pair of you; and keep me straight and honest. . . . a natural Grace follows and I say God pardon me and make me pure. (*Letters* 2: 471)

THE HISTORY

OF

PENDENNIS.

HIS FORTUNES AND MISFORTUNES,

HIS FRIENDS AND HIS GREATEST ENEMY

BY

W. M. THACKERAY,

Author of "Vanity Fair," the "Snob Papers" in Punch, &c. &c.

LONDON: BRADBURY & EVANS, 11, BOUVERIE STREET.

J. MENZIES, EDINBURGH; T. MURRAY, GLASGOW; AND J. M'GLASHAN, DUBLIN.

9. Title page of *Pendennis* (*Works* 3: lvii).

The next day, however, Thackeray wrote to Edward Fitzgerald:

> My dear old cupid. . . . As soon as the book . . . [was] done and the very day when somebody left town I came down to this Mirean Eboad [Brighton]—and am directly much better . . . and have leisure to think of my friend and wish he was here. Come, Eros! Come, boy-god of the twanging bow! Is not Venus thy mother here? Thou shalt ride in her chariot, and by thy side shall be if not Mars at least Titmars. (*Letters* 2: 472)

One letter invokes God and purity while the other invokes Eros and Venus, and the two together reflect the frontispiece and Thackeray's endless struggle with temptation.

Thackeray was fully aware of the discrepancies in his own attitudes; the following, written to his mother in November 1851, reveals his capacity for self-analysis:

> As a man's leg hurts just as much after it's off they say: so you suffer after certain amputations; & though I go about and grin from party to party . . . I have a natural hang dog melancholy within—Very likely it's a woman I want more than any particular one: and some day may be investing a trull in the street with that priceless jewel my heart—It is written that a man should have a mate above all things. The want of this natural outlet plays the deuce with me. Why cant I fancy some honest woman to be a titular Mrs. Tomkins? I think that's my grievance: and could I be suited I should get happy and easy presently. . . . [Yet] say I got my desire, I should despise a woman; and the very day of the sacrifice would be the end of the attachment. (*Letters* 2: 813)

Thackeray's letters and his frontispiece to *Pendennis* all express a similar ambivalence toward desire and social mores. In the novel, the three figures in the frontispiece merge into one character— Laura Bell. It is Laura, not Pen, who contends with desire, rejects Helen's narrow self-righteousness, and reaches a more complex understanding of sexual ethics. In Thackeray's novels, women do not merely represent ideas (the good woman, the fallen woman), they struggle with them too, and Thackeray invests Laura with some of his own moral intelligence.

Unfortunately, Thackeray also identifies to some degree with Warrington, and so *Pendennis* is marred by an unusual authorial obtuseness. When Warrington tells the story of his unhappy marriage and separation and the bleak prospect of living the rest of his life "with my old books and my pipe for a wife" (*Pendennis* 596), he is creating a persona that closely resembles Thackeray himself. Thackeray's obliviousness toward Warrington's responsibilities can only be attributed to his own painful experiences. When Laura hears Warrington's story, she begins to reach for his hand, but stops. The narrator rebukes her—and English women generally:

> Here there came a sigh from somewhere near Warrington in the dark, and a hand was held out in his direction, which, however, was instantly withdrawn, for the prudery of our females is such, that before all expression of feeling, or natural kindness and regard, a woman is taught to think of herself and the proprieties, and to be ready to blush at the very slightest notice; and, checking, as, of course, it ought, this spontaneous motion, modesty drew up again, kindly friendship shrank back ashamed of itself, and Warrington resumed his history. (*Pendennis* 596)

Within a few moments, however, Laura's hand "went out resolutely and laid itself in Warrington's." It is uncharacteristic for Thackeray so unjustly to condemn Laura's brief hesitation while entirely overlooking Warrington's silence about his marriage, maintained even while traveling with the Pendennis family through Europe. It had been clear to all that Laura was falling in love with Warrington, and her relatives encouraged the match (Major Pendennis especially, for he thought single females a nuisance). Nowhere does the narrator acknowledge that Warrington's secrecy is less than "kindly," "friendly," or "spontaneous."

A partial explanation for Thackeray's injustice to Laura lies in his personal identification with Warrington, and his anger at Jane Brookfield's coolness. In 1849, her husband wrote to Jane that "Thackeray stamps and growls at your having written a very chill letter to him. . . . whether I am right or wrong in my prudery, there is no doubt you were right in doing what I wished."[8] But Thackeray's emotional sources go back further. Thirteen years earlier, shortly before their marriage in July 1836, he had written to Isabella Shawe:

> If I have given needlessly vent to my feelings you don't know how often I have smothered them; if I have hurt you by my warmth, have you never wounded me by your coldness?—And which was the most praiseworthy sentiment of the two? mine when I gave up to you

everything—soul and body—or yours when you remembered that there was one thing stronger than love in the world & that—Decorum?—

However, take me or leave me—I never can love you as I have, although you fancy that my love for you was not *"pure"* enough. (*Letters* 1: 319–20)

At issue for Thackeray were three questions: whether the women he loved felt any passion beneath their decorous conduct; how such passion was to be schooled when morality required it; and how to distinguish between true morality and proprieties imposed by "wretched canting Fakeers of Christianism" (*Letters* 2: 615–16).

Having fallen in love with Warrington and learned only later that he was married, Laura enters a period of loneliness and pain. Friendless (except for Lady Rockminster) and homeless, she is viewed as a nuisance by the Major, who "pish'd and psha'd, and said there ought to be convents, begad, for English ladies" (*Pendennis* 602). Recognizing that her lot is "infinitely better" than those of "thousands of unprotected girls" (690), Laura waits patiently for Pen to marry, so that she can "stay home and be Aunt Laura. . . . I am an excellent housekeeper" (693).

Although Thackeray's identification with Warrington led him into certain inconsistencies, the more important fact is that he is writing one of the central emotional struggles of his own life into the character of a woman, Laura Bell. For example, the reader is told that Laura's love has been "schooled into such calmness, that it may be said to have been dead and passed away" (699). But when Pen proposes a second time to Laura and she accepts, the narrator tells us that "very likely" Laura was thinking how strange it was that her love for Warrington had simply vanished (760). With characteristic irony, "very likely" strongly implies that Laura's love for Warrington has not vanished—nor will the narrator let us forget it, even as she marries Pen. This unfulfilled passion is her inheritance from Helen—and from the author.

Thus a second important distinction between Laura and Helen is that Laura learns from her experience of desire whereas Helen does not. Although the narrator tells us that Laura had in fact "done no wrong" (700), Thackeray presents Laura's experience of passion as a *felix culpa* that teaches her sympathy and mercy. When she learns to accept her own vulnerability to illicit sexual desires, Laura overcomes two major faults: the first she shares with Helen, that of being unforgiving and cruel to Fanny; the second is that she has been "changing and unfaithful"—that is, she has loved Warrington after having loved Pen, and she has loved where love is forbidden. Laura's subsequent efforts to help Fanny are an emblem of her new capacity for charity.

Thackeray has recognized and explored what Gabriel Marcel calls "the spirit of excommunication" in Helen Pendennis's religiosity and has opposed it to Major Pendennis's smiling, cynical adaptability to all creeds and practices. The result is that the ideal resides in the middle ground, in what Marcel terms a "spiritual welcoming" based on the recognition that all are members of the "community of sin."[9] This is the insight that Laura's development conveys. She represents a step toward goodness: for greatness, we must turn to her friend of later years, Ethel Newcome. Just as Laura had eclipsed Helen, she will in turn be eclipsed by Ethel.

In both *Pendennis* and *The Newcomes,* not only the tyros but the women characters too are based on actual persons and derived from Thackeray's experience. More remarkably, women characters not only express Thackeray's own deepest moral dilemmas, they reflect at the same time the difficulties that women in particular faced, and Thackeray's insights into representations of women in literature. Ethel Newcome represents an idea toward which all of Thackeray's work has been tending: the idea of the heroine. In order to fully understand how Thackeray constructed these feminist narratives, we must familiarize ourselves further with the story of Caroline Norton.

MARRIAGE AND THE LAW

By the time *The Newcomes* began serial publication in 1853, Thackeray had known Caroline Norton for at least ten, possibly fifteen, years. By 1853, Norton had been separated from her husband, George Norton, for seventeen years, sharing custody of the two surviving boys and receiving an allowance from him. She depended for support also on her brother, on her uncle, and on earnings from her writing. Now she was again engaged in litigation with George. In 1848, Caroline had signed papers that gave George access to a trust fund set up for her by her family. In return, George signed a separation agreement, which Caroline believed to be a contract, permitting Caroline to live separately and promising her a specific allowance. (Ironically, George was still receiving

£1,000 a year from Melbourne's "patronage" appointment.)

When George learned that Melbourne had bequeathed Caroline some money, he stopped paying the allowance. The "contract" Caroline thought he had signed now turned out to be invalid, because husband and wife, being defined legally as one person, could not enter into legal contract. Caroline stopped paying her bills so that her creditors would sue George, and he subpoenaed her bankers and publishers, claiming that her earnings belonged by law to him. He stunned Caroline by publicly repeating, in court, the old accusation of a love affair with Melbourne, using this as justification for not supporting a woman who was still "profiting" from her crimes. George now claimed the copyright to her works, which outraged Norton: "Let him claim the copyright on THIS," she challenged in her *Letter to the Queen,* a scathing attack on George and on male privilege generally. And in *English Laws,* she wrote: "I will never again write, while my copyrights are held to be Mr. Norton's; except on this single subject of the state of the Laws of Protection for Women."[10]

Concurrently, two bills were before Parliament, a Marital Causes Act and a Married Woman's Property Act. Feminists had worked for years to get these bills considered, but the bills languished in committee. Now, impelled again by personal difficulties, Norton reentered the political arena, to support the moribund bills by publishing *English Laws for Women in the Nineteenth Century* (1854) and *A Letter to the Queen on Lord Chancellor Cranworth's Marriage and Divorce Bill* (1855). Some of the claims Norton makes in these documents anticipate arguments John Stuart Mill was to use six years later: that social progress can be measured by the degree of freedom a society accords women, for example; and that women's oppression is similar to slavery, in that it seems natural when people are accustomed to it. But, unlike Mill's work, Norton's *English Laws* is a passionate autobiography as well as a political document—an autobiography in which her sufferings are offered to the public in hope of finding a remedy for other women in similar situations:

> I learnt, too, the Law as to my children—that the right was with the father; that neither my innocence nor his guilt could alter it; that not even his giving them into the hands of a mistress, would give me any claim to their custody. The eldest was but six years old, the sec-

ond four, the youngest two and a half when we were parted. . . .
   What I suffered on my children's account, none will ever know
or measure.[11]

Writing on behalf of Englishwomen generally, Norton used her
own life as a narrative upon which to structure her feminist arguments. In *The Newcomes*, Thackeray uses a narrative that closely
corresponds to Norton's, and for the same purpose.

Clara Newcome resembles Caroline Norton in several ways.
Their names are similar, and Clara signs a letter in an impassioned
way reminiscent of Caroline: "the *wretched, lonely* C. N." (*Works* 13:
255). Both have three children, whom they will lose if they attempt
to escape their marriages. And the "crim. con." suit that Barnes
brings against Clara's lover is similar to the suit George had
brought against Melbourne. Although the Norton-Melbourne
trial had taken place some twenty years earlier, it was again topical,
as Caroline and George battled it out once more in the public
press. Thackeray's readers would have noted the parallels. Thackeray wrote to his mother (on 6–7 March 1855) that he had gone
to the Reform Club to "read the trial of Norton v. Melbourne having a crim. con. affair coming on in the Newcomes" (*Letters* 3:
428).[12]

When Clara runs away with Jack Belsize, Thackeray makes it
clear that she has been forced to choose between staying with an
abusive husband and running away with another man (she is portrayed as being too emotionally exhausted—actually, near complete emotional collapse—to accomplish an escape alone) and
consequent loss of friends, property, and children. Jack, whom
Thackeray presents as a good man who cannot bear to watch
Clara's suffering, is sued by Barnes for criminal conversation. Like
Caroline Norton, Clara is publicly disgraced by the very husband
who had driven her to adopt such desperate measures in the first
place. Thackeray describes the situation in terms both political
and religious:

> Suppose a young creature taken out of her home, and given over to
> a hard master whose caresses are as insulting as his neglect; con-
> signed to cruel usage; to weary loneliness; . . . suppose her schooled
> into hypocrisy by tyranny—and then, quick, let us hire an advocate
> to roar out to a British jury the wrongs of her injured husband, to
> paint the agonies of his bleeding heart. . . . Let us console that

martyr, I say, with thumping damages; and as for the woman—the guilty wretch!—let us lead her out and stone her. (*Works* 13: 230)

This was not Thackeray's first expression of anger at the English legal system. In 1850, he had written a poem entitled "Damages, Two Hundred Pounds" that concludes:

So, God bless the Special Jury! pride and joy of English ground,
And the happy land of England, where true justice does abound!
British jurymen and husbands, let us hail this verdict proper:
If a British wife offends you, Britons, you've a right to whop her.

Though you promised to protect her, though you promised to defend her,
You are welcome to neglect her: to the devil you may send her:
You may strike her, curse, abuse her; so declares our law renowned
And if after this you lose her,—why, you're paid two hundred pound.
(*Works* 15: 277–79)[13]

The primary difference between the Newcomes and the Nortons is that the fictional husband, Barnes Newcome, wins his "crim. con." suit—but this small exercise of authorial license better dramatizes the injustices of the legal system and supports the Marital Causes Act then before Parliament. What Norton had argued, Thackeray demonstrates: the law did not serve to make women better but to make men worse. *The Newcomes* is Thackeray's most direct attack on existing marriage laws and demonstrates their injustice in a way that reflects favorably on Norton, the Divorce Bill's most controversial supporter. The 1850s were crucial years for the women's movement in England. Gradually the Victorian public was beginning to recognize the claims of the female emancipation movement and to accept legislative reform. In 1857, the Marital Causes (or Divorce) Act became law. It established a separate civil court, so that a special act of Parliament was no longer required for divorce, thus making divorce far more accessible to women. And it expanded the grounds upon which women could obtain a divorce, although a double standard regarding adultery remained. Thackeray's novels must be understood in light of these political debates and in context of his friend Norton's writings. Jane Perkins's evaluation of the impact of Norton's *English Laws* also applies to Norton's story as Thackeray presents it in *The Newcomes*:

The impression it made . . . is incalculable, coming as it did at a time when public opinion had so far outstripped the law in its judgment of the rights and wrongs of women that it was ready to be set on fire by the story of a woman who, to use her own words, "had learned the English law piecemeal by suffering under it."[14]

By translating Caroline Norton's history into the powerful medium of fiction, Thackeray caused his readers to identify with women like her, circumventing many prejudices against either her scandal-ridden past or the women's movement in general. Thackeray, who had studied law for a year and found it unbearably dry, now employed that easy and most delightful of teachers, the novel, to advocate legal reform. Thackeray's influence is—like Norton's—incalculable, but it is clear that in *Barry Lyndon, Vanity Fair,* and *The Newcomes,* Thackeray's representations of the destructive effects of nineteenth-century gender ideology supported the reforms that Norton advocated: Infant Custody, Marital Causes, and Married Woman's Property Acts.

In *The Newcomes,* Thackeray created a historical fiction out of the life story of his beautiful, brilliant, unhappy friend, Caroline Norton. The pattern is typical of Thackeray: beginning with characters based on "originals" in life, Thackeray's sympathetic, creative mind and complicated narrative strategies invest certain characters and actions in his novels with great political significance. The next "original" who remains to be recognized is Sally Baxter, a young American woman he had met while he was lecturing in New York.

When he came to write *The Newcomes,* Thackeray decided to relinquish the fictive autobiographical voice he had employed in *Esmond* and *Pendennis.* On 26 July 1853, he wrote to Sarah Baxter apropos of *Pendennis,* which was "advancing very pleasantly": "I am not to be the author of it. Mr. Pendennis is to be the writer of his friend's memoirs and by the help of this little mask . . . I shall be able to talk more at ease than in my own person. I only thought of the plan last night and am immensely relieved by adopting it" (*Letters* 3: 297–98). "This little mask" freed Thackeray from many difficulties of autobiography while still providing all the advantages of a limited ironic first-person narrative. In addition, in *The Newcomes,* Pen's "masculine" point of view is countered by a woman's perspective, coming from Laura Bell (now Pen's wife), who we know learned a great deal more about passion in *Pendennis* than did Pendennis.

Pen learns much of the story through Laura; she visits, writes letters, speaks intimately with people, and sees and hears more than Pen can. Pen, for example, thinks Clara an artless young woman, whereas Laura immediately recognizes Clara's secret love for Jack Belsize. And when Pen does not understand Laura's silent disapproval, she comments, "'The inferior animals have instincts, you know.'" Laura, Pen remarks parenthetically, is often thus "satirical upon the point of relative rank of the sexes" (*Works* 13: 147) and (the reader sees) often disproves Pen's conventional ideas. Thus the competing perspectives provided by this sometimes testy narrator couple allow Thackeray to present Ethel Newcome almost as if suspended and floating between them.

Thackeray had found not only the voice but also the model for a fully realized heroine, in a young woman he met while lecturing in New York. His letters refer, in what could only be a half-serious, avuncular way, to someone he "fell in love with." Sarah Baxter provided Thackeray with the bridge he needed to combine Caroline Gann and Catherine Hayes, Amelia Sedley and Becky Sharp, Rachel and Beatrix Castlewood, and to create the heroine who represented the culmination of all his development thus far: Ethel Newcome. He himself recognized that Sally Baxter uncannily realized his political prescience and his emotional needs: "I have found Beatrix Esmond and have lost my heart to her" (*Letters* 3: 154). Sally Baxter's worldliness did not have the deeper moral connotations that Beatrix's had in *Esmond* but charmed Thackeray, and so she could function as model for a sympathetic yet satirical Becky/Blanche/Beatrix figure: "[T]his pretty one she is 19 years old and already considers herself quite an old & passée young person" (*Letters* 3: 142). To his mother, Thackeray wrote of both his love and his art:

> I have been actually in love for 3 days with a pretty wild girl of 19 (and was never more delighted in my life than by discovering that I could have this malady over again). . . . When I began to write Esmond how miserable I was! I can contemplate that grief now and put it into a book: and the end of my flirtation with Miss Sally Baxter here is that I have got a new character for a novel—though to be sure she is astoundingly like Beatrix. (*Letters* 3: 149)

Eight months later, in July–August 1853, Thackeray wrote to Sarah Baxter (in terms that echo *The Newcomes*) to advise her against marrying for money and a position in society, where people

> never feel love, but directly it's born, they throttle it and fling it un-
> der the sewer as poor girls do their unlawful children—they make
> up money marriages and are content . . . the children lurk upstairs
> with their governess, and when their turn comes are bought and
> sold, and respectable and heartless as their parents before them. . . .
> I was fancying my brave young Sarah (who has tried a little of the
> pomps and vanities of her world) transplanted to ours and a Lon-
> don woman of society. (*Letters* 3: 296–97)

The character who fills Thackeray's "fancy," who is Sally Baxter as "London woman of society," and who refuses to be bought and sold is Ethel Newcome.

Thackeray was living in Rome with his daughters while writing the early numbers of *The Newcomes,* and among his friends were Robert and Elizabeth Barrett Browning and George Lewes and George Eliot (*Works* 12: xli, xlvii). This liberal English society, the manners of Italian women, and the historical perspective given to representations of women in both classical and Christian art in Rome—all may have helped Thackeray to clarify and deepen his discernment of gender issues. Of all Thackeray's female charac-ters, Ethel is best able to assume the role of heroine. That Thack-eray delights in Ethel is clear from the pleasure with which he de-scribes her words, looks, and actions, and one of the chief sources of his delight is her high spirit.

The insipid, passive model of femininity does not stand a chance against her. Even at thirteen, Ethel is gay, agile, "downright Ethel" (*Works* 12: 130); with children she is "loved like a mother al-most, for as such the hearty kindly girl showed herself to them; but at home she was . . . intractable" (*Works* 12: 137). When Lord Kew's horses run wild, Ethel "sat in her place like a man" and Kew twice calls her "a trump" (*Works* 12: 144–45). Colonel Newcome—also a trump, but an old one (*Works* 12: 210)—upon meeting Ethel, thinks to himself: "'What a frank, generous, bright young creature is yonder! . . . How cheery and gay she is; how good to Miss Hon-eyman, to whom she behaved with just the respect that was the old lady's due—how affectionate with her brothers and sisters!'" (*Works* 12: 209).

The terms in which Thackeray praises Ethel describe a character who is neither tribute to nor satire upon conventional images of women. She is a character with both faults and excellencies; she has depth. Writing as Pen but sounding very much like himself, Thackeray describes her:

> [Tall and] of a countenance somewhat grave and haughty, but on occasion brightening with humour and beaming with kindliness and affection. Too quick to detect affectation or insincerity in others, too impatient of dullness or pomposity, she is more sarcastic now than she became when after years of suffering had softened her nature. Truth looks out of her bright eyes, and rises up armed, and flashes scorn or denial, perhaps too readily, when she encounters flattery, or meanness, or imposture. After her first appearance in the world, if the truth must be told, this young lady was popular neither with many men, nor with most women. (*Works* 12: 311)

Thackeray's description leaves room for growth; there is a promise of greatness here. Courageous, high-spirited, kind to children, and honest by nature, Ethel will be "gentled" by experience and achieve that greatness once her high-principled intolerance is moderated by either sympathy or acknowledgment of her own faults, or both. (Clive, in contrast to Ethel, is very popular.) En route, the fierce, courageous woman has gained the author's imaginative sympathy, and the sweet, simple, clinging little woman has been left behind.

Ethel embodies a somewhat aristocratic ideal, with her noble grace, her self-command and dignity, her money. Even after her "conversion," "The fiery temper of former days was subdued in her, but the haughty resolution remained which was more than a match for [Barnes's] cowardly tyranny; besides, she was the mistress of sixty thousand pounds" (*Works* 13: 309). It is a stately composure, not want of feeling, that distinguishes Ethel from Laura when the two friends hear of Clive's impending marriage to Rosey:

> Keziah must have thought that there was something between Clive and my wife, for when Laura had read the letter she laid it down on the table, and . . . burst into tears.
> Ethel looked steadily at the two pictures of Clive and his father. Then she put her hand on her friend's shoulder. "Come, my dear," she said, "it is growing late, and I must go back to my children." And she saluted Mrs. Mason and her maid in a very stately manner, and

left them, leading my wife away, who was still exceedingly overcome. (*Works* 13: 306)

In *Vanity Fair,* Lady Jane exerts some of this same "stately" strength when she confronts Sir Pitt, but Ethel is the most fully developed example of Thackeray's heroine, the beneficiary of the best education society has to offer, simultaneously reflecting and redefining her culture's values. Like Laura, Ethel learns from experience and observation. Her turning point comes after Clara leaves Barnes, and Ethel recognizes that she had nearly entered into the same kind of marriage:

> As I lay awake, thinking of my own future life, and that I was going to marry, as poor Clara had married, but for an establishment and a position in life; I my own mistress and not obedient by nature, or a slave to others as that poor creature was—I thought to myself why should I do this? (*Works* 13: 286–87)

It is no wonder that Clive's impression as an artist is that Ethel would do for a Diana but not a Venus, a noble huntress but not a symbol of languorous love (*Works* 12: 318). R. D. McMaster remarks truly that this "identification with Diana expresses Ethel's divided spirit and complex psychology."[15]

Not Obedient by Nature

Clive's association of women with figures from Greek mythology signals Thackeray's recognition of the extent to which concepts of gender are culturally constituted. One scene in *Pendennis* demonstrates how well Thackeray understood the shaping influence of cultural assumptions, showing Pen at the theater. The scene so closely resembles a scene in Balzac's "Sarrasine" (1830) that we must assume Thackeray either read the Balzac story or was working from some mediating text. "Sarrasine" has been made familiar to many readers through Roland Barthes's analysis in *S/Z,* and this analysis, as well as Barbara Johnson's analysis of both, may be applied to Thackeray's parallel text.

Both Thackeray's and Balzac's scenes evoke the male gaze, and both show young men "falling in love" with staged representations of the feminine ideal. Both scenes interrogate (Barbara Johnson uses the term *deconstruct*) the concept of femininity itself. Balzac's handling of the subject is the more radical challenge to conventional concepts of femininity (the "woman" on stage is actually a castrato, and the man's disillusionment ends in death), but Thackeray accomplishes a similar analysis within the conventions of domestic realism. In "Sarrasine," a young French sculptor, visiting Italy for the first time, attends the theater and beholds the perfect woman:

> Suddenly a burst of applause. . . . She came coquettishly to the front of the stage and greeted the audience with infinite grace. The lights, the general enthusiasm, the theatrical illusion, the glamour of a style of dress which in those days was quite attractive, all conspired in favor of this woman. Sarrasine cried out with pleasure.[16]

Pendennis too is an artist—of sketches and words rather than of clay or marble—and is similarly affected by the crowd's excitement: "The pit thrilled and thumped its umbrellas; a volley of applause was fired from the gallery. . . . Pen's eyes opened wide and bright. . . . Pen this time, flaming with wine and enthusiasm, clapped hands and sang 'Bravo' louder than all" (*Pendennis* 71–72). Balzac's description of this ideal woman/castrato will reveal its full irony only on a second reading:

> At that instant he marveled at the ideal beauty he had hitherto sought in life. . . . La Zambinella displayed to him, united, living, and delicate, those exquisite female forms he so ardently desired, of which a sculptor is at once the severest and the most passionate judge. Her mouth was expressive, her eyes loving, her complexion dazzlingly white. And along with these details, which would have enraptured a painter, were all the wonders of those images of Venus revered and rendered by the chisels of the Greeks. The artist never wearied of admiring the inimitable grace with which the arms were attached to the torso, the marvelous roundness of the neck. . . . This was more than a woman, this was a masterpiece! . . . With his eyes, Sarrasine devoured Pygmalion's statue, come down from its pedestal.[17]

Thackeray's description too alludes to Venus and to a similar list of features:

> Her forehead was vast, and her black hair waved over it with a natural ripple, and was confined in shining and voluminous braids at

the back of a neck such as you see on the shoulders of the Louvre Venus—that delight of gods and men. Her eyes, when she lifted them up to gaze on you, and ere she dropped their purple deep-fringed lids, shone with tenderness and mystery unfathomable. Love and Genius seemed to look out from them and then retire coyly. . . . Who could have such a commanding brow but a woman of high intellect? . . . But it was her hand and arm that this magnificent creature most excelled in. . . . like—what shall we say?—like the snowy doves before the chariot of Venus—it was with these arms and hands that she beckoned, repelled, entreated, embraced her admirers. (*Pendennis* 71–72)

Though illusory, La Zambinella's "feminine" qualities have the power to intoxicate. Balzac's character "was so utterly intoxicated that he no longer saw the theater, the spectators, the actors, or heard the music. Moreover, the distance between himself and La Zambinella had ceased to exist, he possessed her, his eyes were riveted upon her, he took her for his own."[18]

In Thackeray, the scene's sexual implications are more veiled, but his social satire is more explicit, and his dark vision of the gender ideology that animates Pendennis's world—and that Thackeray finally links to death—is similar to Balzac's: "All the house was affected. Foker . . . wept piteously. As for Pen, he was too far gone for that. He followed the woman about and about. . . . Pen's hot eyes saw only Fotheringay, Fotheringay. The curtain fell upon him like a pall" (*Pendennis* 73). Barbara Johnson's explication of Balzac's scene applies equally to Thackeray's text:

> Balzac's fictional narrator makes explicit the narcissistic character of Sarrasine's passion and at the same time nostalgically identifies with it. . . . What [Sarrasine] devours so eagerly in La Zambinella is actually located within himself: a collection of sculpturesque clichés about feminine beauty and his own narcissism.[19]

Thus, whether alluding indirectly to the social and political debate about women and the professions, or whether demonstrating what it means to fall in love with an imaginary woman comprised of a collection of clichés, Thackeray shows that woman's "nature" is in large part a social construct. Thackeray is setting the stage, so to speak, for a redefinition of gender along increasingly liberal lines.

In *Pendennis,* sex-associated characteristics rest fairly lightly on both male and female characters. Statements about "woman's nature" gradually give way to a general sense that gender differences are often externally imposed. For example, the bluestockings who fared so badly under Fitz-Boodle's and Barry Lyndon's narrative control are redeemed in the person of Miss Bunion, a poet who appears at the Bungay dinner party. Thackeray's depiction of this character is partially satirical, but also partially respectful. Although the "gifted being" writes of herself as "a violet, shrinking meanly," she is "large and boney," with "a step heavy as a grenadier's," and she trails straw from the rumpled skirts of her dress and eats and drinks "with a vast appetite" (*Pendennis* 367–69). Her poetry is a Thackerayan parody of literary conventions of the feminine. Miss Bunion's insight into Pen's character is superior to her poetry, however. When she tells him, years later (apparently they have become friends), that he is "neither so solemn, not so stupid, not so pert" as he looks, he can only reply in a tone of "comical gallantry" (*Pendennis* 370). Pen's gallantry is a kind of defensive weapon here; we have seen it also in *Esmond.* Clearly, Thackeray is ambivalent about this intelligent, "masculine" woman writer; that she is not entirely a figure of fun is a mark of his growth.[20]

In Miss Bunion, Thackeray shows that a woman's writings may be scripted for her by society—that is, as a woman Miss Bunion must write as "a violet, shrinking meanly," if she wishes to succeed in the profession. He makes a similar point about the profession of law, showing that it is not nature but society that excludes women from the profession. Mary Poovey has described, in *Uneven Developments,* the ideal of womanhood that operated to hinder women from working outside the home. That ideal envisioned women as noncompetitive, giving of their "labor" (in both senses of the term) only for love. Thus, woman represents emotional connection as opposed to the alienation, isolation, and fragmentation that characterize so much of the Victorian age and that in fact characterize (as Ina Ferris demonstrates) Arthur Pendennis himself as a "representative nineteenth-century man."[21] One scene in particular seems designed to remind the reader that gender ideology, insubstantial though it may be, has the strength of iron bars. Pen is ill, and Laura and Helen have come to town to care for him. Laura has been loaned the room of Pen's neighbor and fellow student, Percy Sibwright. The description of Sibwright's bedroom hints at a certain effeminacy: his bed is "the prettiest little brass bed in the world, with chintz curtains lined with pink" and the room contains a "little exhibition of shiny boots, arranged in trim rows." But this dandy, like dandies generally in Thackeray, is "a gallant lover of the sex," and "a choice selection of portraits of females, almost always in sadness and generally in disguise or *déshabillé,* glittered round the neat walls of his elegant little bower of repose" (544).

In this room, in which "scarce anything told of the lawyer but the wig-box beside the Venus" (544), Laura tries on Sibwright's wig and reads one of his French novels. The image reminds us of the narrowness of a young woman's life and suggests that Laura could be at least as good a lawyer as Sibwright, but Thackeray does not say so. Instead, he asks what Sibwright, "the enraptured rogue," would have said if he could have seen her at such a moment. We know already: he would have encapsulated her in a poem filled with clichés of femininity—just like the portraits that glitter round his walls. Years later, when Laura confesses her "transgressions" to Pen, the scene is framed by two male viewpoints, that of the "gallant lover" Sibwright at its opening, and that of the bemused husband Pen at its close. Laura is hemmed in by watchful male eyes, just as Amelia had been at the opera.

Thackeray understood that women wanted the power to choose a profession (as well as to enjoy a French novel) as freely as men; his daughter Annie had by now become an outspoken witness for women's ambitions. In a letter to Mrs. Fanshawe (the feminist whom Jane Brookfield's husband had ordered her to ignore), Anne wrote in 1852:

> I should like a profession so much not to spend my life crochetting mending my clothes & reading novels—wh seems the employment of English ladies, unless they teach dirty little children to read wh is well enough in its way but no work to the mind . . . as my favorite Miss Martineau says it is far nobler to earn than to save I think I should like to earn very much & become celebrated like the aforesaid Harriet who is one of the only sensible women living besides thee & me.[22]

Thackeray was living with a feminist in his own family by this time, and was surely aware of the implications of scenes such as this of

Laura trying on the lawyer's wig. Thackeray's novel echoe Florence Nightingale's plea: "Why have women passion, intellect, moral activity . . . and a place in society where no one of the three can be exercised?"[23]

PATTERNS OF DEVELOPMENT

When George Eliot pointed out to Mrs. Charles Bray in 1854 that "Lady C is Amelia, Esmond is Dobbin, and Trix is Becky," she was remarking the continuities in Thackeray's exploration of gender ideology.[24] Ethel did not spring from nothing: her characterization is the realization of a series of patterns in Thackeray's fiction—patterns of increasing validation of independence and forcefulness in women, and a growing disparagement of the timid, passive ideal that reaches its logical conclusion in Rosey Newcome's psychic disintegration and death. In the larger Thackerayan pattern, Becky and Ethel are on the same continuum, and Amelia's least attractive qualities find their ultimate expression in Rosey. Qualities that seem valuable feminine characteristics in the early works are shown to be harmful later on. Amelia's devotion to her son, for example, evolves into Helen's sexual jealousy and, finally, into Rachel's passion for Henry Esmond. On the other side, Becky's defiance is echoed in Beatrix's angry resistance to Henry's emotional demands and in Ethel's rejection of both Kew and Farintosh because she is "not obedient by nature." It is obvious that Thackeray's most "modern" heroine, Ethel Newcome, descends from the wicked but lively—"I'm no angel"—Becky Sharp. It is Ethel who declares: "'We are sold, . . . we are as much sold as Turkish women. . . . No, there is no freedom for us. I wear my green ticket, and wait till my master comes. But every day as I think of our slavery, I revolt against it more'" (*Works* 12: 429).

This Thackerayan pattern of evolving female characters—from Amelia to Rosey, from Becky to Ethel—reflects Thackeray's growth from uneasy ambivalence to a clear and strong rejection of many social fictions regarding women. In the early works, for example, Thackeray seems to subscribe, albeit satirically, to the convention that women's lives revolve around men. Thus women tend to be rivals, and their friendship is portrayed as shallow, as is the case with Laura and "dearest Blanche," and with Becky and Amelia. In *Vanity Fair,* the narrator comments:

For the affection of young ladies is of as rapid growth as Jack's bean-stalk, and reaches up to the sky in a night. It is no blame to them that after marriage this *Sehnsucht nach der Liebe* subsides. It is what sentimentalists, who deal in very big words, call a yearning after the Ideal, and simply means that women are commonly not satisfied until they have husbands and children on whom they may center affections which are spent elsewhere, as it were, in small change. (*Vanity Fair* 39)

Similarly, the affection between Helen and Laura in *Pendennis* is merely "such affection as women, whose hearts are disengaged, are apt to bestow upon a near female friend" (*Pendennis* 229), and the friendship between Blanche and Laura springs up like "Jack's bean-stalk . . . to the sky in a night" (248) and dies as rapidly when the two become rivals over Pen.

The obvious source of this estrangement between women is competition for the economic security and the social and emotional validation that only men are able to give. This would seem no more than a realistic representation. But by the time he wrote *The Newcomes,* Thackeray was beginning to challenge even the idea that women are always rivals. Laura teases Arthur about this belief:

You fancy we are all jealous of one another. No protests of ours can take that notion out of your heads. My dear Pen, I do not intend to try. We are not jealous of mediocrity; we are not patient of it. I dare say we are angry because we see men admire it so. You gentlemen, who pretend to be our betters, give yourselves such airs of protection, and profess such a lofty superiority over us, prove it by quitting the cleverest woman in the room for the first pair of bright eyes and dimpled cheeks that enter. (*Works* 13: 147)

Yet Pen persists: when Laura and Ethel meet, he reflects that Ethel's charm has overcome "even female jealousy. Perhaps Laura determined magnanimously to conquer it; perhaps she hid it so as to vex me and prove the injustice of my suspicions" (*Works* 13: 161). The narrative irony is now directed against Pen and the myth of universal female jealousy. Only those who refuse the role of "pretty fond parasite" whose nature it is to "creep about his feet and kiss them" (*Pendennis* 582) are able to care for or about others. As emotional (and economic) dependence on men lessens, Thackeray's women characters begin to form friendships. Laura and Ethel not only become lifelong friends, they also offer aid and comfort to other women. Ethel, for example, despite her love for Clive, is characterized by nobility, not jealousy, when she goes to comfort his sick, weeping wife: "I dare say Clive's words were incoherent; but women have more presence of mind; and now Ethel, with a noble grace which I cannot attempt to describe, going up to Rosey, seated herself by her, spoke . . . of her wish, her hope that Rosey should love her as a sister" (*Works* 13: 484).

The basis of women's power shifts from helplessness and manipulativeness to intelligence, character, and economic independence. If one recalls Becky's questionable modes of living "on nothing a year" and Amelia's pathetic attempts to support and keep her son, the contrast will be clear. Helen Pendennis supports Pen, and Laura pays Pen's debts and lends him money twice; Blanche's mother buys a husband for herself and a title for her son, as—on a smaller scale—Mrs. Bonner uses her life savings to acquire the Clavering Arms and a young husband, Lightfoot. Emily Costigan supports her drunken father by her acting and later through an allowance, and Lady Rockminster takes charge of Laura after Helen's death, and her wealth and social position enable her to push through the marriages of Fanny to Huxter and of Laura to Pendennis when the elderly Mr. Huxter and Major Pendennis oppose them. Fanny's mother, Mrs. Bolton, runs the Shepherd's Inn during the frequent absences of her drunken husband, but her autonomy stops when he returns home, for he beats her. Even poor Madame Fribsby manages to support herself as a milliner, and it is she who exposes Altamont's identity and helps to rid the others of this parasite. And in *Henry Esmond,* Rachel uses her private inheritance to send Harry to college, and the Dowager Viscountess supports him after Lord Castlewood's death.

The tyranny of the fathers depicted in *Vanity Fair* is ending. Fathers may be removed altogether by death, as are Laura's, Pen's, and Foker's fathers, and Captain Shandon. Or they may be controlled through their weaknesses. Many of the men drink heavily, for example: Shandon, Costigan, Strong, Bolton, Armstrong, Clavering, young Huxter . . . the procession is remarkable (Becky Sharp and Pen's laundress are the only women who drink). Or fathers and uncles can be reconciled to events that they first opposed, as are Major Pendennis and Mr. Huxter. The most important father figure in *Pendennis* is Warrington, and (oddly for one of Thackeray's good men) he neither sees nor communicates with his children. Such patterns, combined with the absence of patri-archal figures and the economic independence of women, signal the ascendancy of women in Thackeray's novels.

Thackeray never creates an entirely admirable male figure; the self-deprecatory ironic tone he generally used in speaking and writing about himself is reflected in the fact that no male charac-ter is fully heroic. Some—like Pendennis, Clive Newcome, and Philip Firmin—always remain somewhat boyish. Some—such as Henry Esmond and George Warrington—have a certain stateli-ness but lack the energy, sparkle, and humor of Thackeray's tyros, and they live, finally, secluded lives. His greatest gentlemen, Colonel Dobbin and Colonel Newcome, are men whose intentions are noble but whose mistakes, desires, and drives have harmful consequences for others, which shadow their greatness. Katherine Rogers has remarked that "All of his great characters, with the ex-ception of Colonel Newcome, are women; and many of his keen-est psychological insights appear in his analyses of the bad side of good women and the good side of bad women."[25]

Thackeray's female characters establish a clear pattern of growth, a progression that links Ethel Newcome with Catherine Hayes, and Rosey Mackenzie with Caroline Gann of *A Shabby Gen-teel Story*. The pattern is in one sense dialectical, in that "opposites" such as Becky and Amelia become gradually merged into one an-other. Thackeray's works increasingly challenge conventional im-ages of the good woman: her ignorance of evil, her lack of sexual passion, her frequent recourse to sentiment rather than spiritual or intellectual principle, her emotional susceptibility, and her sub-missiveness and passivity. In place of these qualities, Thackeray gradually endows his good women with some of the characteristics of the bad: intelligence, independence, wit, aggressiveness, pas-sion, courage, unconventionality. It is the extraordinarily named Laura Bell, who is frequently satirical upon the point of male su-periority, whose "dazzling glance of calm scrutiny" unnerves Pen (*Pendennis* 688).

The "good" women in Thackeray's early works—Amelia, Helen, Rachel—are childlike, whereas women who live in the world seem older than their years: Beatrix looks and feels sometimes like her mother's sister, and Ethel, at twenty, feels "sometimes . . . a hun-dred; and . . . so tired" (*Works* 13: 120). Associated with this girl-ishness in good women is a lack of sexual awareness. Amelia, re-peatedly described as pure, loves George in a sentimental, asexual way, and it is not until the fiction of her innocence (her ignorance of George's relationship with Becky) is shattered that she can marry Dobbin. Becky has a high level of sexual awareness; she "plays the game" that men usually win, knowledgeably but with no passion.

Rachel Castlewood's attraction for Henry lies at the heart of *Henry Esmond.* The sexual element is complicated by her maternal feelings and by feelings of rivalry with Beatrix. Long-repressed, guilt-ridden, and finally "sublimated into sentiment" (as Gordon Ray expresses it), Rachel's sexual desire is evaded and denied by Henry as he insists on her angelic purity.[26] And Beatrix, who is cast out by the jealous suspicions of Rachel and Henry, is their too frank, too attractive scapegoat; with her removal, the sexual guilt of Rachel and Henry is washed away and they are free to marry.

In *Pendennis,* Thackeray begins to treat female sexuality more directly; it emerges first as Helen's maternal jealousy. Then Laura's blushes and hesitations before physical contact with Pen or Warrington show that she is awakening sexually. It is only after she has conquered her love for Warrington, a married man, that Laura can understand and forgive Pen and Fanny Bolton. Recognizing and accepting sexual desire is a major step in Laura's spiritual growth. She combines some of Becky's awareness of sex with some of Amelia's capacity to feel emotional attachment and to make ethical distinctions. But whereas Amelia had to learn to feel passion before she could marry, Laura had to learn to discipline it.

Only in *The Newcomes* does a woman's sexuality emerge as a positive value. Pen describes Ethel's beauty: "I watched her as I have watched a beautiful panther at the zoological gardens, so bright of eye, so sleek of coat, so slim in form, so swift and agile in her spring" (*Works* 13: 37). Ethel herself has a kind of interest in good-looking young men that is new to Thackeray's heroines:

> All the time we have been making this sketch Ethel is standing looking at Clive; and the blushing youth casts down his eyes before hers. Her face assumes a look of arch humour. She passes a slim hand over the prettiest lips and a chin with the most lovely of dimples, thereby indicating her admiration of Mr. Clive's mustachios and imperial. (*Works* 12: 310)

There is a remarkable opening up of sexual roles here; Ethel is both attractive and attracted; shyness and assertiveness belong to both men and women; and Ethel is neither wicked nor burdened with sexual guilt, even after Clive's marriage to Rosey.

Similarly, the capacity for clear perception passes from Becky through Beatrix to Laura; Ethel, as a dynamic character, has to grow in perception before she can fully realize her potential. Becky is not truthful—she uses her perceptiveness to manipulate people—but her clear-sightedness gives her an advantage over others, and like the author, she sees that much of social life is role-playing. Thus, she can be an ingenue, shyly interested about India, for Jos, and a witty, cynical gossip for Miss Crawley, or anything else she perceives is wanted. Ethel is less clever but capable of greater depth: she has, Laura tells Pen, "problems that she has to work out for herself, only you, Pen, do not like us poor ignorant women to use such a learned word as problems" (*Works* 13: 282).

Perceptive women in Thackeray's works sometimes seem to speak for the author. When Becky remarks on the moral advantages of wealth—"I could be a good woman if I had five thousand a year" (*Vanity Fair* 409)—she echoes a line in one of Thackeray's letters to his mother (1839): "If I had 3000 a year I think I'd be so [good, sober, and religious] too" (*Letters* 1: 399). And when Becky tells Amelia that her adored George had been a "low-bred Cockney dandy," she helps free Amelia from her illusions, as much as when she tells her that George had wanted Becky to run away with him. Becky can speak the truth when she wants to, and when she does, she seems to speak for Thackeray. After all, much of her education had come through the conversation of her father's friends, artists who probably resembled Thackeray's Bohemian friends. Laura too can speak in Thackerayan terms, as when she reminds Arthur of "dancing-girls [in India] . . . whose calling is to dance, and wear jewels, and look beautiful. . . . Can we cry out against these poor creatures. . . ? It seems to me that young women in our world are bred up in a way not very different" (*Works* 13: 282–83).

Ethel Newcome possesses an unconventional perceptiveness similar to Becky's and to Beatrix's. When she visits the water colour exhibitions with Lady Kew, they stand before one of Mr. Hunt's pieces depicting "with such consummate truth and pathos—a friendless young girl cowering in a doorway, evidently without home or shelter" (*Works* 12: 365). Lady Kew stands admiring—until Ethel laughs. What had moved her was the green ticket attached to the painting and proclaiming "SOLD." Ethel remarks,

10. Initial letter from chapter 16 of *The New-comes*, in which Ethel is engaged (*Works* 13: 212).

"'I think, Grandmamma, . . . we young ladies in the world, when we are exhibiting, ought to have little green tickets pinned on our backs, with "Sold" written on them'" (*Works* 12: 366). Ethel recognizes that sexual relationships are commercialized, in one way or another, on all levels. That evening, Ethel transforms herself into an illustration of the point when she appears at dinner with a stolen green "SOLD" ticket pinned to her dress. Thackeray's comment is: "Let us be perfectly sure, that to whatever purpose Miss Ethel Newcome, for good or evil, might make up her mind, she had quite spirit enough to hold her own" (*Works* 12: 367). Thackeray was to silently repeat the theme with his initial letter for chapter 16 of *The Newcomes* (*Works* 13: 212), showing a young girl being auctioned off before a crowd of men with "Lot 1" written on her dress (see figure 10), and here he has Ethel express the idea outright.

We can never know the debt that Victorian literature owes to Thackeray for his sensitive and groundbreaking portraits of women. Beginning with parody, then exploring the power of institutional pressures over women, Thackeray's writings reflect a growing insight and finally a profound reordering of ideas concerning gender. As conventional standards of femininity are exposed as essentially false and damaging to both men and women, qualities of perceptiveness, strength and energy, frankness, generosity, and liberality replace them. His sense of the novelist's responsibility leads Thackeray inevitably to the Woman Question. En route, he redefines the personal and public aspects of women's lives for his readers. He knew that unless the personal were redefined, the political would not change.

7 / Childbirth, Madness, and Motherhood

Echoes of Ancient Matriarchy

I say the world is full of Miss Nightingales.
—*The Newcomes* (*Works* 13: 287)

Up to this point, I have attempted to demonstrate the liberality of Thackeray's views by examining a variety of rather disparate topics—his satire, parody, and realism, his exploration of subjectivity through ironic first-person narrative, the evolution of his heroines, and parallels between his life and his fiction. Now the time has come to sum up Thackeray's career and to show that Thackeray himself seems finally to have resolved his ambivalences and established a unified and profound view of the power of gender ideology in history and over the individual. Thackeray's last three novels complete the pattern we have been tracing thus far. They are *The Virginians: A Tale of the Last Century* (1857–1859); *The Adventures of Philip on His Way Through the World* (1861–1862); and *Denis Duval* (unfinished, 1864).

In each of these novels Thackeray "dove deeper": to search the hidden roots of his wife's insanity; to redefine the connections between gender and the ability to care for children, an ability that he well knew was not biologically determined nor limited to one sex; and to explore, although only briefly, the intriguing idea of an entirely different kind of social order, one in which women were free moral agents, empowered to carry out their decisions. It was a social order that glimmered on the horizon of the century's social theories, and that could be glimpsed in the classical mythology that Thackeray absorbed with the rest of his classical learning. To accomplish this deepening of concern, Thackeray had to link three major preoccupations of the Victorian age: female insanity; the clichéd but sacrosanct triad of woman, nature, and motherhood;

and the question of how human society evolved from what seemed to many anthropologists to have been matriarchal roots.

It might seem at first glance that Ethel Newcome's strength and sanity have no connection whatsoever to the pathetic mental collapse of Clarisse de Viomesnil in Thackeray's last, unfinished novel *Denis Duval*, except perhaps as antithesis. But in fact, this final novel sets out in a direction that can only be described as both fundamentally consistent with what has come before and yet unprecedented—a perfectly logical inductive leap forward. In *The Newcomes*, Ethel's heroism can be equated with "sanity" in that she is able to make intelligent, responsible decisions and to carry them through, and a key to her moral stature is her ability to take care of others—especially of Clara Newcome's abandoned children. To reach this point, Ethel had to reject not only a mercenary, loveless marriage but also the subordination that she saw as an essential component of marriage as defined by society and the law: determining that she is her "own mistress, and not obedient by nature, or a slave to others as that poor creature [Clara] was," Ethel decides that she will "be the mother to [Clara's] orphans" (*Works* 13: 286–87). Ethel's resistance to women's "slavery"—to being "sold" on the market—serves as emblem for rejection of the marriage, property, and child custody laws that maintain women's dependence, and so a literary concept—heroism—becomes both a legal argument and a radical redefinition of motherhood.

The Newcomes opens with a fable that serves as a perfect metonym for popular images of motherhood. The fable features a wolf:

> He was so cunningly dressed up in sheep's clothing that the very lambs did not know master wolf; nay, one of them, whose dam the wolf had just eaten, after which he had thrown her skin over his shoulders, ran up innocently towards the devouring monster, mistaking him for her mama.
>
> "He he!" says a fox, sneaking around the hedge-paling.... "How absurd these lambs are! Yonder silly little knock-knee'd bahling does not know the old wolf.... He is the same old rogue who gobbled up little Red Riding Hood's grandmother for lunch, and swallowed little Red Riding Hood for supper... He he!"

For a while "the little lambkin" lies "unsuspiciously at the side of the wolf in fleecy hosiery, who did not as yet molest her, being replenished with the mutton her mamma." But just as the wolf begins to think of having lambkin for supper, a donkey in a lion's skin frightens away all the animals, and the lamb survives, only to be led away by a butcher (*Works* 12: 1–5).

Now Thackeray brings in the Critic, who will make some indignant, foolish remarks upon the fable Thackeray has just written, and then, Thackeray tells us, the Critic, "if in a virtuous mood, may indulge in some fine writing regarding the holy beauteousness of maternal affection" (*Works* 12: 5)—as in fact some critics have done regarding Helen Pendennis, one writing "What can we do but simply bow down reverently before the goodness and sweetness of Helen Pendennis?"[1] The fable is an allegory: the fleecy sheep represents women who internalize the misogynistic values of a culture and are devoured from within. On the surface they look like mothers/sheep, but beneath the comfortable exterior is a devouring monster. And foolish critics can respond to images of motherhood only with clichés and sanctimonious sentiment.

The fable in fact represents Thackeray's relationship with critics—and many readers—up to the present day. Conventional assumptions about women are so powerful that they have interfered with our ability to understand his fiction. Such assumptions have clothed Thackeray's women in "fleecy hosiery" and obscured the dangerous reality underneath. Feminism today provides us with the tools to understand Thackeray's fable-novels better.

INSANITY

> In a society that not only perceived women as childlike, irrational, and sexually unstable but also rendered them legally powerless and economically marginal, it is not surprising that they should have formed the greater part of the residual categories of deviance from which doctors drew a lucrative practice and the asylums much of their population.[2]

Isabella Thackeray's insanity, terrible as it was, may be redeemed—may serve her fellow sufferers—as it operates through Thackeray's novels as a force for greater understanding of women's problems. If he appropriated her suffering in any way, it was to put his poor mad wife into his books as a metaphor for women's oppression and to suggest alternatives: legal equality, economic independence, and the development of women's moral and intellectual powers. It is not clear whether Isabella's insanity was caused by cultural and domestic pressures to live up to some feminine ideal or by physical problems such as puerperal fever. Since there is evidence for both conclusions, it seems that the cause may be some combination of cultural and physical factors.

Among the cultural causes, we must recall that Isabella grew up with a domineering mother who was resentful of the low social status in which her husband's death had left her. When Thackeray met Isabella, she was shy, timid, undemonstrative; some would call her withdrawn. She was oddly passive about writing letters. Thackeray seemed to understand her weaknesses: his early letters are sometimes harsh, sometimes sympathetic, but always urge more expressiveness, more activity, more passion, more warmth. He incurred Mrs. Shawe's wrath by insistently reminding Isabella in writing that marriage meant sharing his bed. He believed that Isabella would improve when freed from her mother's dominance.

Isabella's marriage thwarted her mother's ambitions and resulted in what must have been a painful rejection. After the marriage, money was scarce, Isabella was far from being a good manager, and her mother withheld even the small allowance she had promised the couple. This left them entirely dependent on Thackeray's parents—and Thackeray's mother's disapproval of Isabella's incompetence must have added to her sense of abandonment and unworthiness. Isabella depended on Thackeray for society, and her clinging, girlish ways sometimes annoyed him. Thackeray could not long keep up the role of husband to a child bride. In addition, he himself had a lifelong need to be out and about, and a rather fainthearted habit of escaping unpleasant situations by slipping away—and so he left Isabella alone, or with critical female relatives, far too often.

An appendix in Gordon Ray's edition of the *Letters* (1: 518–20) provides a psychiatric case history of Isabella's illness. In it, Dr. Stanley Cobb discusses, as well as he can from the evidence available, the causes of the breakdown. His analysis begins with the fact that Isabella's mother had undergone similar periods of depression after the births of her children and that she was "unstable and difficult." Thus, Isabella may have inherited a tendency toward insanity from her mother. Further, Isabella's environment was made stressful by her mother's difficult personality. Then three pregnancies in four years, with one child dying at eight months, "brought heavy physical burdens. . . . Added to this were the adjustments to marriage and the grief over losing a child." Dr. Cobb implies that Isabella's insanity resulted from a combination of physical and emotional causes, but he does not link her insanity to issues of gender. Thackeray would do better.

After Isabella's insanity began to manifest itself, Thackeray gave enormous amounts of time and energy to helping her. He took ice-water showers with her, tied himself to her while they slept so that if she got out of bed he would wake up, hired nurses to care for Isabella and the children while he wrote, and traveled from doctor to doctor, looking for one who could help. Finally, when the medical and psychiatric theories of his day had been exhausted, rather than put Isabella into a mental institution, he placed her in the home of a kindly, competent woman and her daughter, hoping always for a cure. Isabella continued to alternate between periods of vacant passivity, languor, and depression, and periods of suicidal and murderous rages. Feelings of unworthiness—of being an unfit wife and mother—dominated her mind. Perhaps Isabella's self-hatred was transferred to her daughter on the day when she pushed Annie a little way into the sea in an apparent attempt to drown her.[3] The same kind of impulse will move Clarisse to leave Agnes by the side of the sea in *Denis Duval*.

If there is any way Thackeray can be faulted, it is for his "neglect" in the early years. It was a neglect for which he tried to make amends in becoming his wife's nurse—and in painful hours of introspection that resulted in insights more profound than those of most medical and psychiatric professionals of his age. More than most Victorian analysts of women's mental diseases, Thackeray recognized that gender-specific cultural factors contribute significantly to women's insanity.

Even if Isabella's insanity was due primarily to physical causes, cultural factors certainly played a part, and through his art Thackeray developed these insights into a broad cultural critique. Female insanity occurs five times in Thackeray's fiction. Thackeray was aware both of the symbolic and expressive value of madness in literature and of its implications in life. For him, insanity was a painful reality, and its recurrence in women in his fiction suggests that he was searching for insights into its causes.

The first occurrence of female insanity is Amelia Sedley's in *Vanity Fair*. In describing Amelia, Thackeray conveys a deep compassion that is surely derived from his own experience with Isabella. After hearing of George's death, Amelia:

> spent the first portion of that time in a sorrow so profound and pitiable, that we who have been watching and describing some of the emotions of that weak and tender heart, must draw back in the presence of the cruel grief. . . . Tread silently round the hapless couch of the poor prostrate soul. Shut gently the door of the dark chamber wherein she suffers. (347)

Though it never did so for Isabella, motherhood brings Amelia a restoration to sanity: "how she laughed and wept over [the baby] —how love, and hope, and prayer woke again in her bosom as the baby nestled there. She was safe." But even while acknowledging pathos, Thackeray's keen, detached intelligence resists sentimentalization: not only is George unworthy of such grief, but Dobbin too is implicated in an ambiguous absurdity that attaches to this scenario at its conclusion: "Our friend Dobbin was one of [those who had been constantly with Amelia]. . . . To see Dobbin holding the infant, and to hear Amelia's laugh of triumph as she watched him, would have done any man good who had a sense of humour" (347). The pain and suffering are authentic, Thackeray demonstrates, but they arise to some extent out of delusion and folly that are inextricably linked to concepts of love, personality, and gender.

The second episode of madness occurs in *The Newcomes*. Although Rosey Mackenzie resembles Amelia in her sweet, gentle exterior, in her case, the causes of insanity become more clear. First, she is ruled by a domineering mother well versed in the "womanly" arts of placating men, husband-hunting, jealousy, and petty cruelty to "rival" women. Second, despite her affection for another man (Captain Hoby), Rosey is compelled to marry Clive; and so Rosey learns to feign affection for both mother and husband. The sweet-little-girl qualities that once captivated "spoonies" like Dobbin and Colonel Newcome (and Thackeray himself) become stale as their underlying manipulativeness becomes apparent. Thus, another cause of Rosey's decline becomes Clive's ill-concealed contempt. Despite Clive's joyless indifference to her, Rosey is continually pregnant and has at least two miscarriages

(*Works* 13: 426). There are signs of anorexia. Pen sees her and remarks that "the light of her eyes had gone out" and that she eats almost nothing, despite her "situation" (pregnancy). Pen adds, "poor Rosey was always in a situation" (*Works* 13: 474).

Finally, after an angry scene between Clive and Mrs. Mackenzie, Rosey goes into hysterics and then into labor. She gives birth to a stillborn child and dies. Just as Rawdon Crawley's discovery of Becky with Lord Steyne receives all the critical attention, whereas Lady Jane's similar discovery of her husband with Becky is overlooked, so too is Colonel Newcome's deathbed "Adsum" and "Leonore" frequently discussed, whereas Rosey's dying words are forgotten. But Rosey's death parallels Colonel Newcome's in a similar way, as an analogy—with similar incidents but very different emotional and ethical significance.

The events are narrated by Pen, who has just lost his temper and expressed his long-suppressed anger toward Mrs. Mackenzie. Suddenly he hears Rosey's voice "from an inner apartment, screaming, 'Mamma, Mamma!'" (*Works* 13: 496). Rosey is dying in an inner chamber, with its connotations of the cave, the womb, the inner sanctum.[4] Perhaps it is fear of motherhood, perhaps it is her own unmet need for mothering that makes her cling so to Mrs. Mackenzie. At that moment three generations come together in a primal scene of life-out-of-death. Rosey, who had been given life by Mrs. Mackenzie, is also being devoured by her. The image of Rosey before her mother as "a bird before a boa-constrictor, doomed—fluttering, fascinated" (*Works* 13: 431), conveys also the image of the bird, still whole and alive inside the boa constrictor, in a kind of reverse pregnancy. In this case, the child nourishes the mother from within. Rosey dies, not simply from medical complications, but from the disruption of her psychic life, from weakness and fear that paralyze her mind and kill her will to live. Her madness is both symptom and cause of the impending death.

The third case of female insanity is Clara Pulleyn Newcome, another woman whose mind buckles under the pressures of an unhappy domestic situation. Like Isabella Thackeray, Clara changes from a cheerful (though timid) person into a depressed, withdrawn, and solitary woman. Thackeray's description of Clara resembles some descriptions of his wife after her insanity began.[5] At first, Clara is sweet, dutiful, obedient. But Barnes Newcome's physical and verbal abuse coupled with Clara's frustrated love for

Jack Belsize lead to a breakdown. First she fights Barnes, quarreling and flying into rages, then she seems to enter into a state of depression: "More and more sad does the Lady Clara become from day to day; liking more to sit lonely over the fire; careless about the sarcasms of her husband; the prattle of her children" (*Works* 13: 552). Thackeray does not make clear how far Clara recovers after she runs away with Jack Belsize, but we are told that after the divorce her "whole being, and hope and passion" have centered on a new baby. The apathy and carelessness and incipient insanity have disappeared, with release from a bad marriage.

The fourth instance occurs in *Philip*. Caroline Gann is described as having gone through a period of insanity between the time covered in *A Shabby Genteel Story* and that covered in *Philip*. Much of the book's plot (and the course of Philip's life) depends on Caroline's delusion that Philip Firmin is the reincarnation of her own dead infant, a "mania" common (according to the narrator, Pen) to women who have lost a baby (as had Isabella):

> How came she to love the boy so? Years back, in her own horrible extremity of misery, she could remember a week or two of a brief, strange, exquisite happiness, which came to her in the midst of her degradation and desertion, and for a few days a baby in her arms. . . . It was taken from her, after a few days—only sixteen days. Insanity came upon her, as her dead infant was carried away: —insanity, and fever, and struggle—ah! who knows how dreadful? She never does. . . . But George Brand Firmin, Esq., M.D., knows how very frequent are such cases of mania. (*Works* 18: 240–41)

The characteristically agile narrative shift from Caroline Gann to George Brand Firmin, Esq., M.D., is a fine stroke of irony. Educated and made wealthy by the social and medical establishments whose fringes Caroline lives on, Firmin would "know" her case in an abstract way; in actuality, he is the one who had so degraded and deserted her, years before. After Caroline recovers, she takes up nursing, showing a special talent for helping women in childbirth. Except perhaps on the point of her dead baby's reincarnation as Philip (who as his half-brother may indeed resemble him), she is sane. But Caroline's recovery is no mere return to a previous state; she surfaces from the mind's depths to play a role in *Philip* that would not have been possible before her breakdown. (This will be discussed shortly.)

The last case of insanity in a woman occurs in *Denis Duval.* In this unfinished work, Clarisse de Viomesnil, eighteen years old, obediently marries the man her parents have chosen for her, Vicomte de Barr (later Count de Saverne), age forty-three. Like Amelia, Rosey, and Clara, she is "as gentle, subordinate a slave as ever you shall see in Jamaica or Barbadoes," and of necessity a hypocrite, for "You don't expect sincerity and subservience too" (*Works* 21: 22). When her husband goes to war, she secretly hopes that he will not return and fears that she will go mad when she sees him (*Works* 21: 22–23). During his absence she gives birth to a baby girl, despite her husband's desire for a boy—another "failure." A month later she is dangerously ill of a fever, possibly puerperal fever, which is to last three months.

While in this state, Clarisse has herself and her daughter baptized into the Roman Catholic church. Significantly, both take the name Agnes. St. Agnes was a third-century Roman girl who took a Christian vow of chastity. When she refused to marry she was forced into a house of prostitution and then killed. She was twelve years old at the time. Thackeray could not have chosen the name by accident, especially when it is linked to Roman Catholic baptism or when compared to the name Henry Esmond's mother assumed when she became a nun, Mary Magdalene. When she has partially recovered, Clarisse leaves her husband's house and flies to Ursule Duval in England. Here, as a boy, Denis observes her behavior:

> She was very ill—pale, with a red spot on either cheek, sitting for whole hours in silence, and looking round frightened, as if a prey to some terror. . . . At times, Madame could not bear the crying of the child, and would order it away from her. At other times, she would clutch it, cover it with cloaks, and lock her door, and herself into the chamber with her infant. (*Works* 21: 39)

Clarisse's extreme ambivalence toward her daughter almost results in death. One night, Clarisse leaves the baby lying on a rock by the side of the sea, under a silver moon and vulnerable to the incoming tide. Denis meets her as she returns from this symbolic act of child sacrifice, dressed in white and glimmering and singing in the darkness, and it is Denis who rescues the baby (*Works* 21: 55–56). Finally, after her husband is killed in a duel with de la

Motte, she is possessed by the idea that she will be burned at the stake for the murder of her husband. In his final apostrophe to this poor mad woman, who is almost surely drawn from Isabella, Thackeray wrote:

> All night long we could hear her songs, her screams, her terrible laughter. . . . Oh, pitiful was thy lot in this world, poor guiltless, harmless lady! In thy brief years, how little happiness! For thy marriage portion only gloom, and terror, and submission, and captivity. The awful Will above us ruled it so. Poor frightened spirit! it has woke under serener skies now, and passed out of reach of our terrors, and temptations, and troubles. (*Works* 21: 60)

Denis's narrative evades a full discussion of the sources of Clarisse's madness, but the text reveals it: "submission, and captivity" for her "marriage portion." Before bowing to the divine will, Thackeray traces the human agency that brought this tragedy about: unhappy forced marriage, tyranny at home, suppressed anger, hopeless passivity, childbirth with mixed responses of love and resentment toward the child, and possibly puerperal fever. All of these elements have appeared in earlier works, becoming more intense and frequent in the later ones.

Thackeray repeatedly weaves incidents from life into patterns that invest them with social meaning. At the same time, as he had done with Becky's appearances as Clytemnestra, Thackeray uses allusion and symbol to give the resonance and significance of myth to his scenes: Rosey screaming in the inner chamber, Clarisse offering her daughter to the moon and the sea and expecting to be burned at the stake, Caroline Gann chloroforming Tufton Hunt. One other possible model for Clara Barnes's and Clarisse de Viomesnil's insanity should be mentioned.

Among Thackeray's close friends in the 1830s and 1840s was Saville Morton. Ray states that he was second only to Fitzgerald in Thackeray's circle of friends at that time. Morton had an affair with the wife of a friend, Elliott Bower. In 1852, after the birth of her fifth child, Mrs. Bower developed puerperal fever. In her delirium she raved at her husband, accusing him of physical abuse, clutching a letter from his mistress, and telling him that the child she had borne was not his but Morton's. Then she said to her sister, "Queen of England, drive away this man." Her husband seized a carving knife from the dining room table and stabbed Morton to death. He was acquitted of murder, however, and Mrs. Bower recovered and went into mourning for Morton (*Letters* 1: cli–clii). The incident must have touched Thackeray deeply, especially since the love triangle somewhat resembled his own situation with the Brookfields, and Mrs. Bower's postpartum insanity was so like Isabella's. The undercurrents of rage that erupted into violence in the Bower home reappear in *The Newcomes* and in *Denis Duval* in Barnes's humiliation in the street and in the killing of Clarisse's husband. It is interesting that in Thackeray's scenes, however, it is the husband who is punished, not the lover. Mrs. Bower's address to her sister as the Queen of England is also noteworthy. Victoria must have represented to many women a source of power that was at once matriarchal and patriarchal, what Nina Auerbach calls a "transfigured, mythic presence." Elaine Showalter reports that a great number of Victorian madwomen thought they themselves were the queen.[6] As the only woman with power in the government, the Queen represented, despite her lack of sympathy with the woman's cause, a symbol of the contradictions inherent in Victorian gender ideology.

MARRIAGE

We have seen that in Thackeray's novels, good women become increasingly independent. In order to develop this concept Thackeray had to overcome the stranglehold that the "marriage plot" has traditionally had on the novel. Florence Nightingale once said, "[Marriage] ought to be a sacred event, but surely not the only event, of a woman's life."[7] Thackeray illustrates this truth in a number of works. He frequently shows women refusing marriage altogether: Laura turns down Pendennis's first offer of marriage; Ethel breaks off with both Kew and Farintosh; and Hetty Lambert refuses several offers of marriage, including Harry Warrington's. Other models of independent single women are the milliner Madame Fribsby in *Pendennis,* Martha Honeyman in *The Newcomes,* and Caroline Gann in *Philip.* Thackeray objected to novelistic conventions of romantic love (recall that in *A Shabby Genteel Story,* novels were Caroline Gann's primary source of ideas; later in *Philip* she cannot understand how Pendennis, a married man, could write such things) and to what Rachel Brownstein calls "the novel's long marriage to the marriage-plot." Thackeray seems to have recognized the degree to which, in Carolyn Heilbrun's words, "Marriage, in fiction even more than in life, has been the woman's adventure, the object of her quest, her journey's end."[8] Laura's and Ethel's refusals of marriage in *Pendennis* and *The Newcomes* are not invalidated by their later marriages: Laura and Pen achieve an egalitarian marriage only after a great deal of mutual growth, and Ethel and Clive marry only in fable land.

Thackeray wrote at a time of great agitation concerning marriage laws; as we have seen, *The Newcomes* supported passage of the Matrimonial Causes Act of 1857. In his next four novels, Thackeray shows that the marriage laws then in force could make mothers weak both in mind and body and legally powerless to give their children even an identity, except by submitting to or circumventing the laws that gave men entire power over them and their children. In *Philip,* Thackeray again raises the question of what constitutes a marriage. When the Twysdens try to prove Caroline Gann's marriage to Firmin valid so that Philip (born of Firmin's second marriage) will be illegitimate and they can inherit his mother's fortune, their attorney Mr. Bond goes to Caroline to "restore her to her rights." Bond recapitulates what had happened to Caroline in Thackeray's earlier, unfinished *Shabby Genteel Story:*

> You are the lawful wife of George Brand Firmin. . . . In the year 1827, you, Caroline Gann, a child of sixteen, were married by a clergyman whom you know, to George Brand Firmin. . . . And though he thought the marriage was not binding upon him, binding it is by Act of Parliament and judges' decision. (*Works* 18: 286)

And Caroline, who "seemed to be very well versed in the law of the transaction," replies: "'You mean, sir, . . . that if me and Mr. Brandon was married to each other, he knowing that he was only playing at marriage, and me believing that it was all for good, we are really married.'" The answer is yes. Then Caroline takes the only step available to her to invalidate the marriage: she declares that she had always known that the marriage was false.

Obviously, Caroline's primary motive is to see that Philip inherits his mother's fortune as a legitimate son. And yet, her statement that she knew that the marriage was false echoes Dobbin's words to Amelia, that he "knew all along" she was unworthy of his love. The suggestion that people engage in activities—love affairs, marriages, friendships—while aware of negative elements, even of essential inauthenticity, is one of Thackeray's important subtexts. More importantly, when Caroline resigns her claim to a legitimate marriage, she also gives up the possibility of being perceived— justly—as the innocent victim of a deceptive seducer and takes to herself, in the eyes of the world, the guilt that attaches to women in illicit sexual unions. Acknowledgment of one's own failures is a requisite for growth in Thackeray's works (vide Laura in *Pendennis* and Ethel in *The Newcomes*); here, Caroline takes on sins not truly her own, for in *A Shabby Genteel Story* she really was a naive sixteen-year-old tricked into a false marriage. By accepting this "guilt," Caroline makes the marriage laws seem a matter of mere legalistic technicalities rather than of morality; and by sacrificing the legitimacy of her own dead baby, she gives Philip his maternal inheritance and a radically different "legitimacy."

And what, the reader may ask, of Laura Bell? What does she do while Ethel refuses to marry, Clara escapes a bad marriage, and Caroline denies ever having been married? Ina Ferris demonstrates that after *Pendennis* (that is, in *The Newcomes* and *Philip*), Laura is cast in an increasingly negative light.[9] Just as her baby worship becomes increasingly cloying, her ideas become increasingly conformist. Laura, who had once thought for herself, begins to adhere rigidly to abstract principles that disregard suffering and moral complexity and keep women in subjection. Soon after Caroline Gann has denied her own marriage on a fine point of law, Laura speaks up for the sanctity of marriage. First, the reader should recall that in *The Newcomes* Laura had urged Clive and Rosey to stay together despite their misery, and in fact the discord in that household led indirectly to the deaths of both Rosey and Colonel Newcome. Then her advice to Clara, couched in terms of a threatening dream, was to stay with Barnes.

Here, in *Philip*, Laura "fires up" because Agnes Twysden, engaged to Philip, is flirting with Woolcomb, whom she will later marry. Pendennis, the narrator, is consistently ironic as he describes his wife's indignation, and some of that irony is deflected onto her religious principles: this "enthusiast" "would persecute to death almost" anyone "who would break love's sacred laws":

> In her creed, if not in her church, marriage is a sacrament, and the fond believer never speaks of it without awe.

> Now, as she expects both parties to the marriage engagement to keep that compact holy, she no more understands trifling with it than she could comprehend laughing and joking in a church. (*Works* 18: 295)

But Thackeray's narrative undermines Laura's view when Pen points out that, if she were a Mormon, she would have to submit to certain other customs. The view of marriage as a holy sacrament is undercut by such narrative strategies, as well as by the dramatic evidence—the soul-destroying marriages of Clara Newcome, of Philip's mother, and, eventually, of Agnes Twysden and Clarisse de Saverne too.

And yet, Laura's view retains some validity within the logic of the text, in the character of Madame de Florac, Colonel Newcome's "Leonore." As a girl obediently marrying the man her parents had chosen, she too finds herself in an unhappy marriage. But by an almost saintly subjugation of self-will, such as Laura recommends to Clara, she manages to live an exemplary life. Though not happy in earthly terms, she is a noble woman; Lady Kew cannot be rude to her, and Clive brings to this woman who had spent her whole life waiting for death a copy of Sassoferato's "Virgin and Child." But her nobility is not meant to be an argument for a social system that forces dependent women into marriage. Thackeray has Madame de Florac interpret her own biography as a warning against loveless marriage: "Better poverty, Ethel—better a cell in a convent, than a union without love. Is it written eternally that men are to make slaves of us?" (*Works* 13: 123–24). Whereas Thackeray can see the potential for holiness or greatness in women whose spirits are not crushed by marriage, he never loses sight of the injustices in the legal, social, and economic situation of women, and he understands that women are too often forced to choose between one kind of martyrdom and another. Thackeray does not entirely reject Laura's view of marriage, but he certainly does qualify it.

MATRIARCHY

Ethel Newcome's willingness to step in and take over the care of Clara's abandoned children is sometimes interpreted as a diminution of the fiery Ethel to a conventional motherly heroine. Some see the conclusion even as a punishment. I see it rather as a part of a larger pattern in which women gain independence and power and in which maternal values are invested with some of that power. The two concepts are inextricably linked; despite women's actual legal and political powerlessness in Victorian life, in the novels, Thackeray creates power structures and value systems that can only be called matriarchal.

I use the word *matriarchal* advisedly here. Gerda Lerner, in *The Creation of Patriarchy,* maintains that the term is often used so vaguely as to be almost meaningless, and it would seem, from her painstaking definition, that a better phrase would be "a possibly matrilineal, matrilocal society, in which women share power with men and are held in high esteem." I certainly do not mean to suggest that matriarchy as a feminist ideal denotes a mirror image, or inversion, of patriarchy. Such a society has apparently never existed. But the term *matriarchy* has validity nevertheless. First, it serves as a shorthand phrase for what Lerner designates a "society built on maternalist principles."[10] And it connotes the kind of society described so warmly by J. J. Bachofen in his *Das Mutterrecht* (1861), whose title can mean the rule of the mothers or the mother power. Bachofen and his followers—most notably Friedrich Engels, Charlotte Perkins Gilman, Elizabeth Cady Stanton, and Robert Briffault—came too late to have influenced Thackeray.[11] However, the idea that primal maternal instinct is the source of human altruism and community is found in writers closer to Thackeray such as Herbert Spencer and Walter Bagehot, and it echoes what Kate Millet terms "two favorite Victorian themes—the Home and the Goodness of Women." It is somewhat surprising to learn from George Boas that "Bachofen's theory of a matriarchal society out of which modern patriarchal societies evolved was accepted pretty generally among sociologists until about the beginning of the twentieth century."[12]

The theory of matriarchal origins derives from three sources: the evolutionary view of social organization that became so important during the nineteenth century; evidences in mythology of early goddess-centered religions; and anthropological studies that posited that in early societies the male role in conception would not be recognized, and therefore women would appear to have absolute, mysterious power over life and death, and kinship systems would of necessity flow through the mother. It should be pointed out that Thackeray, like Engels, is one of the few writers to contest the idea that patriarchy is an advance over matriarchy, or that maternal behavior is the exclusive characteristic of the biological mother.

Again unlike many nineteenth-century theorists, Thackeray redefines the connections between gender and caring for children. His works are filled with children who have lost one or both parents: young George Osborne and Rawdon Crawley, Arthur Pendennis, Frank and Beatrix Castlewood, Rosey Mackenzie, and Harry and George Warrington have all lost their fathers; and Catherine Hayes, Becky Sharp, Laura Bell, Henry Esmond, and Denis Duval are all orphans. Even as early as *Vanity Fair,* Thackeray had made clear how varied mothers' responses to their children could be: Becky's indifference contrasts with Amelia's doting fondness, and Rawdon and Lady Jane take over the mothering role that Becky rejects. In *The Newcomes,* few mothers actually "mother." Lady Kew is too imperious, Ethel's mother too weak, Mrs. Mackenzie too parasitical. And in the next generation, Rosey is too weak, and Clara too depressed, to care for children. Thackeray had himself lost a father at an early age and had been separated from his mother. It is likely that growing up with neither father nor mother, and then acting as both mother and father to his own daughters, led Thackeray to redefine concepts of parenthood. In Thackeray's works, "mothering" is not limited to the female biological parent, nor do actual mothers always act in a motherly way.

Although it is only occasionally mothers who mother, as a principle, however, "maternalism" is crucial to Thackeray's works. Lady Jane, Sarah Mason (who gave the boy Thomas Newcome "years of love, and fidelity, and constancy" [*Works* 12: 23]), Martha Honeyman, Ursule Duval—all are ennobled by their care for children not their own. And men gain in moral stature according to how they treat children: William Dobbin, Rawdon Crawley, Colonel Newcome, Clive Newcome. Thus, when Ethel steps in to take care of Clara's children, she is not being conventionally feminine, as has been charged. It is in fact the independence she gains by breaking off with Farintosh and by keeping her fortune her own that enables her to do this clearly important work. The conventional heroine is rarely able to give of herself this way. Even Jane Eyre sends Adèle away to school because "my time and care were now required by another—my husband needed them all."[13] It is Thackeray who links maternal behavior with female independence and power.

And, by extending the boundaries of "mothering" to include men, Thackeray is creating a setting in which men and women can be companions. In Carolyn Heilbrun's words, when men also "mother," boys do not have to reject intimacy to attain malehood. They will have been initiated into "intimacy and nurturance" by males they can imitate.[14] In *Vanity Fair,* Rawdon's feelings regarding his son parallel Amelia's, witness his grief at sending the boy to school, his intense interest in the boy's friends and schoolmasters, his eager visits. It is the revelation of these feelings that gains him Lady Jane's respect. And in *The Newcomes,* Thackeray describes the Colonel's love for his son as lover-like in its intensity (*Works* 12: 268). Later, Clive takes over the same role for Boy: "It was touching to see the eagerness and tenderness with which the great strong man now assumed the guardianship of the child. . . . 'He inherited that loving heart from his father,' Laura said, 'and he is paying over the whole property to his son'" (*Works* 13: 500). Just as Laura Bell in Percy Sibwright's attorney's wig signified Thackeray's recognition that women could perform more roles than custom allowed, so does Colonel Newcome's appearance as Clive's parent show that men could be more tender and nurturing to children than was usually expected. Thackeray saw himself as a lover of children; in 1856 he wrote to Annie from Philadelphia: "I think Granny and I and you have all got the love of children famously developed."[15]

In the opening pages of *The Newcomes,* cultural clichés about motherly love are ironically reduced to a stock response of the critics. These critics—confused by the fable in which the lamb lies down beside the wolf in sheep's clothing who has just eaten her mother—will, "if in a virtuous mood," discourse on "the holy beauteousness of maternal affection." That is, they fail to recognize that while they idealize her, the mother has been devoured, and a predator takes her place by her children. In the novel, Clara most resembles the sheep and Barnes the wolf, and it is Ethel who becomes shepherdess and restores order. After Clara leaves Barnes, "Miss Ethel had to take command of the whole of this demented household, hysterical mamma and sister, mutineering servants, and shrieking abandoned nursery, and bring young people and old to peace and quiet" (*Works* 13: 280). Thackeray does not let us forget how conventional even his good men are: even Colonel

Newcome thinks Ethel's broken engagement and her taking over the care of Clara's children a deserved punishment (*Works* 13: 303, 315). George Warrington, whom Laura had once loved, prefers Rosey to Ethel as a "little placid wife; a nice little simple creature, who is worth a dozen Ethels" (*Works* 13: 346). Ethel has to endure such disapproval because she rejects the passive, feminine role that would have made her as ineffectual as Clara and Rosey.

Ethel's behavior, and the value with which the narrative invests it, provides a subtext—never fully developed—in which maternal values transcend those of the patriarchal society. One characteristic of this subtext is, as we have seen, that maternal behavior becomes the norm—men and women both care for children, whether the children are their own or not; they give generously of their affection to all children; families become "open" rather than "closed" systems as the bonds between adults and children are extended further and resources are shared. And, unlike Bachofen, who praises matriarchal societies even as he designates them a "lower" order of social organization, Thackeray does not place a higher value on patriarchy. Nor does he overvalue "the holy beauteousness of maternal affection."

The second characteristic of the maternalist subtext is that women have power. Ethel, as we have seen, assures her own legal and economic independence by *not* marrying and then takes in Clara's children. But Thackeray goes further. Women also frequently control inheritances; they rule families; they work to support those families if they are not wealthy; and sometimes make their own "laws," in opposition to those of the patriarchy. For example, inheritances begin to depend more frequently on women. In *Vanity Fair* and *Henry Esmond*, men must hold most of the wealth and the rights of inheritance (secretly in Esmond's case), but in *Pendennis*, Helen and Laura provide Pen's income until he begins to earn money for himself. In *The Newcomes*, Lady Kew seems a reincarnation of *Vanity Fair*'s Miss Crawley, except that Lady Kew leaves her money to a woman, Ethel. And Ethel, finding a letter in which Colonel Newcome's stepmother had expressed a wish (which was never carried out) to leave a legacy to Clive, devises a method of transferring £6,000 of her own money to him, without his learning the true source.

In *The Virginians*, Thackeray opposes two matriarchies: one, in England, is presided over by Beatrix Castlewood Tusher; the other, in America, is ruled by Rachel Esmond Warrington, the daughter-editor of Esmond's memoirs. Beatrix and Rachel have power, but they cannot use it well because both are ruled from beyond the grave by Henry Esmond. While he lived, Esmond had neglected both these half-sisters in favor of their mother, Rachel Castlewood, and now a rage of jealousy endlessly fuels their enmity. Rather than reject the male-centered values of the patriarchy, they have internalized them. They will go to their graves longing always for one very flawed man's exclusive love. In other cases, as with Laura, Ethel, and Caroline, when women attain psychological emancipation, they use their liberty to benefit others.

Philip Firmin is twice cheated out of his inheritance by men and twice restored to it by women. The first man, Colonel Baynes, signs away the principal of Philip's mother's estate to Philip's father. The second man—Philip's father, Dr. Firmin—secretly uses up Philip's inheritance and then escapes to America, from whence he sends his son begging letters. The ultimate inversion of fatherly love occurs when Firmin forges Philip's name and embezzles £368 from him.

Women, however, bring Philip prosperity. His mother's money and his maternal uncle's bequest come through the female line and, even more significantly, would not have been his had not Caroline repudiated the validity of her marriage to Firmin. And it is Caroline who saves Philip from having to pay on the forged check by chloroforming Tufton Hunt and stealing the paper (she had been given the chloroform to help women in childbirth).[16] Thackeray's illustrations highlight the importance of this incident: the chapter begins with an initial letter drawn by Thackeray that represents Joan of Arc with sword unsheathed (see figure 11).[17] The analogy is clear: Joan of Arc fought to restore Charles VII to the throne as Caroline now fights to restore Philip to his maternal inheritance. Frederick Walker's illustration of the scene is entitled "Judith and Holofernes"; Judith, heroine of the Book of Judith, saved the city of Bethulia from Nebuchadnezzar's general, Holofernes, by going to his camp, seducing him, and when Holofernes fell into a drunken sleep, beheading him with his own sword. Both stories depict women who use violence to repel invasion by outsiders, to protect what might be considered an extension of the family—the nation or the tribe. Thackeray uses these narratives to suggest a broader vision of what women can do, and

11. Initial letter from chapter 19 of *Philip*, in which Caroline Gann chloroforms Tufton Hunt (*Works* 19: 296).

indeed, have done. Like Lady Morgan in *Woman and Her Master*, Thackeray draws upon historical narratives to rewrite the "script" for Victorian women.

When Caroline Gann denies the validity of her marriage to Firmin, she does in some senses become Philip's "mother": she has legitimized his birth and ensured his inheritance. When she assaults Tufton Hunt, who performed the false marriage, she frees Philip from the burden of his father's crimes and perhaps achieves some measure of retribution for herself. Each time she performs an apparently immoral action, she restores order and achieves results that must be considered moral, as the innocent are protected from evildoers (or the lamb is protected from the wolf).

The world of the fathers is here even more sordid than in *Vanity Fair*. Actual fathers are all destructive in some way: Colonel Baynes is careless with Philip's inheritance; Dr. Firmin steals from his own son; old Mr. Gann, Caroline's father, is a parasite. Thackeray's critique extends to patriarchal institutions: the law that entraps Mrs. Firmin in an unhappy marriage and nearly delegitimizes Philip; educational and economic institutions that give men power and money (note that Caroline Gann works for two doctors, Firmin and Goodenough—one is evil, the other good, but both are more powerful than she); and legal and social codes that declare children nonexistent unless they are born within the official family of some male (recall that Barnes's ragged, dirty, illegitimate children are removed from church by the police as he marries Clara).

In this Thackeray resembles Elizabeth Gaskell, whose "Lizzie

Leigh" (1850) conveys a similar protest against patriarchal definitions of legitimacy. In Gaskell's story, a mother is separated from her "fallen" daughter until the death of her husband allows her to express her own, higher, standard of morality. It is only women who lovingly take in the abandoned illegitimate child and its mother, while men reject both. To the women, Gaskell shows, the stigma of illegitimacy is less important than the child's need. Just as the three generations of women are about to be reunited, the child dies in a fall indirectly caused by a drunken old man who is supported by his daughter. Like Gaskell's story, Thackeray's novels *Philip* and *Denis Duval* directly challenge the morality of laws and conventions that declare unmarried women legal non-entities and their children outcasts.

In *Philip*, Caroline Gann's work as a midwife is invested with several kinds of meaning. Economically, it gives her an independence unusual to women and even allows her to support the father (another parasitical father) who had turned her away after George Firmin abandoned her. Socially, it unites her with mothers of all classes into a kind of maternal sisterhood; she is much in demand, because she understands the sufferings of women so well, and she moves in a subculture of women whose medical care is increasingly dominated by powerful male physicians like George Firmin. And as a "fallen woman," Caroline represents a view of motherhood that is deeply sympathetic to the helplessness of women within patriarchy, and that is an implicit protest against damning judgments of them and their children as sinners and bastards.

Caroline's work as midwife recurs in *Denis Duval* in the nursing practice of Ursule Duval. In both cases, work gives independence and dignity. Ursule, who lives with her father-in-law and her son, Denis, dominates her home; when Clarisse escapes the patriarchal enclosure of her moody, incessantly moralizing husband, she goes to the "matriarchy" presided over by Ursule, her foster-sister. Ursule has to endure a great deal of gossip and scandal after Clarisse's arrival, but she is not disturbed. Her strength lies in the maternal bond—both had been nursed by Ursule's mother. And midwifery provides her with another culture and therefore an alternative system of values.

Thackeray was well read in the classical literature of Greece and Rome, and may well have reasoned about ancient matriarchal societies in the same way that Bachofen did—by observing vestiges of ancient matriarchal traditions in the art, myths, and literature of an otherwise patriarchal classical culture. Thackeray may have concluded—as Bachofen did—that in a maternalist ethos all children would be legitimized by their mothers. And, given power, the mothers would presumably infuse their institutions with values derived from maternal behavior. Bachofen describes the matriarchal stage of civilization as a period of freedom, equality, and open kinship networks, as opposed to the closed hierarchical system of patriarchal society. A passage from *Das Mutterrecht* provides evidence of the kind of reasoning Thackeray might have employed:

> The relationship which stands at the origin of all culture, of every virtue, of every nobler aspect of existence, is that between mother and child; it operates in a world of violence as the divine principle of love, of union, of peace. Raising her young, the woman learns earlier than the man to extend her loving care beyond the limits of the ego to another creature. . . . Woman at this stage is the repository of all culture, of all benevolence, of all devotion, of all concern for the living and grief for the dead.[18]

In these final novels, too, Thackeray's allusiveness suggests an ahistorical reading of culture. Bachofen had characterized ancient matriarchies as ruled by the spirit of the goddess Demeter. In her search for her lost child, in her descent into the underworld of madness, and in her nursing of Philip, Caroline Gann resembles Demeter, and the parallel is worth pursuing for a moment. According to tradition, Demeter, goddess of agriculture and family life, left heaven to seek her daughter Persephone, who had been stolen by Hades (Pluto). While searching for her lost daughter, Demeter stopped to nurse a sick boy, just as Caroline nurses Philip. The boy, Triptolemus, later established the temple where the Eleusinian Mysteries were conducted. These rites were believed to give initiates a vision of the eternal source of life. Ancient myths frequently associate women with agriculture, with the moon and its cycles, and with the mysteries of life and death, and so it seems do Thackeray's last two novels. When Tufton Hunt—who in the disguise of a priest had pretended to marry Caroline to George Firmin years ago—comes to Caroline at night (when the moon has power) to assault her and rob her son (as she feels Philip to be), he finds himself lying in the street in a mysterious state of twilight sleep (chloroform).

In *Denis Duval*, Thackeray uses ancient symbols of maternity in the scene in which Clarisse leaves Agnes at the edge of an incoming tide under a silver moon: the sea is traditionally a source of life and resembles the "sea" within the womb to which Clarisse, and perhaps Isabella Thackeray, wished to return her daughter. The moon is allied with the menstrual cycle in women; silver was believed to have a magical power to ward off evil; and Clarisse, returning from the sea, "glimmering" in her white nightclothes and singing, seems almost to have returned from a sacred ritual, a sacrifice.[19] Clarisse's repeated attempts to have herself and her daughter transformed in some way, either by water (the double baptism, in which both receive the name Agnes, and the attempted drowning) or by fire (she imagines she will be burned at the stake, like a witch or a heretic), represent a search for a new life, a new source of power, a new religion.

In these last novels, Thackeray begins to explore the idea of an entirely different kind of social order, one in which women are strong, free moral agents, an ideal social order that glimmered on the horizon of his century's social theories. To accomplish this, Thackeray merged Victorian concepts of womanhood with scientific ideas of social evolution and with classical narratives to create an alternative vision of motherhood that allied it with independence, strength, and sanity.

Thackeray challenged Victorian concepts of femininity and femaleness by insisting that the glorification of motherhood and family on which so much Victorian culture rested was subverted by an ideology that idealized female weakness and absolved or alienated men from just, responsible social relations. Society, he shows, aggressively encodes female weakness into law and teaches female psychological dependency as a "Natural" virtue.

Because Thackeray was aware of so many ancient and modern images of women (Clytemnestra, Iphigenia, Diana, Venus, Judith, Mary, Mary Magdalene, Scheherazade, Fidelio, Joan of Arc, Demeter) that provided alternatives to Victorian ideals of womanhood, he presented women in his novels whose maternal instinct is not idolized as an exclusively private and domestic gift (nor is it exclusive to women). And he translated his affirmation of maternal values into acceptance of shared power, and an expanded sense of caring for children as a function of community, including the potential for males to be as loving as women are strong. Time and again, his novels prove that laws and customs that weaken women harm all of society. Beginning with a murderess and moving through the figure of a remarkable heroine to two strong, independent midwives, Thackeray's women characters contributed extraordinary testimony to the feminist movement.

CONCLUSION

In the final analysis, Thackeray's novels reflect a trend in Victorian culture toward an increasing consciousness of gender issues and an acceptance of feminist perspectives. As with so many other "modern" issues, little we argue about today has not already been debated by the Victorians, in different words perhaps, but often with such subtlety and power that their works can still be read not only as historical documents but as inspiration for our own struggles—John Stuart Mill on women, Cardinal Newman on the idea of a university, and George Eliot on the individual in the social web of history stand as cases in point. Conditions for women have changed, thanks to the work of our Victorian forebears, but many of the issues have not.

Contemporary criticism has just begun in the last thirty years to recognize the complexity and the quality of the Victorians' critique of gender issues. Thus, studies of gender in a variety of authors (Trollope, Dickens, Hardy, George Eliot) have recently emerged, along with some excellent studies of Victorian gender ideology in general. The irony is that, until recently, we "moderns" seem to have been missing one of the most important aspects of the Victorian novel: its brilliant analysis of the relations between men and women.

It has been my purpose in this book to contribute to our increasing appreciation of the Victorian novel by providing a reading of Thackeray that shows how his characterizations of women began with sympathetic insight and grew from there. Whereas most feminist critics seem to ignore Thackeray, misread him as regressive, touch on only one or two works, or discuss Thackeray only briefly in works of a broader scope (Moers, Auerbach, or Poovey, for example), this study has focused exclusively and comprehensively on Thackeray. Drawing on the work of Thackeray scholars, feminist critics, and theorists in a variety of fields, I have attempted to follow one particular thread through the totality of his writings in order to reveal an important pattern.

Not all of Thackeray's works have received equal attention here, but neither do all of his works give equal prominence to the subject of gender ideology. I have attempted to survey the canon of Thackeray's works to locate and discuss those works, or portions of works, that fit this particular pattern. En route, I have drawn from Thackeray's life and letters and from comments by his contemporaries and have attempted to locate Thackeray's works in the larger discourse of the day, particularly to situate them next to the life and polemical writings of Caroline Norton. I have found that the more I learned of Thackeray, the more certain I became of my conclusions. I am confident that, although I have not said nearly all that can be said on the subject, readers of Thackeray will continue to confirm this principle of Thackerayan scholarship for themselves: that Thackeray was a brilliant and conscious (albeit not necessarily a systematic) partisan of the women's movement of his day. How much effect he had we can never know, but it is certain that his works were meant to focus attention on the injustice of women's social position and to bring home to readers an often new perspective on their own individual lives.

Notes

INTRODUCTION

1. Geoffrey Tillotson, *Thackeray the Novelist* (Cambridge, Mass.: Cambridge University Press, 1974), 5.

2. Peter Shillingsburg, "Thackeray's(?) Amelia," *Thackeray Newsletter* 39 (May 1994): 7–9.

3. Citations of *Pendennis* are from *The History of Pendennis: His Fortunes and Misfortunes, His Friends and His Greatest Enemy*, ed. Donald Hawes with an introduction by J. I. M. Stewart (London: Viking Penguin, 1972), and further references will be given parenthetically in the text by page number.

4. Peter L. Shillingsburg, *Pegasus in Harness: Victorian Publishing and W. M. Thackeray* (Charlottesville: University Press of Virginia, 1992), 212.

5. W. K. Wimsatt, Jr., and M. C. Beardsley, "The Intentional Fallacy," *Sewanee Review* 54 (1946): 468–88.

6. Elaine Showalter, *The Female Malady: Women, Madness, and English Culture, 1830–1980* (New York: Pantheon Books, 1985), and Phyllis Chesler, *Women and Madness* (Garden City, N.Y.: Doubleday, 1972).

7. William Makepeace Thackeray, *The Letters and Private Papers of William Makepeace Thackeray*, ed. Gordon Ray, 4 vols. (Cambridge: Harvard University Press, 1945–1946), 2: 423–25. Future references will be given parenthetically in the text as *Letters*, followed by volume and page number.

8. Hans-Georg Gadamer, *Truth and Method*, trans. and ed. Garrett Barden and John Cumming (New York: Crossroad, 1984), 336.

9. Elizabeth K. Helsinger, Robin Lauterbach Sheets, and William Veeder, *The Woman Question: Society and Literature in Britain and America, 1837–1883*, 3 vols. (New York: Garland, 1983), 1: xi. Ruth apRoberts is quoted from an address on "Teaching Victorian Literature" presented at the MLA conference in New York on 28 December 1986.

10. *Letters of Thomas Carlyle to his Youngest Sister*, ed. Charles Townsend Copeland (Boston: Houghton, Mifflin and Co., 1899), 86, cited in Gordon Ray, *The Buried Life* (London: Oxford University Press, 1952), 20.

11. John Stuart Mill, *The Subjection of Women* (Cambridge, Mass.:

MIT Press, 1970), 15.

12. Helsinger et al., *The Woman Question*, 1: ch. 5; Mary Poovey, *Uneven Developments: The Ideological Work of Gender in Mid-Victorian England* (Chicago: University of Chicago Press, 1988), ch. 6. Mill's response to Ruskin is from Helsinger et al., *The Woman Question* 1: 101.

13. Lady Morgan [née Sydney Owenson], *Woman and Her Master: A History of the Female Sex from the Earliest Period*, 2 vols. (London: David Bryce, n.d.).

14. Lionel Stevenson, *The Wild Irish Girl: The Life of Sydney Owenson, Lady Morgan* (New York: Atheneum, 1969), 48. See also Lionel Stevenson, "*Vanity Fair* and Lady Morgan," *PMLA* 48 (1933): 547–51.

15. George Eliot to John Blackwood, 11 June 1857, in *George Eliot's Life*, ed. J. W. Cross, 2 vols. (New York: Harper & Bros., 1885), 1: 331. (See Tillotson, *Thackeray the Novelist*, 288–95, for a discussion of George Eliot's debt to Thackeray.) Charlotte Brontë, "Author's Preface" to *Jane Eyre*, ed. Richard J. Dunn (New York: W. W. Norton, 1971), 2.

16. Barbara Bodichon cited in Helsinger et al., 3: 76.

17. [Lady Eastlake (née Elizabeth Rigby)], "Review: *Vanity Fair, Jane Eyre*, and *The Governesses' Benevolent Institution—Report for 1847*," *Quarterly Review* 84 (1848): 153–85 (174).

18. [Kirk, John F.], "Thackeray, as a Novelist," *North American Review* 77 (July 1853): 213, 212, 213.

19. [Luyster, I. M.], "The Women of Thackeray," *Christian Examiner* 69 (September 1860): 171, 178–79, 171.

20. Dorothy Van Ghent, *The English Novel: Form and Function* (New York: Rhinehart & Co., 1953), 147–48. Maria DiBattista, "The Triumph of Clytemnestra: The Charades in *Vanity Fair*," *PMLA* 95 (1980): 827. Eve Kosofsky Sedgwick, *Between Men: English Literature and Male Homosocial Desire* (New York: Columbia University Press, 1985), 148. Gordon Ray, *Thackeray: The Age of Wisdom 1847–1863* (New York: Farrar, Straus and Giroux, 1972), 182. Nina Auerbach, *Woman and the Demon: The Life of a Victorian Myth* (Cambridge, Mass.: Harvard University Press, 1982), 100.

21. Katherine M. Rogers, "The Pressures of Convention on Thackeray's Women," *Modern Language Review* 67 (1972): 257–63. Richard Barickman, Susan MacDonald, and Myra Stark, *Corrupt Relations: Dickens, Thackeray, Trollope, Collins, and the Victorian Sexual System* (New York: Columbia University Press, 1982), 164–65.

22. See Poovey, *Uneven Developments;* Deborah Valenze, "Cottage Religion and the Politics of Survival," in *Equal or Different: Women's Politics, 1800–1914*, ed. Jane Rendall (New York and Oxford: Basil Blackwell, 1987), 31–56; and Brian Heeney, *The Women's Movement in the Church of England* (New York and Oxford: Clarendon Press, 1988).

23. M. Jeanne Peterson, *Family, Love, and Work in the Lives of Victo-*

rian Gentlewomen (Bloomington: Indiana University Press, 1989).

24. Erna Olafson Hellerstein, Leslie Parker Hume, and Karen M. Offen, eds., *Victorian Women: A Documentary Account of Women's Lives in Nineteenth-Century England, France, and the United States* (Stanford: Stanford University Press, 1981), 11.

25. My overview of the historical realities is based upon Estelle B. Freedman and Erna Olafson Hellerstein's introduction to part 2, "The Adult Woman," in ibid., 118–33, and Leslie Parker Hume and Karen M. Offen's introduction to part 3, "The Adult Woman—Work," in ibid., 272–91.

26. Ibid., 122. See also excerpt from Martineau's autobiography in ibid., 153–55.

27. Mary Wollstonecraft, *A Vindication of the Rights of Woman: With Strictures on Political and Moral Subjects,* ed. Miriam Brody Kramnick (Harmondsworth, Middx., England: Pelican Books, 1975), 146, 155–56; Hellerstein et al., *Victorian Women,* 124.

28. Michel Foucault, *The History of Sexuality,* trans. Robert Hurley, 3 vols. (New York: Random House, 1978), 1: 156–59. (Originally published as *La Volounté de savior* [Paris: Editions Gallinard, 1976].)

29. Hellerstein et al., *Victorian Women,* 19–20. Ray Strachey, *"The Cause": A Short History of the Women's Movement in Great Britain* (Port Washington, N.Y.: Kennikat Press, 1969), describes the movement for women's higher education from a fascinating, "insider's" point of view.

30. Poovey, *Uneven Developments,* 1–15.

31. Mikhail Bakhtin, *Problems of Dostoevsky's Poetics,* ed. and trans. Caryl Emerson (Minneapolis: University of Minnesota Press, 1984), 90.

32. Rosemary Radford Reuther, *Sexism and God-Talk: Toward a Feminist Theology* (Boston: Beacon Press, 1983), 99–109 (108).

33. Ibid., 102–3.

34. Hellerstein et al., *Victorian Women,* 15.

35. Reuther, *Sexism and God-Talk,* 101.

36. William Makepeace Thackeray, *The Works of William Makepeace Thackeray,* ed. Anne Thackeray Ritchie and Leslie Stephen, 26 vols. (New York: AMS, 1968), 13: 123–24. Future references will be given parenthetically in the text as *Works,* followed by volume and page number.

37. Linda Alcoff, "Cultural Feminism versus Post-Structuralism: The Identity Crisis in Feminist Theory," *Signs: Journal of Women in Culture and Society* 13 (1988): 405–36 (413, 414). I am grateful to my friend and colleague Susan Ross for bringing this excellent article to my attention.

38. Mill, *Subjection of Women,* 22. Alcoff, "Cultural Feminism," 419.

39. Alcoff, "Cultural Feminism," 434, quotes Teresa de Lauretis, ed., "Introduction," *Feminist Studies/Critical Studies* (Bloomington: Indiana University Press, 1986), 8.

40. Alcoff, "Cultural Feminism," 431. [Coventry Patmore], "Fielding and Thackeray," *North British Review* 24 (November 1855): 201, cited in John Loofbourow, *Thackeray and the Form of Fiction* (New York: Gordian Press, 1976), 109.

CHAPTER 1. THE FORMATIVE YEARS

1. Gordon Ray, *Thackeray: The Uses of Adversity, 1811–1846* (New York: Farrar, Straus and Giroux, 1972), 214.

2. Manuscript letter, 14 February 1856, quoted in Ray, *Buried Life,* 91.

3. See Thackeray, *Letters,* 1: cxii–cxiv; Ray, *Buried Life,* 101–3; and Ray, *Uses of Adversity,* 52–59. See also Ann Monsarrat, *An Uneasy Victorian: Thackeray the Man* (New York: Dodd, Mead, 1980), 7–8, 10, 15–16.

4. Monsarrat, *Uneasy Victorian,* 114–15.

5. See Chester M. Jones, M.D., "The Medical History of William Makepeace Thackeray," attached as Appendix 28 to Thackeray, *Letters* 4: 453–59.

6. Manuscript letter to Kate Perry, 7 December 1852, quoted in Ray, *Buried Life,* 95–96.

7. Most of this summary of Thackeray's career is based on Monsarrat, *Uneasy Victorian,* 36–54. See also "How Thackeray Lost His Patrimony," Appendix 4 to *Letters* 1.

8. Ray, *Uses of Adversity,* 191–92.

9. Quotations are from Monsarrat, *Uneasy Victorian,* 342; *Punch,* 27 January 1844, cited in Ray, *Uses of Adversity,* 364–65.

10. For a full discussion of Thackeray and Norton, see Micael Clarke, "William Thackeray's Fiction and Caroline Norton's Biography: Narrative Matrix of Feminist Legal Reform," *Dickens Studies Annual* 18 (1989): 1–15.

11. Ray, *Age of Wisdom,* 74–75.

12. Lionel Stevenson, *The Showman of Vanity Fair: The Life of William Makepeace Thackeray* (London: Chapman & Hall, 1947), 156, 383.

13. Eastlake is quoted in Alice [Marreco] Acland, *Caroline Norton* (London: Constable, 1948), 208–9. Acland does not indicate the source of these quotations, except insofar as to list Eastlake's *Journals and Correspondence,* ed. C. E. Smith, 2 vols. (1895), in her bibliography.

14. Acland, *Caroline Norton,* 156–57.

15. George Meredith, *Diana of the Crossways* (New York: Norton, 1973), 15–16.

16. Acland, *Caroline Norton,* 22–23. See also Lois Josephs Fowler, "Caroline Norton" in *Dictionary of Literary Biography,* ed. Ira B. Nadel and William E. Fredeman (Detroit, Mich.: Gale Research, 1983), 21: 235.

17. Caroline Norton, *English Laws for Women in the Nineteenth Cen-*

tury, in *Selected Writings of Caroline Norton: Facsimile Reproductions,* ed. James O. Hoge and Jane Marcus (Delmar, N.Y.: Scholars' Facsimiles and Reprints, 1978), 51.

18. Acland, *Caroline Norton,* 103.

19. Norton, *English Laws,* 51; Acland, *Caroline Norton,* 135.

20. W. C. Brownell, *Victorian Prose Masters* (New York: C. Scribner's Sons, 1901), 46, cited in Ray, *Buried Life,* 2.

21. Elizabeth Drew, *The Enjoyment of Literature* (New York: W. W. Norton, 1935), 118–19, cited in Ray, *Buried Life,* 6.

CHAPTER 2. EARLY WORKS

1. Shillingsburg, *Pegasus in Harness,* 36–38.

2. James H. Wheatley, *Patterns in Thackeray's Fiction* (Cambridge, Mass.: MIT Press, 1969), 25–26, 8.

3. John W. Dodds, "Thackeray as a Satirist Previous to *Vanity Fair,"* *Modern Language Quarterly* 2 (1941): 163.

4. Miriam M. H. Thrall, *Rebellious Fraser's: Nol Yorke's Magazine in the Days of Maginn, Thackeray, and Carlyle* (New York: AMS Press, 1966), 64.

5. [John Hamilton Reynolds], "William Ainsworth and *Jack Sheppard,"* *Fraser's Magazine* 21 (February 1840): 227–45 (227). References will henceforth be given parenthetically in the text. For a full discussion, see Micael Clarke, "A Mystery Solved," *Victorian Periodicals Review* 23 (1990): 50–54.

6. Thackeray, *Catherine,* in *Fraser's Magazine* 22 (February 1840): 211.

7. *William Makepeace Thackeray: Contributions to the* Morning Chronicle, ed. Gordon Ray (Urbana: University of Illinois Press, 1955), 73–74.

8. Vineta Colby, *Yesterday's Woman: Domestic Realism in the English Novel* (Princeton, N.J.: Princeton University Press, 1974), 33. This book offers a full and appreciative account of women's contributions to the novel as a genre.

9. Ibid., 53, 55.

10. Patrick Brantlinger, *The Spirit of Reform: British Literature and Politics, 1832–1867* (Cambridge, Mass.: Harvard University Press, 1977), 35–40.

11. Loofbourow, *Form of Fiction,* 4, 15.

12. Cited in Thrall, *Rebellious Fraser's,* 74.

13. Quotations are from "A. Z.," "Some Recollections of Thackeray," *Lippincott's Magazine* 7 (1871): 107; Thrall, *Rebellious Fraser's,* 72; John Sutherland, "Introduction" to Thackeray, *Vanity Fair* (New York: Oxford University Press, 1983), ix.

14. Ray, *Uses of Adversity,* 230–31. See also Loofbourow, *Form of Fiction,* chapters 2–3 for an extensive discussion of the centrality of parody

to Thackeray's work through *Esmond.*

15. Jerome Hamilton Buckley, *The Victorian Temper: A Study in Literary Culture* (New York: Random House, 1964), 6.

16. Monsarrat, *Uneasy Victorian,* 114–15.

17. Robert A. Colby, "*Catherine:* Thackeray's Credo," *Review of English Studies* 15 (1964): 381.

18. Helsinger et al., *The Woman Question* 1: 5. For the Martineau incident, see her *Autobiography,* ed. Maria Weston Chapman (Westmead, England: Gregg International Publishing, 1969), 2: 376.

19. "Our Batch of Novels for Christmas, 1837," *Fraser's Magazine* 17 (January 1838): 79, quoted in Helen Heineman, *Mrs. Trollope: The Triumphant Feminine in the Nineteenth Century* (Athens: Ohio University Press, 1979), 152, 285 n. 14.

20. Colby, *"Catherine,"* 393–94. See also Robert Colby, *Thackeray's Canvass of Humanity: An Author and His Public* (Columbus: Ohio State University Press, 1979), 167.

21. Juliet McMaster, *Thackeray: The Major Novels* (Manchester: Manchester University Press, 1971), 189–91.

22. Nicholas A. Salerno, "*Catherine:* Theme and Structure," *American Imago* 18 (1961): 159–66.

23. Colby, *"Catherine,"* 395.

24. Ray, *Uses of Adversity,* 234–36. Ray attributes Thackeray's preoccupation with seduction during this period to "some unrecorded episode in Isabella's history [with Edward Marlborough Fitzgerald] a fuller knowledge of which might help to explain her mental break-down" (ibid., 478 n. 16). In 1848, Thackeray wrote to Fitzgerald, "Ever since I heard that fatal story about poor Isabella I could not find it in me to show a confidence wh existed no more. Nor in spite of your denials can I resist Kinglake's testimony against you. I dont mean as regards the injury past. I wish to God I could say not guilty" (*Letters* 2: 237). This is not Edward J. Fitzgerald, Thackeray's good friend, who translated the *Rubáiyát of Omar Khayyám.* In 1848, Thackeray wrote to Edward J., "Your namesake they say has been stabbed. . . . I am afraid that he is recovering. The world does not contain a greater villain" (*Letters* 2: 366).

25. José Ortega y Gasset, "First Installment on the Dehumanization of Art," in *Contemporary Literary Criticism,* ed. Robert Con Davis (New York: Longman, 1986), 40.

26. Ray, *Uses of Adversity,* 333.

27. Ibid., 334–35.

28. Caroline Norton, *A Letter to the Queen on Lord Chancellor Cranworth's Marriage and Divorce Bill, by Pearce Stevenson, Esq.,* in *Selected Writings,* 105.

29. Wayne Booth, *The Rhetoric of Fiction,* 2d ed. (Chicago: University of Chicago Press, 1983), 158–59. Wheatley, *Patterns,* 41.

30. Ray, *Uses of Adversity,* 346. The first three chapters, for instance,

contain two minor asides; the last three contain eight, some of which are major disquisitions.

31. *The Luck of Barry Lyndon*, ed. Martin J. Anisman (New York: New York University Press, 1970, a reproduction of the original 1844 text), 2.1.312. Subsequent references to this work will be given parenthetically in the text (as part, chapter, and page number).

32. It is not clear whether Thackeray made, supervised, or approved the changes to the second edition. Ray refers to them as Thackeray's (*Uses of Adversity*, 487 n. 24, and *Buried Life*, 131 n. 60). However, Thackeray did not like the new title and wrote to his publishers to ask why it had been changed, which leads some scholars to conclude that some or all of the textual changes were made by someone else (see Colby, *Thackeray's Canvass*, 224 n. 3).

33. Ray, *Buried Life*, 131 n. 60.

34. Ray, *Uses of Adversity*, 128–29.

35. See Sandra M. Gilbert and Susan Gubar, *The Madwoman in the Attic: The Woman Writer and the Nineteenth-Century Literary Imagination* (New Haven and London: Yale University Press, 1979), part 3, "How Are We Fall'n?: Milton's Daughters," 147–310, for a wide-ranging, imaginative, and provocative discussion of the meaning of the Fall for nineteenth-century women readers. Gilbert and Gubar call it "Milton's and Western culture's central tale of the fall of woman and her shadow self, Satan" (255). The title of this section is taken from Anne Finch, "How are we Fall'n? fall'n by mistaken rules / And Education's more than Nature's Fools" (219: taken from "The Introduction," *Poems of Anne Countess of Winchelsea*).

36. Wheatley, *Patterns*, 50; Reuther, *Sexism and God-Talk*, 152; Morgan, *Woman and Her Master*.

37. Anisman, "Introduction," 23, cites Jesse Foot, *The Lives of Andrew Robinson Bowes, Esq., and the Countess of Strathmore* (London, ca. 1810). It is not known whether Thackeray read this work or whether he heard the story from a friend, John Bowes (Ray, *Uses of Adversity*, 339–40).

38. Anisman, "Introduction," 26.

39. See Ray, *Uses of Adversity*, 339–45; Colby, *Thackeray's Canvass*, 201–27; and Anisman, "Introduction," 23–42.

40. For a thorough discussion of the status of women under the law, see Lee Holcombe, *Wives and Property: Reform of the Married Women's Property Law in Nineteenth-Century England* (Toronto: University of Toronto Press, 1983). For a bibliography of some of the works addressing these debates, see Barbara Kanner, "The Women of England in a Century of Social Change, 1815–1914: A Select Bibliography," in *Suffer and Be Still: Women in the Victorian Age*, ed. Martha Vicinus (Bloomington: Indiana University Press, 1972), 173–206, and "The Women of England in a Century of Social Change, 1815–1914: A Select Bibliography, Part II," in *A Widening Sphere: Changing Roles of Victorian Women*, ed. Martha Vicinus

(Bloomington: Indiana University Press, 1977), 199–318. For a succinct description of the many facets of the ongoing debate, see Helsinger et al., *The Woman Question* 2: 3–55.

41. Acland, *Caroline Norton*, 65.

42. Norton, *A Plain Letter to the Lord Chancellor on the Infant Custody Bill, by Pearce Stevenson, Esq.,* in *Selected Writings,* 46.

43. Anisman, "Introduction," 30–31, cites Gordon Ray's unpublished doctoral dissertation, "Thackeray and France" (Harvard University, 1940), 238–41, for the source of this tale.

44. Engels is cited in György Lukács, "Reportage or Portrayal?" in *Essays on Realism,* ed. Rodney Livingstone, trans. David Fernbach (Cambridge, Mass.: MIT Press, 1980), 49. Tolstoy is cited in ibid., 60. Vineta Colby expresses a similar idea with regard to the silver fork novel that transformed type characters into characters typical of their social class, by showing that these novels linked characters' lifestyles to their often unconsciously held "ideals, tastes, and values" (*Yesterday's Woman,* 53–55).

45. Edward Bulwer-Lytton, *England and the English* (London: R. Bentley, 1833), bk. 4, ch. 2., quoted in Colby, *Yesterday's Woman,* 57–58.

46. Carlyle is cited in Ray, *Uses of Adversity,* 420, as having reflected, "Nobody in our day wrote, I should say, with such perfection of style" (quoted in T. Wemyss Reid, *The Life, Letters, and Friendships of Richard Monckton Milnes, First Lord Houghton* [London: Cassell, 1890], 1: 421).

CHAPTER 3. *VANITY FAIR:* BACKGROUNDS

1. Some early critics and readers favored Becky over Amelia and set off the debate about Thackeray's preference for wicked women. The arguments are summed up through the early 1960s in Andrew Von Hendy's "Misunderstandings about Becky's Characterization in *Vanity Fair,*" *Nineteenth-Century Fiction* 18 (1963): 279–83. Amelia inspires a similar range of reactions. A "polyphonic reading" is provided in Peter Garrett's chapter on *Vanity Fair* in *The Victorian Multi-Plot Novel: Studies in Dialogical Form* (New Haven: Yale University Press, 1980).

2. Loofbourow, *Form of Fiction,* 4.

3. Roland Barthes, *S/Z,* trans. Richard Miller (New York: Hill and Wang, 1974), 145.

4. *Vanity Fair: A Novel without a Hero,* ed. Geoffrey and Kathleen Tillotson (Boston: Houghton Mifflin, Riverside Edition, 1963), 80. Page references will henceforth be given parenthetically in the text.

5. Deborah A. Thomas, *Thackeray and Slavery* (Athens: Ohio University Press, 1993), 60.

6. Thackeray's artistic growth accords with the views expressed by "J. R." (identified in *Wellesley Index* as John Robertson) in an article entitled

"Criticism on Women" (*Westminster Review* 32 [1839]: 454–75), in two ways. The article attacks men who abuse and slander women who "dared to differ from them in politics" (459): the author's list includes Caroline Norton, Lady Morgan, Maria Edgeworth, and Harriet Martineau, all of whose views are to some extent supported in *Vanity Fair*. The article anticipates the novel again in its discussion of the current "lax morality prevalent on the subject of satire" (470). The mistake many satirists of the day make, "J. R." states, is to narrow their intellectual positions to anger and intolerance (472–73).

7. Stevenson, "*Vanity Fair* and Lady Morgan," 550–51.

8. Barbara Hardy, *The Exposure of Luxury: Radical Themes in Thackeray* (Pittsburgh, Pa.: University of Pittsburgh Press, 1972), 16.

9. F. Anne Payne, *Chaucer and Menippean Satire* (Madison: University of Wisconsin Press, 1981), 14.

10. Ibid.

11. Loofbourow, *Form of Fiction*, contains impressive analyses not only of Thackeray's use of classical conventions (although he does not discuss Menippean satire), but also of his parody of fashionable fiction and chivalric romance in *Vanity Fair*. Parody is an essential element of Menippean satire. Bulwer-Lytton is explicitly parodied in a passage (later removed) that begins, "The night was dark and wild—the clouds black— black—ink-black." Besides Loofbourow and Wheatley, see also Tillotson, "Preface" and "Appendix," *Vanity Fair*, xvii n. 8, and 672.

12. Wheatley, *Patterns*, 65, 66.

13. One of Thackeray's sources for Osborne appears in his letters. In 1846 Thackeray met "Lord Fitzroy Somerset walking in St. James's Park . . . and absolutely crying. He had just quarreled with his son about a marriage before receiving news of the poor fellow's death, in that tremendous carnage [the Crimean War]" (*Letters* 2: 232).

14. Payne, *Chaucer and Menippean Satire*, 5, 4, 11–12, 35.

15. Gilbert and Gubar, *Madwoman in the Attic*, 205–6, 338; Ellen Moers, *Literary Women: The Great Writers* (New York: Anchor Books, 1977), 64; Eastlake, "Review," 171.

16. *Women, the Family, and Freedom: The Debate in Documents*, ed. Susan Groag Bell and Karen M. Offen (Stanford: Stanford University Press, 1983), 1: 271.

17. Eastlake, "Review," 176–77.

18. See Poovey, *Uneven Developments*, 126–36, for a discussion of the "conservatism and the potential subversiveness of Eastlake's position" (134).

19. Robert Colby, *Fiction with a Purpose: Major and Minor Nineteenth-Century Novels* (Bloomington: Indiana University Press, 1967), 192–203. Poovey, *Uneven Developments*, 127.

20. Thackeray's portrayal of Brontë's last days, presented without either attribution or comment, is haunting: "One evening, at the close of 1854, as Charlotte Nicholls sat with her husband by the fire, listening to the howling of the wind about the house, she suddenly said to her husband, 'If you had not been with me, I must have been writing now.' She then ran upstairs, and brought down, and read aloud, the beginning of a new tale. When she had finished, her husband remarked, 'The critics will accuse you of repetition.' She replied, 'Oh! I shall alter that. I always begin two or three times before I can please myself.' But it was not to be" (*Cornhill* 1 [April 1860]: 485–87). Modern readers can only wonder what made Brontë stop writing during the last several years of her life.

21. [Harriet Martineau], "Middle-Class Education in England: Girls," *Cornhill Magazine* 10 (1864): 553–54.

22. Maria Edgeworth and Richard Lovell Edgeworth, *Practical Education* (New York: Garland, 1974), 2: 551, 1: 168.

23. [Lady Eastlake (née Elizabeth Rigby)], "The Englishwoman at School," *Quarterly Review* 146 (1878): American edition, 27.

24. See Anne Thackeray Ritchie, "Introduction" to *Vanity Fair*, in *Works* 1: xv. Thackeray's feelings about the school he attended at Chiswick are also reflected in this scene.

25. Boswell, *Life of Johnson* (London: Oxford University Press, 1969), 327. Johnson did, however, oppose the "common notion that a woman would . . . be the worse wife for being learned" (406).

26. [Edward Bulwer-Lytton], "The Spirit of Society in England and France," *Edinburgh Review* 52 (1831): 374–87.

27. Eastlake, "The Englishwoman at School," American edition, 22–23.

28. Edgeworth and Edgeworth, *Practical Education* 2: 548.

CHAPTER 4. *VANITY FAIR:* DYNAMICS

1. Charlotte Brontë to W. S. Williams, 29 March 1848. The letter is reproduced in full in Clement K. Shorter, *Charlotte Brontë and Her Circle* (Westport, Conn.: Greenwood Press, 1970), 413–14.

2. Van Ghent, *The English Novel*, 151.

3. Martha Vicinus, "Introduction: The Perfect Victorian Lady," in *Suffer and Be Still: Women in the Victorian Age* (Bloomington: Indiana University Press, 1972), ix–xv.

4. For an article on female "hypocrisy" viewed in contemporary terms (that is, as double-discourse), see Lisa Jadwin, "The Seductiveness of Female Duplicity in *Vanity Fair*," *SEL* 32 (autumn 1992): 663–87.

5. John K. Mathison, "The German Sections of *Vanity Fair*," in *Nineteenth-Century Fiction* 18 (1963): 235–46. See also George J. Worth, "More

on the German Sections of *Vanity Fair*," *Nineteenth-Century Fiction* 19 (1965): 402–4. Robert T. Bledsoe, "*Vanity Fair* and Singing," *Studies in the Novel* 13 (spring–summer 1981): 51–63, provides a contrary reading. Bledsoe argues that "in each case, Thackeray's musical allusions are used to express intense hostility toward the two women" (56). For an appreciative overview of Thackeray's knowledge of opera and the significant uses to which he put it, see Joe K. Law, "Thackeray and the Uses of Opera," *Review of English Studies* 39 (November 1988): 502–12.

6. Ray, *Age of Wisdom*, 277.

7. Sigmund Freud, "On the Universal Tendency to Debasement in the Sphere of Love," in *The Complete Psychological Works of Sigmund Freud*, ed. James Strachey and Anna Freud (London: Hogarth Press, 1957), 11: 178–90 (183).

8. Eastlake, "The Englishwoman at School," American edition, 22–23.

Chapter 5. *Henry Esmond* and Eighteenth-Century Feminism

1. Ray, *Buried Life*, 97, cites a letter dated 13–15 July 1853 (in *Letters* 4: 435), in which Thackeray regrets that *Henry Esmond* is not popular and he puts off taking pains and writing any more "careful books" until after his fortune is made; hence, this is by implication a careful book that does not sell. Thackeray's "very best I can do" is cited in Ray, *Buried Life*, 78.

2. Charlotte Brontë, letter to W. S. Williams, her editor at Smith, Elder, dated 10 November 1852, quoted in Elizabeth Gaskell, *The Life of Charlotte Brontë*, ed. Alan Shelston (Harmondsworth, England: Penguin Books, 1975), 486.

3. George Eliot is cited from *The George Eliot Letters*, ed. Gordon S. Haight (New Haven, Conn.: Yale University Press, 1954–1955), 2: 67.

4. *The History of Henry Esmond*, ed. John Sutherland (New York: Penguin Books, 1970), 75. Future references will be given parenthetically in the text by page number.

5. Ray, *Buried Life*, 95.

6. Sedgwick, *Between Men*, 148. René Girard, *Deceit, Desire, and the Novel: Self and Other in Literary Structure*, trans. Yvonne Freccoro (Baltimore: Johns Hopkins University Press, 1965), 3.

7. Monsarrat, *Uneasy Victorian*, 278. See also chapters 14, 15, and 19.

8. Ms. in the British Museum. For a full transcription of the poem, see Monsarrat, *Uneasy Victorian*, 211–12.

9. Monsarrat, *Uneasy Victorian*, 200, cites Charles Brookfield and Frances Brookfield, *Mrs. Brookfield and Her Circle* (London:· Pitman, 1905), 1: 13.

10. Sedgwick, *Between Men*, 147–48.

11. Auerbach, *Woman and the Demon*, 100.

12. Critical discussions of the subjectivity of the narrative point of view in *Esmond* include Wolfgang Iser, *The Implied Reader: Patterns of Communication in Prose Fiction from Bunyan to Beckett* (Baltimore: Johns Hopkins University Press, 1974), 130–34; Loofbourow, *Form of Fiction*, chapters 6–9; McMaster, *The Major Novels*, 109–25; Jane Millgate, "History *versus* Fiction: Thackeray's Response to Macaulay," in *Costerus*, n.s. 2 (1974): 43–58; Ray, *Buried Life*, chapter 6, and *Age of Wisdom*, chapter 6; Elaine Scarry, "*Henry Esmond:* The Rookery at Castlewood," in *Literary Monographs* 7 (1975): 1–43; and John E. Tilford, "The Love Theme of *Henry Esmond*," in *PMLA* 67 (1952): 684–701.

13. John A. Sutherland, *Thackeray at Work* (London: Athlone Press, 1974), 72.

14. Christina Crosby, *The Ends of History: Victorians and "The Woman Question"* (New York and London: Routledge, 1991), 44–68, skillfully analyzes *Esmond* as "an ironic counter-text not only to Macaulay's *History* . . . but also to the whole nineteenth-century historical project" (45). She goes on to label Thackeray's text as "feminized" history because it "contests disciplined history by focusing precisely on what the latter must eliminate" (60). Crosby's use of the term *feminized* is problematic: indeed Crosby cites two Victorians, Bagehot and Trollope, who remark that Thackeray's mind was like a woman's, a statement that is, for good reason, almost impossible to make today. Crosby bases her analysis of *Esmond* as "feminized history" on the centrality *Esmond* gives to intimate private life, on the novel's contestation of the idea of history as a "positive record" of persons and events, and on its insistence that history is "a problem . . . that is all too often taken for a solution" (67–68).

15. George Brimley, "Thackeray's *Esmond*," *Spectator* 25 (6 November 1852): 1066–67. For Thackeray's opinion of the review, see Ray, *Age of Wisdom*, 188.

16. Scarry, *"Henry Esmond,"* 43.

17. Iser, *Implied Reader*, 130.

18. Lionel Stevenson, "Thackeray's Dramatic Monologues," collected in *From Smollett to James: Studies in the Novel and Other Essays Presented to Edgar Johnson*, ed. Samuel Mintz, Alice Chandler, and Christopher Mulvey (Charlottesville: University Press of Virginia, 1981), 155.

19. John Sutherland, "Introduction," in Thackeray, *Henry Esmond*, 21–22.

20. For evidence of the thoroughness of Thackeray's readings in seventeenth- and eighteenth-century history, see Edgar Harden, *Thackeray's "English Humourists" and "Four Georges"* (Newark: University of Delaware, 1985), and his article on "The Writing and Publication of *Esmond*," in *Studies in the Novel* 13 (1981): 79–92; Lidmila Pantůčková, *W. M. Thackeray as a Critic of Literature*, Brno Studies in English 10–11 (Brno: Universita J. E. Purkyně, 1972); Sutherland, "Introduction," to Thackeray,

Henry Esmond, and John Sutherland, "Thackeray's Notebook for *Henry Esmond,*" in *Costerus,* n.s. 2 (1974): 193–215.

21. [Judith Drake], *An Essay in Defence of the Female Sex* (London: A. Roper and E. Wilkinson, 1696), 23. The title is listed (among others) in Joseph Grego, *Thackerayana: Notes and Anecdotes* (New York: Haskell House, 1971), 197–98. Thackeray's edition of *An Essay in Defence of the Female Sex* is dated 1697; the edition I cite, apparently a second edition, was printed in 1696 for A. Roper and E. Wilkinson in Fleet Street. Regarding the attribution of Drake's *Essay,* see Joan Kinnaird, "Mary Astell: Inspired by Ideas," in *Feminist Theorists: Three Centuries of Key Women Thinkers,* ed. Dale Spender (New York: Pantheon, 1983), 28 n. 2, who cites Florence Smith, *Mary Astell* (New York: Columbia University Press, 1916), 173–82, 186.

22. Harden, *Thackeray's "English Humourists,"* 100; 234 n. 4; 28.

23. Lady Mary Wortley Montagu, *The Letters and Works of Lady Mary Wortley Montagu,* ed. Lord Wharncliff (New York: AMS Press, 1970), 2: 465. For her response to Pope's proposal, see Robert Halsband and Isobel Grundy, "Biographical Anecdotes," in *Lady Mary Wortley Montagu: Essays and Poems* (Oxford: Oxford University Press, 1977), 37. Harden, *Thackeray's "English Humourists,"* 100; 234 n. 4.

24. Kinnaird, "Mary Astell," 38.

25. Harden, *Thackeray's "English Humourists,"* 217. Kinnaird, "Mary Astell," 31, identifies the object of Steele's compliment.

26. "Mary Astell," *Dictionary of National Biography* (1917), 674.

27. Mary Astell, *Some Reflections Upon Marriage, with Additions* (1730; New York: Source Book Press, 1970), 62.

28. [Drake], *Essay,* 23. References to this work will henceforth be given parenthetically in the text.

29. Wollstonecraft, *A Vindication of the Rights of Woman,* 83, 114.

30. Robert Halsband, *The Life of Lady Mary Wortley Montagu* (Oxford: Clarendon Press, 1956), 71–72.

31. Thackeray's remark is from Harden, *Thackeray's "English Humourists,"* 127. Sarah's remark is quoted in Karl von den Steinen, "The Discovery of Women in Eighteenth-Century English Political Life," in *The Women of England from Anglo-Saxon Times to the Present,* ed. Barbara Kanner (Hamden, Conn.: Archon, 1979), 230.

32. Priscilla Wakefield, *Reflections on the Present Condition of the Female Sex* (New York: Garland Publishing, 1974), 68–69. Charlotte Smith, *Desmond: A Novel* (New York: Garland Publishing, 1974), 1: iii.

33. Astell, *Reflections Upon Marriage,* 65–66.

34. Ibid., 39.

35. Thackeray cited in Ray, *Age of Wisdom,* 462 n. 5.

36. Dudley Flamm, *Thackeray's Critics: An Annotated Bibliography of British and American Criticism, 1836–1901* (Chapel Hill: University of North

Carolina Press, 1966), 13.

37. John E. Tilford, Jr., "The Love Theme of *Henry Esmond*," *PMLA* 67 (1952): 692.

38. Freud, "Debasement," *Works* 11: 186.

39. Ibid., 11: 183.

40. William Baker, *The Libraries of George Eliot and George Henry Lewes* (British Columbia, Canada: University of Victoria, 1981), 114. Written to Mrs. Charles Bray on 19 May 1854. We should note that, years later in her autobiography, Martineau claimed she was "unable to read *Vanity Fair*, from the moral disgust it occasions," but that she spoke to Thackeray about "Dobbin's admirable turning of the tables on Amelia." Perhaps she meant "unable to read" metaphorically; or perhaps she knew the story of *Vanity Fair* through hearsay. She went on to write that "*Pendennis* much increased my respect and admiration; and *Esmond* appears to me *the* book of the century. . . . I have read it three times" (*Autobiography* 2: 376).

CHAPTER 6. THE EMERGENCE OF THE THACKERAYAN HEROINE

1. Ray, *Uses of Adversity*, 111. For a discussion of Mrs. Carmichael-Smyth as original for Helen Pendennis, see Ray, *Buried Life*, chapter 4. For the card playing, see Ray, *Uses of Adversity*, 110.

2. Ray, *Age of Wisdom*, 87–88.

3. Robert Bledsoe, "*Pendennis* and the Power of Sentimentality: A Study of Motherly Love," *PMLA* 91 (1976): 871–83.

4. These words of Thackeray's from an unpublished letter are cited in Ray, *Buried Life*, 91.

5. Catherine Peters, *Thackeray's Universe: Shifting Worlds of Imagination and Reality* (New York: Oxford University Press, 1987), 179. Peters cites F. C. Burnand, *Records and Reminiscences* (London: Methuen, 1904), 1: 237. The further information is taken from Ronald Pearsall, *The Worm in the Bud: The World of Victorian Sexuality* (Toronto: Macmillan, 1969), 248–49.

6. See Auerbach, *Woman and the Demon*, 86–96, for a discussion of the "fluid interchange" between angels and demons in Thackeray's fiction.

7. Martin Meisel, *Realizations: Narrative, Pictorial, and Theatrical Arts in Nineteenth-Century England* (Princeton, N.J.: Princeton University Press, 1983), 327. See also Joan Stevens, "Thackeray's Pictorial Capitals," in *Costerus*, n.s. 2 (1974), 116.

8. Ray, *Age of Wisdom*, 86.

9. Gabriel Marcel, *The Mystery of Being*, trans. René Hague (Chicago: Henry Regnery, 1960), 2: 193. See also McMaster, *The Major Novels*, 66–69, who accounts for the dichotomy between Helen and the Major in terms of knowledge rather than sympathy.

10. Norton, *A Letter to the Queen*, 73. Norton, *English Laws for Women*, 73.

11. Norton, *English Laws for Women*, 49–50.

12. I am indebted to Robert Colby for pointing out this passage. The connection between the Norton and the Newcome cases is indicated in Colby, *Thackeray's Canvass*, 390 n. 22.

13. "Damages, Two Hundred Pounds," in *The Ballads of Policeman X* (*Works* 15: 277–79). Thackeray's poem is consistent with other criticism of the power invested by the law in husbands and fathers. In 1846, he wrote to Edward M. Fitzgerald that, "To separate [your children] from [your wife] would be the greatest crime of all. She has a right to keep them, & *to take any steps to keep them*" (*Letters* 2: 236).

14. Jane Gray Perkins, *The Life of Mrs. Norton* (London: John Murray, 1910), 239.

15. R. D. McMaster, *Thackeray's Cultural Frame of Reference: Allusion in "The Newcomes"* (Montreal and Kingston: McGill-Queen's University Press, 1991), 37.

16. Reproduced in Barthes, *S/Z*, 237.

17. Ibid., 237–38.

18. Ibid., 239.

19. Barbara Johnson, "The Critical Difference: BartheS/BalZac," in *The Critical Difference: Essays in the Contemporary Rhetoric of Reading* (Baltimore: Johns Hopkins University Press, 1980), 9–10.

20. Robert Colby has pointed out to me that "Miss Bunion" is believed to be a caricature of the Fraserian and poet "L.E.L."

21. See Mary Poovey's chapter on *Copperfield, Pendennis,* and the professionalization of writing in *Uneven Developments*. Ina Ferris's discussion may be found in her *William Makepeace Thackeray* (Boston: Twayne Publishers, 1983), 49.

22. Quoted in Ray, *Age of Wisdom*, 205.

23. From Florence Nightingale, "Cassandra," in her unpublished "Suggestions for Thoughts to Searchers After Religious Truth" (written 1852; privately printed and circulated 1859), in Strachey, *"The Cause,"* 396.

24. Baker, *Libraries*, 114.

25. Rogers, "The Pressures of Convention," 263. This is the only work I am aware of that deals with this question directly and exclusively, but Rogers's conclusion differs from mine. Although she wrote that "Thackeray excelled in the representation of women," she concludes that in works after *Vanity Fair* Thackeray yielded to contemporary conventions and presented lifeless stereotypes. I hope in this study to present sufficient evidence for another conclusion.

26. Ray, *Age of Wisdom*, 193.

CHAPTER 7. CHILDBIRTH, MADNESS, AND MOTHERHOOD

1. Ray, *Buried Life*, 56, cites Thomas Hood, "Thackeray and His

Female Characters," *Englishwoman's Domestic Magazine*, n.s. 8 (1864), 162, as typical of most reviewers' reactions. Ray's own reaction to Helen Pendennis is, curiously, to give less credence to "what Thackeray shows Mrs. Pendennis to be" and more to "what he says about her" as Thackeray's actual evaluation of Helen Pendennis's character.

2. Showalter, *The Female Malady*, 73. Showalter's work has been very helpful in situating Isabella Shawe's insanity in its cultural and medical contexts, and in assessing Thackeray's place in the literature of female madness.

3. Ray, *Uses of Adversity*, 254.

4. See Gilbert and Gubar, *The Madwoman in the Attic*, especially chapter 3, "The Parables of the Cave."

5. See "Thackeray, Isabella," in the index to Thackeray, *Letters* 4: 567, for a complete list, vividly descriptive in itself, of all references in Thackeray's letters to his wife's illness.

6. Auerbach, *Woman and the Demon*, 188. Showalter, *The Female Malady*, 87–90.

7. Nightingale, "Cassandra," 413.

8. Rachel Brownstein, *Becoming a Heroine: Reading about Women in Novels* (New York: Viking, 1982), 81. Carolyn Heilbrun, *Reinventing Womanhood* (New York: W. W. Norton, 1979), 171.

9. Ina Ferris, "The Demystification of Laura Pendennis," *Studies in the Novel* 13 (1981): 122–32.

10. Gerda Lerner, *The Creation of Patriarchy* (New York: Oxford University Press, 1986), 30–31, 26.

11. Bachofen's full title is *Das Mutterrecht: Eine Untersuchung über die Gynaikokratie der alten Welt nach ihrer religiosen und rechtlichen Natur* (The mother right: an examination of the gynocracy of the ancient world in its religious and lawful nature) (Stuttgart, 1861). The English edition is trans. by Ralph Manheim (Princeton: Princeton University Press, 1967). Lerner cites the following as deriving from Bachofen's theory: Charlotte Perkins Gilman, *Women and Economics* (1861); the speeches of Elizabeth Cady Stanton; Lewis Henry Morgan, *Ancient Society* (1877); Friedrich Engels, *The Origin of the Family, Private Property, and the State* (1884); and Robert Briffault, *The Mothers: A Study of the Origins of Sentiments and Institutions*, 3 vols. (New York, 1927). See Lerner, *The Creation of Patriarchy*, 21–27.

12. Kate Millet, *Sexual Politics* (New York: Avon Books, 1971), 98. Millet points out that only Engels attacked patriarchy. George Boas, "Preface," *Myth, Religion, and Mother Right: Selected Writings*, by Johann Jakob Bachofen, trans. Ralph Manheim (Princeton, N.J.: Princeton University Press, 1967), xviii.

13. Brontë, *Jane Eyre*, 396.

14. Heilbrun, *Reinventing Womanhood*, 189–95.

15. Quoted in Anne Thackeray Ritchie, "Introduction" to *The Virginians,* in *Works* 16: xxi.

16. I am grateful to Robert Colby for pointing out that Thackeray's physician, Sir Henry Thompson, published an article on surgery entitled "Under Chloroform" in *Cornhill Magazine* (April 1860): 499–504. And in 1848, Jane Brookfield wrote to Thackeray that she had been dosed "with *chloroform* as a medicine and it is very soothing" (*Letters* 2: 479). Thackeray certainly was up-to-date here.

17. Gerald C. Sorensen, "Thackeray Texts and Bibliographical Scholarship," *Costerus,* n.s. 2 (1974): 281, states that Thackeray drew the ornamental initials and Frederick Walker provided the illustrations for *Philip.* Sorensen cites John R. Harvey, *Victorian Novelists and Their Illustrators* (London: Sidgwick and Jackson, 1970), 82.

18. Bachofen, *Myth, Religion, and Mother Right,* 79.

19. For discussions of the meaning of the sea and silver, see Robert Briffault, *The Mothers: A Study of the Origins of Sentiments and Institutions* (London: Allen and Unwin, 1959), chapter 19; or Nor Hall, *The Moon and the Virgin: Reflections on the Archetypal Feminine* (New York: Harper & Row, 1980), 10, 79–83, 146.

Bibliography

"A.Z." "Some Recollections of Thackeray." *Lippincott's Magazine* 7 (January 1871): 106–10.

Acland, Alice [Marreco]. *Caroline Norton*. London: Constable, 1948.

Alcoff, Linda. "Cultural Feminism versus Post-Structuralism: The Identity Crisis in Feminist Theory." *Signs: Journal of Women in Culture and Society* 13 (1988): 405–36.

Anisman, Martin J. Introduction to Thackeray, *The Luck of Barry Lyndon*. New York: New York University Press, 1970.

apRoberts, Ruth. "Teaching Victorian Literature." Address given at the Modern Language Association conference, New York, on 28 December 1986.

"Astell, Mary." *Dictionary of National Biography*. London: Oxford University Press, 1917.

Astell, Mary. *A Serious Proposal to the Ladies for the Advancement of their True and Greatest Interest*. 1718. New York: Source Book Press, 1970.

———. *Some Reflections Upon Marriage, with Additions*. 1730. New York: Source Book Press, 1970.

Auerbach, Nina. *Woman and the Demon: The Life of a Victorian Myth*. Cambridge, Mass.: Harvard University Press, 1982.

Bachofen, Johann Jakob. *Myth, Religion, and Mother Right: Selected Writings*. Translated by Ralph Manheim. 1861. Princeton, N.J.: Princeton University Press, 1967. (Originally published as *Das Mutterrecht: Eine Untersuchung über die Gynaikokratie der alten Welt nach ihrer religiosen und rechtlichen Natur* [Stuttgart, 1861].)

Baker, William. *The Libraries of George Eliot and George Henry Lewes*. British Columbia, Canada: University of Victoria, 1981.

Bakhtin, Mikhail. *Problems of Dostoevsky's Poetics*. Edited and translated by Caryl Emerson. Minneapolis: University of Minnesota Press, 1984.

Barickman, Richard, Susan MacDonald, and Myra Stark. *Corrupt Relations: Dickens, Thackeray, Trollope, Collins, and the Victorian Sexual System*. New York: Columbia University Press, 1982.

Barthes, Roland. *S/Z*. Translated by Richard Miller. New York: Hill and Wang, 1974.

Bell, Susan Groag, and Karen M. Offen, eds. *Women, the Family, and Freedom: The Debate in Documents.* 2 vols. Stanford: Stanford University Press, 1983.

Blake, Robert. *Disraeli.* New York: St. Martin's, 1967.

Bledsoe, Robert T. "*Pendennis* and the Power of Sentimentality: A Study of Motherly Love." *PMLA* 91 (1976): 871–83.

———. "*Vanity Fair* and Singing." *Studies in the Novel* 13 (spring–summer 1981): 51–63.

Boas, George. "Preface" to *Myth, Religion, and Mother Right: Selected Writings,* by Johann Jakob Bachofen. Translated by Ralph Manheim. 1861. Princeton, N.J.: Princeton University Press, 1967.

Booth, Wayne. *The Rhetoric of Fiction.* 2d ed. Chicago: University of Chicago Press, 1983.

———. *A Rhetoric of Irony.* Chicago: University of Chicago Press, 1974.

Boswell, [James]. *Life of Johnson.* 1799. London: Oxford University Press, 1969.

Brantlinger, Patrick. *The Spirit of Reform: British Literature and Politics, 1832–1867.* Cambridge, Mass.: Harvard University Press, 1977.

Briffault, Robert. *The Mothers: A Study of the Origins of Sentiments and Institutions.* 3 vols. 1927. Abridged reprint, London: Allen and Unwin, 1959.

Brimley, George. "Thackeray's *Esmond.*" *Spectator* 25 (6 November 1852): 1066–67.

Brontë, Charlotte. "Author's Preface" to *Jane Eyre.* Edited by Richard J. Dunn. 1847. New York: W. W. Norton, 1971.

Brookfield, Charles, and Frances Brookfield. *Mrs. Brookfield and Her Circle.* 2 vols. London: Pitman, 1906.

Brownell, W. C. *Victorian Prose Masters.* New York: C. Scribner's Sons, 1901.

Brownstein, Rachel. *Becoming a Heroine: Reading about Women in Novels.* New York: Viking, 1982.

Buckley, Jerome Hamilton. *The Victorian Temper: A Study in Literary Culture.* New York: Random House, 1964.

Bulwer-Lytton, Edward. *England and the English.* London: R. Bentley, 1833.

[———]. "The Spirit of Society in England and France." *Edinburgh Review* 52 (1831): 374–87.

Burnand, F. C. *Records and Reminiscences.* London: Methuen, 1904.

Carlyle, Thomas. *Letters of Thomas Carlyle to his Youngest Sister.* Edited by Charles Townsend Copeland. Boston and New York: Houghton, Mifflin & Co., 1899.

Chesler, Phyllis. *Women and Madness.* Garden City, N.Y.: Doubleday, 1972.

Clarke, Micael. "A Mystery Solved: Ainsworth's Criminal Romances Censured in *Fraser's* by J. Hamilton Reynolds, not Thackeray." *Victorian Periodicals Review* 23 (summer 1990): 50–54.

———. "Thackeray's Barry Lyndon: An Irony against Misogynists." *Texas*

Studies in Literature and Language 29 (1987): 261–77.

———. "Thackeray's *Henry Esmond* and Eighteenth-Century Feminism: A Double Vision of Feminist Discourse and Literary Narrative." *Works and Days: Essays in the Socio-Historical Dimensions of Literature and the Arts* 5 (1987): 85–107.

———. "William Thackeray's Fiction and Caroline Norton's Biography: Narrative Matrix of Feminist Legal Reform." *Dickens Studies Annual* 18 (1989): 1–15.

Colby, Robert A. "*Catherine:* Thackeray's Credo." *Review of English Studies* 15 (1964): 381–96.

———. *Fiction with a Purpose: Major and Minor Nineteenth-Century Novels.* Bloomington: Indiana University Press, 1967.

———. *Thackeray's Canvass of Humanity: An Author and His Public.* Columbus: Ohio State University Press, 1979.

Colby, Vineta. *Yesterday's Woman: Domestic Realism in the English Novel.* Princeton, N.J.: Princeton University Press, 1974.

[Cornwallis, Caroline Frances]. "The Property of Married Women." *Westminster Review* 66 (1856): 331–60. (American edition, pages 181–97.)

Crosby, Christina. *The Ends of History: Victorians and "The Woman Question."* New York and London: Routledge, 1991.

Cross, J. W., ed. *George Eliot's Life.* 2 vols. New York: Harper & Bros., 1885.

de Beauvoir, Simone. *The Second Sex.* Translated and edited by H. M. Parshley. 1959. New York: Random House, 1974.

de Lauretis, Teresa, ed. *Feminist Studies/Critical Studies.* Bloomington: Indiana University Press, 1986.

DiBattista, Maria. "The Triumph of Clytemnestra: The Charades in *Vanity Fair.*" *PMLA* 95 (1980): 827–37.

Dodds, John W. "Thackeray as a Satirist Previous to *Vanity Fair.*" *Modern Language Quarterly* 2 (1941): 163–78.

[Drake, Judith]. *An Essay in Defence of the Female Sex.* London: A. Roper and E. Wilkinson, 1696.

Drew, Elizabeth. *The Enjoyment of Literature.* New York: W. W. Norton, 1935.

Eastlake, Lady (née Elizabeth Rigby). "The Englishwoman at School." *Quarterly Review* 146 (1878): 40–69. (American edition, pages 21–37.)

[———]. "Review: *Vanity Fair, Jane Eyre,* and *The Governesses' Benevolent Institution—Report for 1847.*" In *Quarterly Review* 84 (1848): 153–85.

Edgeworth, Maria, and Richard Lovell Edgeworth. *Practical Education.* 2 vols. 1798. New York: Garland, 1974.

Eliot, George. *The George Eliot Letters.* Edited by Gordon S. Haight. 2 vols. New Haven: Yale University Press, 1954–1955.

———. "Silly Novels by Lady Novelists." *Westminster Review* 66 (October

1856): 442–61.

———. "Woman in France." *Westminster Review* 62 (October 1854): 448–73.

Ennis, Lambert. *Thackeray, the Sentimental Cynic.* Evanston, Ill.: Northwestern University Press, 1950.

Ferris, Ina. "The Demystification of Laura Pendennis." *Studies in the Novel* 13 (1981): 122–32.

———. *William Makepeace Thackeray.* Boston: Twayne Publishers, 1983.

Flamm, Dudley. *Thackeray's Critics: An Annotated Bibliography of British and American Criticism, 1836–1901.* Chapel Hill: University of North Carolina Press, 1966.

Foucault, Michel. *The History of Sexuality.* Translated by Robert Hurley. 3 vols. New York: Random House, 1978. (Originally published as *La Volounté de savoir* [Paris: Editions Gallinard, 1976].)

Fowler, Lois Josephs. "Caroline Norton." In *Dictionary of Literary Biography,* edited by Ira B. Nadel and William E. Fredeman, 64 vols. to date, 21: 234–38. Detroit, Mich.: Gale Research, 1983.

Freud, Sigmund. "On the Universal Tendency to Debasement in the Sphere of Love." In *The Complete Psychological Works of Sigmund Freud,* edited by James Strachey and Anna Freud, 24 vols., 11: 178–90. London: Hogarth Press, 1957.

Gadamer, Hans-Georg. *Truth and Method.* Translated and edited by Garrett Barden and John Cumming. New York: Crossroad, 1984. (Originally published as *Wahrheit und Methode,* 1960.)

Garrett, Peter K. *The Victorian Multi-Plot Novel: Studies in Dialogical Form.* New Haven: Yale University Press, 1980.

Gaskell, Elizabeth. *The Life of Charlotte Brontë.* Edited by Alan Shelston. 1857. Harmondsworth, Middx., England: Penguin Books, 1975.

———. "Lizzie Leigh." In *Mrs. Gaskell's Works,* 8 vols., 7: 386–417. London: Smith, Elder, and Co., n.d.

Gilbert, Sandra M., and Susan Gubar. *The Madwoman in the Attic: The Woman Writer and the Nineteenth-Century Literary Imagination.* New Haven and London: Yale University Press, 1979.

Girard, René. *Deceit, Desire, and the Novel: Self and Other in Literary Structure.* Translated by Yvonne Freccoro. Baltimore: Johns Hopkins University Press, 1965.

Grego, Joseph. *Thackerayana: Notes and Anecdotes.* 1901. New York: Haskell House, 1971.

Gulliver, Harold Strong. *Thackeray's Literary Apprenticeship.* 1934. Valdosta, Georgia: Norwood Editions, 1977.

Hall, Nor. *The Moon and the Virgin: Reflections on the Archetypal Feminine.* New York: Harper & Row, 1980.

Halsband, Robert. *The Life of Lady Mary Wortley Montagu.* Oxford: Clarendon Press, 1956.

Halsband, Robert, and Isobel Grundy. "Biographical Anecdotes." *Lady Mary Wortley Montagu: Essays and Poems.* Oxford: Oxford University Press, 1977.

Harden, Edgar. *Thackeray's "English Humourists" and "Four Georges."* Newark: University of Delaware, 1985.

———. "The Writing and Publication of *Esmond.*" *Studies in the Novel* 13 (1981): 79–92.

Hardy, Barbara N. *The Exposure of Luxury: Radical Themes in Thackeray.* Pittsburgh, Pa.: University of Pittsburgh Press, 1972.

Harvey, John R. *Victorian Novelists and Their Illustrators.* London: Sidgwick and Jackson, 1970.

Heeney, Brian. *The Women's Movement in the Church of England.* New York and Oxford: Clarendon Press, 1988.

Heilbrun, Carolyn. *Reinventing Womanhood.* New York: W. W. Norton, 1979.

Heineman, Helen. *Mrs. Trollope: The Triumphant Feminine in the Nineteenth Century.* Athens: Ohio University Press, 1979.

Hellerstein, Erna Olafson, Leslie Parker Hume, and Karen M. Offen, eds. *Victorian Women: A Documentary Account of Women's Lives in Nineteenth-Century England, France, and the United States.* Stanford: Stanford University Press, 1981.

Helsinger, Elizabeth K., Robin Lauterbach Sheets, and William Veeder. *The Woman Question: Society and Literature in Britain and America, 1837–1883.* 3 vols. New York: Garland, 1983.

Holcombe, Lee. *Wives and Property: Reform of the Married Women's Property Law in Nineteenth-Century England.* Toronto: University of Toronto Press, 1983.

Hood, Thomas. "Thackeray and His Female Characters." *Englishwoman's Domestic Magazine* 8 (1864): 157–64.

Horstman, Allen. *Victorian Divorce.* New York: St. Martin's, 1985.

Iser, Wolfgang. *The Implied Reader: Patterns of Communication in Prose Fiction from Bunyan to Beckett.* Baltimore: Johns Hopkins University Press, 1974. (Originally published as *Der Implizite Leser: Kommunikationsformen des Romans von Bunyan bis Beckett* [Munich: Wilhelm Fink, 1972].)

Jadwin, Lisa. "The Seductiveness of Female Duplicity in *Vanity Fair.*" *Studies in English Literature* 32 (autumn 1992): 663–87.

Johnson, Barbara. "The Critical Difference: BartheS/BalZac." *The Critical Difference: Essays in the Contemporary Rhetoric of Reading.* Baltimore: Johns Hopkins University Press, 1980.

Kanner, Barbara, ed. *The Women of England from Anglo-Saxon Times to the Present.* Hamden, Conn.: Archon, 1979.

———. "The Women of England in a Century of Social Change, 1815–1914: A Select Bibliography." In *Suffer and Be Still: Women in the Victorian Age*, edited by Martha Vicinus. Bloomington: Indiana University Press, 1972.

———. "The Women of England in a Century of Social Change, 1815–1914: A Select Bibliography, Part II." In *A Widening Sphere: Changing Roles of Victorian Women*, edited by Martha Vicinus. Bloomington: Indiana University Press, 1977.

Kinnaird, Joan. "Mary Astell: Inspired by Ideas." In *Feminist Theorists: Three Centuries of Key Women Thinkers*, edited by Dale Spender, 28–39. New York: Pantheon, 1983.

[Kirk, John F.]. "Thackeray, as a Novelist." *North American Review* 77 (July 1853): 199–219.

Law, Joe K. "Thackeray and the Uses of Opera." *Review of English Studies* 39 (November 1988): 502–12.

Lerner, Gerda. *The Creation of Patriarchy*. New York: Oxford University Press, 1986.

Lewes, George. "The Lady Novelists." *Westminster Review* 58 (July 1852): 129–41.

Loofbourow, John. *Thackeray and the Form of Fiction*. 1964. Reprint, New York: Gordian Press, 1976.

Lukács, György. "Reportage or Portrayal?" In *Essays on Realism*, edited by Rodney Livingstone, translated by David Fernbach. Cambridge, Mass.: MIT Press, 1980.

[Luyster, I. M.]. "The Women of Thackeray." *Christian Examiner* 69 (September 1860): 167–90.

McMaster, Juliet. *Thackeray: The Major Novels*. Manchester: Manchester University Press, 1971.

McMaster, R. D. *Thackeray's Cultural Frame of Reference: Allusion in "The Newcomes."* Montreal and Kingston: McGill-Queen's University Press, 1991.

Marcel, Gabriel. *The Mystery of Being*. Translated by René Hague. 2 vols. 1950. Chicago: Henry Regnery, 1960.

Martineau, Harriet. *Autobiography*. Edited by Maria Weston Chapman. 3 vols. 1877. Reprint in 2 vols., Westmead, England: Gregg International Publishers, 1969.

[———]. "Middle-Class Education in England: Girls." *Cornhill Magazine* 10 (1864): 549–68.

Masek, Rosemary. "Women in an Age of Transition: 1485–1714." In *The Women of England from Anglo-Saxon Times to the Present*, edited by Barbara Kanner, 138–82. Hamden, Conn.: Archon, 1979.

Mathison, John K. "The German Sections of *Vanity Fair*." *Nineteenth-Century Fiction* 18 (1963): 235–46.

Meisel, Martin. *Realizations: Narrative, Pictorial, and Theatrical Arts in Nineteenth-Century England*. Princeton, N.J.: Princeton University Press, 1983.

Meredith, George. *Diana of the Crossways.* Introduction by Lois Josephs Fowler. 1885. New York: Norton, 1973.

Mill, John Stuart. *The Subjection of Women.* 1869. Cambridge, Mass.: MIT Press, 1970.

Millet, Kate. *Sexual Politics.* 1969. New York: Avon Books, 1971.

Millgate, Jane. "History *versus* Fiction: Thackeray's Response to Macaulay." *Costerus,* n.s. 2 (1974): 43–58.

Moers, Ellen. *Literary Women: The Great Writers.* 1963. New York: Anchor Books, 1977.

Monsarrat, Ann. *An Uneasy Victorian: Thackeray the Man.* New York: Dodd, Mead, 1980.

Montagu, Lady Mary Wortley. *The Letters and Works of Lady Mary Wortley Montagu.* Edited by Lord Wharncliff. 2 vols. 1861. New York: AMS Press, 1970.

Morgan, Lady (née Sidney Owenson). *Woman and Her Master: A History of the Female Sex from the Earliest Period.* 2 vols. London: David Bryce, n.d.

Nightingale, Florence. "Cassandra." In "Suggestions for Thoughts to Searchers After Religious Truth." Written 1852. Privately printed 1859. Reprinted as Appendix 1 to Ray Strachey, *"The Cause,"* 395–418.

Norton, Caroline. *English Laws for Women in the Nineteenth Century.* 1854. In *Selected Writings.*

———. *A Letter to the Queen on Lord Chancellor Cranworth's Marriage and Divorce Bill. By Pearce Stevenson, Esq.* 1855. In *Selected Writings.*

———. *A Plain Letter to the Lord Chancellor on the Infant Custody Bill, by Pearce Stevenson, Esq.* 1839. In *Selected Writings.*

———. *Selected Writings of Caroline Norton: Facsimile Reproductions.* Edited by James O. Hoge and Jane Marcus. Delmar, N.Y.: Scholars' Facsimiles and Reprints, 1978.

Nussbaum, Martha Craven. *Love's Knowledge: Essays on Philosophy and Literature.* New York: Oxford University Press, 1990.

[Ogle, Nathaniel]. "The Custody of Infants Bill." *Fraser's Magazine* 19 (February 1839): 205–14.

[Oliphant, Margaret]. "The Laws Concerning Women." *Blackwood's Magazine* 79 (1856): 379–87.

Ortega y Gasset, José. "First Installment on the Dehumanization of Art." In *Contemporary Literary Criticism,* edited by Robert Con Davis, 33–43. New York: Longman, 1986. (Originally pubished as *La Deshumanización del arte e ideas sobre la novela* [Madrid: Revista de Occidente, 1925].)

Owenson, Sidney. *See* Lady Morgan.

Pantůčková, Lidmila. *W. M. Thackeray as a Critic of Literature.* Brno Studies in English 10-11. Brno: Universita J. E. Purkyně, 1972.

[Patmore, Coventry]. "Fielding and Thackeray." *North British Review* 24 (November 1855): 197–216.

Payne, F. Anne. *Chaucer and Menippean Satire.* Madison: University of Wisconsin Press, 1981.

Pearsall, Ronald. *The Worm in the Bud: The World of Victorian Sexuality.* Toronto: Macmillan, 1969.

Perkins, Jane Gray. *The Life of Mrs. Norton.* c. 1909. London: John Murray, 1910.

Peters, Catherine. *Thackeray's Universe: Shifting Worlds of Imagination and Reality.* New York: Oxford University Press, 1987.

Peterson, M. Jeanne. *Family, Love, and Work in the Lives of Victorian Gentlewomen.* Bloomington: Indiana University Press, 1989.

———. "The Victorian Governess: Status Incongruence in Family and Society." In *Suffer and Be Still: Women in the Victorian Age,* edited by Martha Vicinus, 3–19. Bloomington: Indiana University Press, 1972.

Phelan, James. "*Vanity Fair:* Listening as a Rhetorician—and a Feminist." In *Out of Bounds: Male Writers and Gendered Criticism,* edited by Laura Claridge and Elizabeth Langland, 132–47. Amherst: University of Massachusetts Press, 1990.

[Phillimore, J. G.]. "Women's Rights and Duties." *Blackwood's Magazine* 54 (1843), 373–97.

Poovey, Mary. *Uneven Developments: The Ideological Work of Gender in Mid-Victorian England.* Chicago: University of Chicago Press, 1988.

Ray, Gordon N. *The Buried Life.* London: Oxford University Press, 1952.

———. *Thackeray: The Age of Wisdom, 1847–1863.* 1958. New York: Farrar, Straus and Giroux, 1972.

———. *Thackeray: The Uses of Adversity, 1811–1846.* 1955. New York: Farrar, Straus and Giroux, 1972.

———. "Thackeray and France." Ph.D. diss., Harvard University, 1940.

———. *William Makepeace Thackeray: Contributions to the* Morning Chronicle. Urbana: University of Illinois Press, 1955.

Reid, T. Wemyss. *The Life, Letters, and Friendships of Richard Monckton Milnes, First Lord Houghton.* 2 vols. London: Cassell, 1890.

Reuther, Rosemary Radford. *Sexism and God-Talk: Toward a Feminist Theology.* Boston: Beacon Press, 1983.

[Reynolds, John Hamilton]. "Hints for a History of Highwaymen." *Fraser's Magazine* 9 (March 1834): 279–87.

———. "William Ainsworth and *Jack Sheppard.*" *Fraser's Magazine* 21 (February 1840): 227–45.

Rigby, Elizabeth. *See* Lady Eastlake.

[Robertson, John ("J. R.")]. "Criticism on Women." *Westminster Review* 32 (1839): 454–75.

Rogers, Katherine M. "A Defense of Thackeray's Amelia." *Texas Studies in Literature and Language* 11 (1970): 1367–74.

———. "The Pressures of Convention on Thackeray's Women." *Modern Language Review* 67 (1972): 257–63.

Salerno, Nicholas A. "*Catherine:* Theme and Structure." *American Imago* 18 (1961): 159–66.

Scarry, Elaine. "*Henry Esmond:* The Rookery at Castlewood." *Literary Monographs* 7 (1975): 1–43.

Schnorrenberg, Barbara A., and Jean E. Hunter. "The Eighteenth-Century Englishwoman." In *The Women of England from Anglo-Saxon Times to the Present,* edited by Barbara Kanner, 183–228. Hamden, Conn.: Archon, 1979.

Sedgwick, Eve Kosofsky. *Between Men: English Literature and Male Homosocial Desire.* New York: Columbia University Press, 1985.

Shanley, Mary Lyndon. "'One Must Ride Behind': Married Women's Rights and the Divorce Act of 1857." *Victorian Studies* 25 (1982): 355–76.

Shillingsburg, Peter L. *Pegasus in Harness: Victorian Publishing and W. M. Thackeray.* Charlottesville and London: University Press of Virginia, 1992.

———. "Thackeray's(?) Amelia." *Thackeray Newsletter* 39 (May 1994): 7–9.

Shorter, Clement K. *Charlotte Brontë and Her Circle.* 1896. Westport, Conn.: Greenwood Press, 1970.

Showalter, Elaine. *The Female Malady: Women, Madness, and English Culture, 1830–1980.* New York: Pantheon Books, 1985.

Smith, Charlotte. *Desmond: A Novel.* 3 vols. 1792. New York: Garland, 1974.

Smith, Florence. *Mary Astell.* New York: Columbia University Press, 1916.

Sorensen, Gerald C. "Beginning and Ending: *The Virginians* as a Sequel." *Studies in the Novel* 13 (1981): 109–21.

———. "Thackeray Texts and Bibliographical Scholarship." *Costerus,* n.s. 2 (1974): 267–85.

Spender, Dale, ed. *Feminist Theorists: Three Centuries of Key Women Thinkers.* New York: Pantheon, 1983.

Stevens, Joan. "Thackeray's Pictorial Capitals." *Costerus,* n.s. 2 (1974): 113–40.

Stevenson, Lionel. *The Showman of Vanity Fair: The Life of William Makepeace Thackeray.* London: Chapman and Hall, 1947.

———. "Thackeray's Dramatic Monologues." In *From Smollett to James: Studies in the Novel and Other Essays Presented to Edgar Johnson,* edited by Samuel Mintz, Alice Chandler, and Christopher Mulvey, 134–56. Charlottesville: University Press of Virginia, 1981.

———. "*Vanity Fair* and Lady Morgan." *PMLA* 48 (1933): 547–51.

———. *The Wild Irish Girl: The Life of Sydney Owenson, Lady Morgan.* 1936. New York: Atheneum, 1969.

Strachey, Ray. "*The Cause*": A Short History of the Women's Movement in Great Britain. 1928. Reprint, Port Washington, N.Y.: Kennikat Press, 1969.

Sutherland, John A. Introduction and notes to Thackeray, *The History of Henry Esmond*. Harmondsworth, Middx., England: Penguin Books, 1970.

―――. Introduction and notes to Thackeray, *Vanity Fair*. New York: Oxford University Press, 1983.

―――. *Thackeray at Work*. London: Athlone Press, 1974.

―――. "Thackeray's Notebook for *Henry Esmond*." *Costerus*, n.s. 2 (1974): 193–215.

Thackeray, William Makepeace. "Catherine: A Story." Seven installments, published in *Fraser's Magazine* 19 (May 1839) through 21 (February 1840).

―――. "Damages, Two Hundred Pounds." In *The Ballads of Policeman X. Works* 15: 277–79.

―――. "A Grumble about the Christmas Books, by Michael Angelo Titmarsh." *Fraser's Magazine* 35 (January 1847): 111–26.

―――. "Half-a-Crown's Worth of Cheap Knowledge." *Fraser's Magazine* 17 (March 1838): 279–90.

―――. *The History of Henry Esmond*. Edited by John Sutherland. New York: Penguin Books, 1970.

―――. *The History of Pendennis: His Fortunes and Misfortunes, His Friends and His Greatest Enemy*. Edited by Donald Hawes with an introduction by J. I. M. Stewart. London: Viking Penguin, 1972.

―――. *The Letters and Private Papers of William Makepeace Thackeray*. Edited by Gordon N. Ray. 4 vols. Cambridge: Harvard University Press, 1945–1946.

―――. *The Luck of Barry Lyndon*. Edited by Martin J. Anisman. New York: New York University Press, 1970.

―――. "On Some French Fashionable Novels: With a Plea for Romances in General." In *The Paris Sketch Book. Works* 22: 95–115.

―――. "Our Batch of Novels for Christmas, 1837." *Fraser's Magazine* 17 (January 1838): 79–103.

―――. *Vanity Fair: A Novel without a Hero*. Edited by Geoffrey and Kathleen Tillotson. Boston: Houghton Mifflin Riverside Edition, 1963.

―――. *The Works of William Makepeace Thackeray*. Edited by Anne Thackeray Ritchie and Leslie Stephen. 26 vols. London: Smith, Elder, 1910–1911. Reprint, New York: AMS, 1968.

Thomas, Deborah A. *Thackeray and Slavery*. Athens: Ohio University Press, 1993.

Thrall, Miriam M. H. *Rebellious Fraser's: Nol Yorke's Magazine in the Days of Maginn, Thackeray, and Carlyle*. 1934. New York: AMS Press, 1966.

Tilford, John E., Jr. "The Degradation of Becky Sharp." *South Atlantic Quarterly* 58 (1959): 603–8.

―――. "The Love Theme of *Henry Esmond*." *PMLA* 67 (1952): 684–701. (Reprinted in *Thackeray: A Collection of Critical Essays*, edited by

Alexander Welsh, 127–46. Englewood Cliffs, N.J.: Prentice-Hall, 1968.)

Tillotson, Geoffrey. *Thackeray the Novelist.* 1954. Cambridge, Mass.: Cambridge University Press, 1974.

Tillotson, Geoffrey, and Kathleen Tillotson. Introduction and notes to Thackeray, *Vanity Fair.* London: University of London, Riverside Edition, 1963.

Valenze, Deborah. "Cottage Religion and the Politics of Survival." In *Equal or Different: Women's Politics, 1800–1914,* edited by Jane Rendall, 31–56. New York and Oxford: Basil Blackwell, 1987.

Van Ghent, Dorothy. *The English Novel: Form and Function.* New York: Rhinehart & Co., 1953.

Vicinus, Martha, ed. *Suffer and Be Still: Women in the Victorian Age.* Bloomington: Indiana University Press, 1972.

———. *A Widening Sphere.* Bloomington: Indiana University Press, 1977.

von den Steinen, Karl. "The Discovery of Women in Eighteenth-Century English Political Life." In *The Women of England from Anglo-Saxon Times to the Present,* edited by Barbara Kanner, 229–58. Hamden, Conn.: Archon, 1979.

Von Hendy, Andrew. "Misunderstandings about Becky's Characterization in *Vanity Fair.*" *Nineteenth-Century Fiction* 18 (1963): 279–83.

Wakefield, Priscilla. *Reflections on the Present Condition of the Female Sex.* 1798. Reprint, New York: Garland, 1974.

Wheatley, James H. *Patterns in Thackeray's Fiction.* Cambridge, Mass.: MIT Press, 1969.

Wimsatt, W. K., Jr., and M. C. Beardsley. "The Intentional Fallacy." *Sewanee Review* 54 (1946): 468–88.

Wollstonecraft, Mary. *A Vindication of the Rights of Woman: With Strictures on Political and Moral Subjects.* 1792. Reprint, edited by Miriam Brody Kramnick. Harmondsworth, Middx., England: Pelican Books, 1975.

Worth, George J. "More on the German Sections of *Vanity Fair.*" *Nineteenth-Century Fiction* 19 (1965): 402–4.

Index